American Indians in American History, 1870–2001

———— A Companion Reader ————

EDITED BY STERLING EVANS

Foreword by Donald L. Fixico

PRAEGER

Westport, Connecticut
London

Library of Congress Cataloging-in-Publication Data

American Indians in American history, 1870–2001 : a companion reader / edited by
Sterling Evans ; foreword by Donald L. Fixico.
    p. cm.
   Includes bibliographical references and index.
   ISBN 0–275–97263–1 (alk. paper)—ISBN 0–275–97277–1 (pbk. : alk. paper)
   1. Indians of North America—History—19th century. 2. Indians of North
America—History—20th century. 3. Indians of North America—Government relations.
I. Evans, Sterling, 1959–
E77.A54 2002
970.004'97—dc21   2001051373

British Library Cataloguing in Publication Data is available.

Library of Congress Catalog Card Number: 2001051373
ISBN: 0–275–97263–1
    0–275–97277–1 (pbk.)

First published in 2002

Praeger Publishers, 88 Post Road West, Westport, CT 06881
An imprint of Greenwood Publishing Group, Inc.
www.praeger.com

Printed in the United States of America

⬥ ™

The paper used in this book complies with the
Permanent Paper Standard issued by the National
Information Standards Organization (Z39.48–1984).

10 9 8 7 6 5 4 3 2 1

For
Lois Risling (Hupa, Yurok)
whose work for American Indians has
probably never been fully recognized or appreciated
and for
Alex and Shelby
in hopes that their generation
will be better informed than was mine

Contents

Contents

Contents

Foreword

This book is the first scholarly effort as a companion reader to represent American Indians properly as a part of U.S. history. Unfortunately it is evident that the indigenous peoples of this continent have been misrepresented in American history, completely neglected, or given scant attention in textbooks. This collective effort orchestrated by Sterling Evans attempts to correct this wrongful portrayal of the native peoples of the United States. It is important for those individuals who are learning about American history to understand that the American experience is a history inclusive of various minorities and women. Without accurate American Indian representation, American history is incorrect and presented with bias.

In order to better understand American Indians as a part of the American experience, it is imperative to understand the views of American Indian people. In this book, seven of the essays are written by American Indian scholars. The remaining essays are written by scholars who have a thorough understanding of American Indians and their cultures. As a whole, this anthology addresses significant issues and major events directly involving Indian people and their communities. From these seventeen essays, much can be learned about and from American Indians about the importance of life and familiar themes of survival, assimilation, cultural retention, acculturation, and cultural adaptation.

American Indians possess certain cultural values and perspectives that have proven to be incongruent with the American mainstream society. In Part I, Raymond Pierotti (Comanche) and Daniel R. Wildcat (Yuchi), and Robert M.

Utley described these cultural differences as reasons for a clash of cultures. In Part II, Elizabeth James-Stern, Margaret Connell Szasz, L.G. Moses and Russel Barsh describe the cultural resistance of American Indians to assimilation into American society. Their work raises such questions as, Why have federal policies tried to change the indigenous peoples of America after demilitarizing them and forcing them onto nearly 300 reservations? In Part III, the late D'Arcy McNickle (Salish-Kutenai) and Tom Holm (Cherokee, Creek) describe the survival of American Indians during the Great Depression, and Native patriotism in World War II. No one really asks about American Indians during the Great Depression nor do people know about the extent of Indian men and women serving in the war for the United States. In Part IV, Peter Iverson and Liza Black describe the deliberate effort to dissolve Indian legal rights by severing the U.S.–Indian trust relations and by urbanizing Indian people. Termination and relocation of native peoples to cities were the most negative actions of the United States toward Indian people in the twentieth century. In Part V, Thomas Clarkin, Kent Blansett (Cherokee), and Daniel C. Swan explain the emergence of a new Indian identity of resilient pride in tribal and in urban communities due to activism and self-determination. In Part VI, Devon Mihesuah (Choctaw), Walter R. Echo-Hawk (Pawnee) and Roger C. Echo-Hawk (Pawnee), Christopher L. Miller, and Donald L. Fixico (Shawnee, Sac and Fox, Creek and Seminole) address pertinent issues confronting American Indians throughout Indian Country in their efforts to preserve identity, tribal rights, and natural resources.

The meaning of life from various Indian points of views is described in this collection of essays, confirming that the natural environment is essential to the mental health of Indian people. Their identities and the core of their cultural beliefs are related to the earth, and the ways of their people have survived and persist in the face of many federal programs and government policies threatening to alter the lives of Indian people. From these strengths are drawn lessons for all of us to incorporate into our lives as Americans amid a growing energy crisis of decreasing fossil fuels and tremendous usage of electricity and water, while breathing polluted air in many cities. Finally this book is more than a political history of Indian-white relations in conflict. It also contains insights into a native ethos about the environment, indigenous beliefs, and tribal ways concerning the importance of life that are an unseen but a significant part of the American experience.

Donald L. Fixico
Bowlus Distinguished Professor of American Indian History
Director of Indigenous Nations Studies, University of Kansas

Preface

Most Americans learning the history of their country over the past 225 years were exposed to very little of the history of American Indians. This has improved remarkably in the last twenty or so years with much-needed revisionism in writing and interpreting First Nations history and including that story into the overall national experience in U.S. history courses. Still, the role of American Indians in mainstream history courses even today is often sidestepped, ghettoized, or at best, underplayed. Likewise, most history textbooks are not set up to include in-depth discussion of the history and implications of U.S. policies toward American Indians and usually neglect the reactions of Native Americans themselves.

This anthology's goal is to correct those shortcomings. It is designed especially to provide a means for teachers, instructors, or professors of U.S. history courses—particularly the survey dealing with Reconstruction to the present—to include various aspects of American Indian history in the larger context. It is organized chronologically to follow the format used by most instructors in their class lectures, and to accompany the time periods covered by the course textbooks. And although it cannot cover *every* aspect of First Nations history in this time period, it can be used as a point of departure, and includes an extensive list of sources for additional study after each section. With that in mind, and following the example of most edited collections designed for undergraduate students, the footnotes have been excluded from the text. The book consists of seventeen essays that can be used in tandem with other materials or readings in the class. Some are written by people familiar to many in the profession and whose work has been seminal in their respective areas. Others are by younger scholars—providing new voices to the ongoing historiography of American Indians. Seven of the essays were written by American Indian scholars, some well established, some new to their professions.

To date there is no companion reader on American Indian history *designed specifically* to accompany a college U.S. history course that covers this time period. Other anthologies either cover the entire span of U.S. history from colonial or early America to the present and are aimed toward an upper-level academic audience, or tend to be more narrowly focused, either geographically, temporally, or topically. Thus *American Indians in American History, 1870–2001* reaches out to the students in the lower-level history survey courses. It is also unique in that in its examination of important policy questions there is also discussion of cultural, environmental, and gender issues. It is, therefore, a book to be used by instructors like me—people who are not necessarily Native Americanists but who seek to include the history of American Indians in their U.S. survey classes.

The book is divided into six parts. Part I deals with the inherent clash of cultures as America expanded westward. The clash is seen in opposing views on the environment, eloquently explained in a chapter by Raymond Pierotti and Daniel Wildcat, and in the military expeditions against Indians, detailed in a chapter by Robert Utley. Part II discusses several aspects of what happened next in the late nineteenth and early twentieth centuries. The U.S. government attempted to assimilate American Indians with the Dawes Act (chapter covering a case study, by Elizabeth James-Stern), and through boarding-school education (chapter by Margaret Connell Szasz). Many Native Americans reacted against such policies by becoming involved with the Ghost Dance Movement (see chapter by L.G. Moses). How all this played out in federal policymaking in the Progressive Era is the topic of Russel Barsh's chapter.

Part III examines the lives of American Indians during the Great Depression of the 1930s (D'Arcy McNickle's chapter on the Indian New Deal), and during World War II (Tom Holm's contribution entitled "Fighting a White Man's War"). The 1940s and 1950s witnessed changes in policy, as discussed in Part IV. There, Peter Iverson's chapter deals with "termination" and relocation, and Liza Black's examines the role of American Indians in Hollywood movies. With the 1960s and 1970s (the years covered in Part V) came "self-determination" and Indian activism. In this section, Thomas Clarkin discusses policy changes during the 1960s, Kent Blansett provides a case study of the beginnings of the Red Power movement, and Daniel Swan looks at American Indian rights via the peyote religion and the Native American Church.

Preface

Finally, Part VI has four different chapters that add to the reader's understanding of recent and contemporary American Indian issues. The first, by Devon Mihesuah, examines the evolving place of American Indian women in history. Next, Walter Echo-Hawk and Roger Echo-Hawk discuss the questions of museum artifacts and repatriation. The third chapter, by Christopher Miller, deals with the history and complexities of Indian reservation gaming and casinos. And, as the book began by looking at American Indians' relationship to the environment, it so closes with an essay by Donald Fixico on natural resources and conflict in Indian country.

Thus, the book is designed to balance the history of federal Indian policy with Native American cultural responses. As editor, I wish all the best to professors, students, and other readers in reaching a better understanding of such a truly vital part of American history.

ACKNOWLEDGMENTS

The birthplace of this anthology was the American Indian Civics Project at Humboldt State University in northern California. The project's goal was to develop ways to infuse the teaching of American Indian civics (history, government, economics) into the mainstream curriculum of K-12 and college/university education. It was funded by a generous four-year grant from the W.K. Kellogg Foundation, whose support of American Indians is greatly appreciated.

Many people helped bring the book together, and I am grateful for their assistance and support. First, at Humboldt State, Lois Risling and Lily Owyang were the project's codirectors, who worked tenaciously to ensure its success. Delores Nason McBroome, the project's curriculum coordinator, originated the idea for this anthology and worked in many ways to see it to fruition. I deeply appreciate her advice, encouragement, and especially her enthusiasm all along the way. Cynthia Gourley, a graduate student here, was my research assistant and was extremely helpful in compiling ideas for the contributions to be used. Nancy Hill provided her ever-essential secretarial support for such a project, and Sheri L. Evans did her usual outstanding job of word-processing the entire manuscript (and showing patience and warm encouragement during its various phases!).

Others deserving credit are Rita Napier, for opening my mind in many ways to the history of American Indians when I was a graduate student at the University of Kansas; all the contributors and publishers who agreed to have their work published or re-released here; Donald L. Fixico for his support of the project; and Cynthia Harris, who as editor for Praeger Publishers, believed in this book and was extremely helpful to work with. My thanks to all.

S. E.,
Blue Lake, CA

1

The 1870s and 1880s: The Clash of Cultures

American Indians in the 1870s and 1880s faced daunting challenges as the U.S. government continued its ongoing colonization efforts to occupy more lands and to subdue the Native peoples who were already living on them. With the Civil War squarely behind them, and with thoughts and reflections on America's centennial in front of them, Americans were in the process of attempting to reconstruct the South and expand into the West. The Homestead Act of 1862 and the construction of transcontinental railroads encouraged thousands of eastern and midwestern farmers and speculators to flood into the Great Plains to try their luck at farming, or to invest in land cheaply and sell it for profit. And as mining and cattle booms erupted from California to Colorado, from Texas to Montana, and from Nevada to South Dakota, more and more eastern Americans came into contact with the environment and peoples of the American West.

But the contact was more of a clash. It was a clash of cultures, of values, of ideas, and of world views. The clash was manifested in the creation of a variety of different zones of interactions, sometimes called frontiers, between westward-moving Americans and First Nations people. There was a mining frontier, a livestock frontier, a farming frontier, a military frontier, a missionary frontier, and a disease frontier—all of which radically changed, but certainly never ended, the American Indians' ways of living from the Great Plains to the West Coast.

Two of these clashes are discussed in the chapters here. The first, by Raymond Pierotti and Daniel Wildcat, examines the important difference between Native Americans' and Anglo Americans' views of nature. "Being Native to This Place" deals with an American Indian outlook on the environment and on the religious or spiritual context of understanding it, as opposed to a more materialistic and domineering environmental viewpoint espoused by European Americans. It compares the emerging mid-nineteenth-century scientific theory of natural selection to that which was readily understood by Indians, and concludes by offering a view from the standpoint of the wolf.

The second chapter studies the clash on the military frontier. Here, Robert Utley examines the American Indian responses to the treaties that forced them onto reservations throughout the West. Like any other colonial power in history, the United States called on its army to maintain the peace and to prevent deprivations from occurring against people moving into frontier regions. The clash resulted in the Indian wars, including that of the Little Bighorn, which took place in the same year as the nation's centennial celebration, 1876. "Wars of the Peace Policy, 1869–1886," then, takes us from the Modocs in northeastern California to the Kiowas of the southern Plains, to the Cheyennes and Sioux of the northern Plains, and to the Apaches of the Southwest to understand a vital aspect of American Indians and their reactions to U.S. policy.

For more information on these and other aspects of frontier clashes, interactions, and American Indian responses, see the For Further Reading list at the end of Part I.

1

Being Native to This Place
Raymond Pierotti and Daniel R. Wildcat

Being native to a place requires one to live with nature. It is built on a worldview directly opposite to the dominant Western worldview, which assumes humans live above, on, separated, or in opposition to nature. Those today who continue or struggle to live with nature—with the geography and biology of the place where they live—can count themselves among the few who are truly native to a place. American Indians, casinos and all, retain a profound sense of what it means to be native to a place. Even today as we speak about "Indian Country," we are not merely speaking of a state of mind but of places and spaces.

Indian Country, with its myriad of contradictions and problems, continues to reflect, no matter how deeply buried, the foundation of a worldview relevant to how and where human beings ought to live. Those wanting to embrace a comfortable and romantic image of the Rousseauian "noble savage" will, however, be disappointed. Living with nature has little to do with the often voiced "love of nature," "closeness to nature," or desire "to commune with nature" one hears today. Those desirous of dancing with wolves will first have to learn to live with wolves.

Learning to live with nature is the foundation of what it means to be native to a place. Understanding this point suggests why oral, ceremonial, and social traditions are so critical to Native identity. It is not through formal pedagogy

This chapter was originally a paper presented at the Hall Center for the Humanities Colloquium on Nature and Technology, University of Kansas, Lawrence, KS, September 6, 1996.

that the lessons required to be native to a place are learned, but instead through the custom and habit of the community: a community not only profoundly ecologically understood, but encompassing a sphere of politics and ethics many in the Western philosophic tradition are only beginning to understand.

Living with nature requires a return to very ancient worldviews that suggest radically different paradigms related to politics, economics, and ethics than those dominant in modern societies. Being native to a place requires for most people on the planet a rearrangement of the customs and habits of their daily life. Fortunately, this wisdom is still possessed by premodern indigenous peoples and miraculously by many indigenous Native Americans, particularly traditional Native scholars recognized in their own communities as elders or wisdom keepers.

Being native to a place is expressed in the ability to experience a sense of place and spatial notion of life that casts off the modern view that "space," not just "outer-space," exists to be conquered. The cultural diversity of indigenous Native Americans is a reflection of their intimate ties to the land and the biology of the places that they call home—of their sense of place. Native American cultures capture more fully than any other cultural groups in the Americas what it means to be native to a place. Not surprisingly, Native peoples have considerable insights into nature.

Our essay will suggest that in at least two major areas of what is thought of as Western science, that is, ecology and evolution, Native peoples understood the basic principles, had developed sophisticated concepts, and had a substantial body of knowledge relative to these branches of science well before Europeans had developed such principles and concepts. In short, modern Western science is only just beginning to catch up with ancient Native American wisdom.

Native peoples developed these ideas because, unlike modern Western societies, they never lost sight of the fact that their very existence depended on understanding ecology. Native peoples' profound understanding of ecology, the nature of individuality, and resulting differences in survival and reproduction led them to develop ideas nearly identical to evolution through natural selection. More importantly, Native knowledge in these two areas of science has something to contribute to the further development and understanding of these concepts.

NATIVE PEOPLES AND ECOLOGY

One feature separating Native peoples from other American minorities, and which in fact forms the dominant culture, is that the First Americans do not have an immigrant experience within their heritage. They and their recent ancestors did not come to North America as imported labor or slaves, to escape religious or political persecution, to seek increased economic opportunities, or any other of the variety of reasons that brought ancestors of most Americans to these shores.

This absence of an immigrant experience yielded a very different view of land use and resource management than occurs in many other cultures. The worldviews and cultures of peoples of the First Nations evolved in the environments of the continent we now call North America. These peoples depended upon the animals and plants of these environments for food, clothing, shelter, and companionship. As a result, they developed strong ties to the fish, the land animals, the forests, the grasslands, and to the very land of North America. Because these places and beings existed and changed along with them for tens of thousands of years, their sense of place and tendency to think spatially as opposed to thinking temporally, in time, was profound.

As Native peoples evolved in North America, they had to learn how to obtain food and shelter from the land. Each species had at least one ability or characteristic that set each of them apart from other species and that enhanced their chances of survival as individuals. Humans had understanding and intelligence, but lacked the speed, horns, teeth, claws, and strength of other species. The way for humans to survive and prosper was to pay careful attention and learn as much as possible about the strengths and weaknesses of all the other organisms, so that they could take them as food and avoid being taken by them as food.

The body of knowledge that was acquired through this careful observation was passed on to others through detailed stories, which had to be repeated constantly so that the knowledge would be passed on intact and future generations would retain the knowledge acquired by their ancestors. Several themes emerged through these stories. First, it was realized that all things are connected. This was not simply an empty phrase, but a realization that it was impossible for any single organism to exist without the connections that it had to many other organisms.

Humans could not exist without the food they obtained from deer, moose, bison, or wapiti (elk). Yet at the same time these plant-eating animals could not exist without the plants that they took in as food. The humans also used plants as food, and sometimes learned which plants to eat by watching what was eaten by the plant-eating animals. As children, we learned that if you had to gather plants for food, you could go into the field and watch what the cows were eating. We learned that the plants the cows ate were good for humans to eat as well.

Our Native ancestors had a vastly more rich knowledge of the same kind; they observed that other organisms killed and ate the plant eaters. Wolf, cougar, bear, coyote, fox, wolverine and badger were good hunters from whom much could be learned. These predators were recognized for their power, and humans recognized a kinship with them since, like the predators, the humans also depended upon the taking of life for their food.

Taking the lives of other organisms and consuming their tissues in order to sustain one's own body tissues establishes the connectedness of living things. By eating parts of other organisms, you are demonstrating that they are made of the same materials of which you are made. The amino acids, fats, carbohydrates that made up the plant or animal upon which you feed are exactly the same as those that make up your own body, and will be taken into your body and used in the same way as they were used by others. These molecules, along with key nutrients, cycle constantly through living things as they feed upon one another. And when living things die and decompose, their elements are returned to earth and water, where they can be taken up by plants or fungi and used to build the bodies of these organisms.

This connectedness—the recognition that macromolecules and nutrients are taken up by plants and fungi, which are eaten by plant eaters, which in turn are eaten by flesh eaters—is a fundamental tenet of the Western science of ecology, where it is called cycling. The idea of a cycle, or circle, of life is not a mystical, ethereal concept based upon great mysteries, but a practical recognition of the fact that all living things are connected. In fact, the principle of cycling goes beyond animals and plants, since nutrients such as phosphorus, nitrogen, calcium, manganese, and sodium also cycle through water, soil, rocks, and the atmosphere. Thus the Native idea that humans and other living things are also connected to earth, water, air, and the sun also reveals an understanding of the physical and geochemical aspects of ecology.

Along similar lines, the understanding that plant eaters depend upon plants for life, that flesh eaters depend upon plant eaters for life, and that plants, plant eaters, and flesh eaters who are not killed and eaten will die and their substance will be broken down and returned to earth to be taken up by plants is another tenet of ecology called trophic dynamics. Although our ancestors lacked the technical vocabulary of modern ecology, they had this knowledge thousands of years before modern ecology was born. What passes today as the science of ecology is nothing more than a restatement of what traditional indigenous North American ceremonies and oral traditions teach: We human beings are shaped by our participation in the sacred circle of life (the great cycle), or what John Mohawk calls "the complex web of life." The Native concept—all things are connected—is basically equivalent to the science of ecology.

The word ecology comes from the Greek word *oikos*, which means "house" and denotes habitat, environment, and domestic relations. At an intellectual level, Western science acknowledges the connectedness of things by implying that ecology is the study of the place where one lives. People of the First Nations have a similar concept in that they do not think of nature as "wilderness," but as home—the place where they became human beings, as Luther Standing Bear has described it. The major difference is that among peoples shaped by Western Civilization few but ecologists recognize the connectedness of animate with inanimate things, and among all living organisms, whereas among the first peoples, all believed in these connections and arranged their lives to show respect for these connections.

For Native peoples this insight has profound implications for their conceptions of politics and ethics. Although deep ecologists and some Western philosophers are exploring the area of environmental ethics today, this is ancient terrain for the First Americans. Unlike the dominant Western political and ethical paradigms, which find knowledge of how human beings ought to act imbedded in the life of one's social, that is, human relationships, our ancestors found their knowledge of how to behave from their membership in a community (ecosystem) consisting of many other-than-human persons, for instance, four-legged persons, winged persons, plant persons, and so forth. In short, while Western thought, following Aristotle's lead, defines politics and ethics as exclusively human realms, Native thought and, more importantly, our cultural practices have defined politics and ethics as existing in the realm of ecosystems. Considerable evidence exists to support a case for a general indigenous model of politics and ethics that when not explicitly stated is evident in the ceremonial and social life of Native peoples.

The best illustration of how Native peoples include many other natural objects and living beings as members of their community is found in Native clan names and totems. It is frustrating constantly to hear non-Native peoples speaking romantically of the Indians' "closeness to nature" or "love of nature." The relationship is more profound than most people can imagine and for many, the implications of this relationship will imply uncomfortable consequences.

To be Wildcat, Bear, or Deer clan means that you are kin to these other persons—they are your relations, your relatives. Ecological connectedness is culturally and ceremonially acknowledged through the traditional clan names, totems, and ceremony. Since in nearly all of our Native creation stories animal- and plant-persons existed before human persons, these kin exist as our elders. These animal- and plant-elders, as much as our human elders, are our teachers. They are respected members of our community. Aristotle proposed that our values—guiding how we ought to live—are learned from our fellow community members. From an indigenous perspective Aristotle's basic reasoning was right, but his notion of community and its membership was wrong.

Native people would argue that it makes no sense to limit the notion of politics and ethics to only human beings. How we human beings live will indeed reflect the communities we belong to; however, by limiting the definition of "persons" to human beings Aristotle created a false and far too narrow sense of community and the corresponding spheres of political and moral life. The inclusion of other living beings and natural objects into a category of "persons," which includes human beings, requires a notion of politics and ethics inclusive of these other community members. As Native peoples our clan identities exist to, among other things, reinforce this important insight. We persons, inclusive of plant- and animal-persons and the human beings, are all related: this is the new insight of ecology and environmental science, and the very ancient wisdom of our traditional indigenous scholars or elders.

The Western concept of ecology and the Native concept of connectedness are very similar, but the Native tradition is much older. Western ecology was not recognized as a science until the early part of the twentieth century, and several of its major concepts were described by American naturalists who had experience with Native peoples, for example, Merriam, Clements, and Grinnell. The science of ecology in Europe tended to focus on the study of individual species, often ignoring interactions that were not direct. Early twentieth-century European ecology functioned as if it were possible to understand a species without also understanding its connection to all the other aspects of its environment. In contrast, in North America ecologists developed the concepts of ecological communities, ecosystems, succession, and nutrient cycles. It is possible that some of these early ideas even came from discussions between nineteenth-century American ecologists and the First Americans with whom they encountered and worked.

The relationships to nature of people of the First Nations have often been described by peoples imbued with the western tradition in simple terms like "harmony with nature" or "love of nature." Such descriptions too often project a rather amorphous, sentimental, and romanticized character onto this relationship, but overlook the empirical knowledge of the lives of plants and animals that was such a major component of the daily lives of Native peoples. The attitudes and relationships of Native people to other organisms result from having evolved as distinct cultures in strong association with those other creatures, and experiencing them on a daily basis. Perhaps the best way to think of this knowledge borne of experience is that Native people lived their lives as though the lives of other organisms mattered, that is, that all other living organisms should be taken seriously. They experienced these other creatures in their roles as parents, as offspring, and ultimately as persons within a shared community. They realized their own lives were intimately intertwined with those of these other organisms. Most importantly, they recognized that the human being, "man," is not the measure of all things. Rather, humans exist as but one small part of a very complex ecosystem, unlike the Western view of nature, which sees human beings above the rest of nature.

Recognizing connectedness and the meaningfulness of other lives did not mean, however, that animals or plants should not be taken or used for food or clothing. In fact, Native people were dependent upon them for these very reasons. Instead, each taking should be accompanied by recognition of the fact that the take represents loss of life to a fellow being whose life had meaning on its own terms. Such a perspective leads inescapably to these conclusions: (1) lives of other organisms should not be taken frivolously; and (2) other life forms exist on their own terms and were not put here only for use by humans.

Europeans often develop a love of nature because they love a particular cat or dog, or perhaps animals in general. As a result, they often imbue these animals with human emotions and thoughts—they anthropomorphize them, which leads them to oppose the taking of other animals through hunting, and to refuse to eat meat. Such Europeans often assume that their attitudes are similar to those of Native peoples, since they think opposing hunting, or eating a vegetarian diet brings them closer to "harmony with nature."

These individuals are often shocked when they realize that Native peoples regard hunting, fishing, and meat-eating to be a part of strong cultural traditions, even when the animal being hunted is endangered or subject to federal regulation, for exammple, bowhead whales and Florida panthers. This conflict of views results because Europeans fail to realize that Native people do not anthropomorphize animals. Instead Native peoples recognize that the lives of animals and plants exist on their own terms and have value independent of any we human beings place on them. Consequently, being taken as food is a common fate of species within their natural environment, for example, deer, moose, and so forth. The lives of human beings and their families often depended upon taking the life of the animal. In such situations, the Native persons understood themselves as predators, as part of the world of the prey, and as connected to the prey in a profound experiential sense. By contrast, Europeans identify with the prey in an extremely anthropocentric and psychological sense—they react as if they or their human loved ones were the ones being taken for food.

This attitude of Europeans also manifests itself in the form of hostility towards all predators. As a result, wolves, cougars, and bears are viewed as creatures of evil, capable of "slaughter of helpless prey" and as marauders. In medieval times, Europeans even captured and hanged wolves that took livestock as if the predators were human criminals who had committed murder. To this day, Western culture demands the killing of any individual predator that attacks a human, even including sharks and crocodiles. In contrast, Native peoples identified with the predators, for as hunters who had to rely upon knowledge of prey they recognized the connection between themselves and the wolf, the bear, or the lion. They also recognized themselves as potential prey for other large carnivores. This knowledge of connectedness and of ecological similarity allows Natives to respect the predator, since they know how difficult it is to take lives, and that the predator feels most connected to the prey when it has taken its life.

Until very recently within the Western tradition the only individuals who understood this connectedness between predators and prey were scientists studying ecology. One of the fundamental tenets of ecological theory is that predators cannot exist without prey, and that prey populations are often regulated and prevented from overeating their food supplies by predators. In his essay, "Thinking like a Mountain," Aldo Leopold argues that if deer fear the wolf then a mountain must also fear its deer, since without the wolf to limit the number of deer, the deer could kill the vegetation, and even risk the mountain itself through erosion. Thus, the connectedness of all things can be understood not only as a Native belief, but as the fundamental concept of ecology; and ecology can be thought of as being the roots of indigenous North American traditional knowledge.

NATIVE TRADITION EVOLUTION AND CREATION

In a similar vein, Native peoples also recognized that all things are related. This idea emerged from the concept of connectedness, since it is obvious that if you can take another organism into your body and have it become part of you, you and it must be made of the same material and are thus related. The relatedness of all things is one of the central tenets of the Western science of evolution, since we now know that all organisms on Mother Earth contain DNA and RNA, which contain the instructions that allow individual organisms to develop in a way that makes them resemble their parents, but not be identical to them.

The idea that each organism is an individual with unique qualities is both a basic understanding of Native perception and a fundamental tenet of Charles Darwin's theory of evolution through natural selection. To examine this point in more detail, consider a statement of Okute (Shooter), a Lakota:

Animals and plants are taught by Wakan Tanka what they are to do. Wakan Tanka teaches the birds to make nests, yet the nests of all birds are not alike. Wakan Tanka gives them merely the outline. Some make better nests than others. . . . Some animals also take better care of their young than others. . . . All birds, even those of the same species are not alike, and it is the same with animals, or human beings. The reason Wakan Tanka does not make two birds, or animals, or human beings exactly alike is because each is placed here to be an independent individual and to rely upon itself.

In his book *The Origin of Species*, Charles Darwin laid out three conditions that are necessary for natural selection to occur and lead to evolutionary change: (1) There must be variation among individuals; (2) this variation must have an effect upon the ability of individuals to survive and reproduce; and (3) this variation must be heritable, that is, capable of being passed from one generation to the next. Only the first two of these are necessary for natural selection to occur, and if the variation can be passed between generations then evolution has occurred. Okute describes similar phenomena in his statement: (1) Great emphasis is placed upon variation among individuals; in fact variation is the major theme of his statement, and (2) This variation leads some individuals to build better nests or take better care of their young, that is, to reproduce more successfully as a result of this variation. Thus Okute has described the process of natural selection in the context of traditional Lakota knowledge. The only difference between the statements made by Darwin and Okute is that Okute does not discuss this variation being passed between generations.

Native peoples also understood evolutionary relationships between groups of organisms. Comanches would not eat the flesh of dogs because dog was "brother" to coyote and wolf, who were sacred figures in Comanche belief. This recognition is exactly the same as recognizing that wolves, dogs, and coyotes are each others' closest evolutionary relations. The Koyukon people of Alaska recognize both ecological and evolutionary relationships between different organisms.

The strong ties of Native peoples to the land led them to a non–human-centered view of nature, which can be seen in their creation myths. A major difference between native and western views of the world is that in nearly all Western views of the world, creators (and tricksters, who are often the same) tend to be human, or human in form. In contrast, in native myths creators are typically animals, for instance, raven (Haida, Koyukon), wolf (Comanche), and bear (Menominee). Thus, the key question we must ask ourselves is, How would it change your world view if the entity that created your world or culture was not a human, or even human-like?

One consequence of viewing your creator as non-human-like is that you would not be troubled by the idea that humans like yourself came from organisms that would not be recognized as human. In fact, the clan systems of many First Nations are a means of acknowledging the relatedness of humans and non-humans. Viewing animals as creators also implies that the animals existed before the humans did, since to be a creator it is necessary to exist before your creation does. Manuel Iron Cloud (Oglala Lakota) explains: "Sungmanitu Tanka Oyate, the Big Dog from the Wilderness People, were a nation long before human beings realized and declared themselves a nation."

The meaning of the term "creation" has led to confusion between Native and western peoples. Western religious practice based upon the Bible uses the concept of creation to argue that God created all organisms within a short period of time, and that these organisms have remained unchanged since the time of creation. For this reason, western creationists argue that evolution, as described by Darwin and other western scientists, cannot have occurred since it assumes change in organisms over time. This Biblical view of nature is antithetical to views held by Native peoples, since in its essence it argues that all things are not related—in fact, humans were specially created in the image of God to have dominion over the birds of the air and the beasts of the field. Despite this apparent belief, many nonscientists of European descent practice evolutionary principles when they breed domestic animals or plants to make them produce more food for humans, that is, bend these organisms away from their natural way, and change one form of animal into a different form (This process is called artificial selection, as opposed to natural selection). What fundamentalist Christians oppose most strongly is the idea that humans are related to animals. They cannot accept that other creatures have their own reasons for living, their own families, and that they do not exist solely for the benefit of humans, since the Bible tells them that they have dominion over these other organisms.

The First Nations also have creation stories, which tell about how specific peoples came to recognize themselves as distinct cultures, separate from other groups. These stories typically recognize the importance of non-humans in the development of a distinct culture, for example, the Comanche or Lakota describe how they learned to hunt from wolf, or the Koyukon tell how they live in the world that Raven made. Unfortunately, a tendency has arisen among biblically oriented religious instructors to co-opt these stories and imbue them with Christian religious symbolism, for example, *Black Elk Speaks*. This practice has been employed to take Native peoples away from traditional beliefs and to turn them from their connection with nature and their recognition of the relatedness of all things. Unlike the Bible, creation stories of the first peoples do not deal with the exact time when these events happened, since they happened so long ago that they exist "on the other side of memory," as Joseph Marshall has explained it. Instead, these stories emphasize that the natural world and its creatures helped shape humans into what they have become, which is an evolutionary view of the origins of humans and their cultures.

It is possible to reinterpret the western creation story of "Adam and Eve" as a story about how idyllic life was for human beings prior to the "discovery of knowledge," which led humans to invent agriculture (Cain the horticulturalist and Abel the pastoralist). The Bible is quite vague about where the women came from that bore Cain children after he killed his brother Abel. Following this logic, the "fall of mankind" could be seen as resulting from losing connection to nature, that is, leaving the Garden of Eden and embarking upon the domestication of animals and plants only for human use. Original Sin could be interpreted as changing from being a hunter and living life as though the lives of other organisms mattered into becoming a farmer or herdsman who manipulates other beings solely for the purpose of benefiting humans.

The tendency to identify the beginning of human civilization with this Biblical "fall of man" (the beginning of agriculture?) results in the fundamental temporal orientation of western civilization. The experiences of Adam, or Moses, are presumed to have meaning today because in this largely abstract nongeographical or spatial sense of history their history is now our history. As a result, such traditions derive instructions for living in the modern world, regardless of place, from written words, which may be hundreds, or even thousands of years old—for example, the Bible or Koran—and totally unrelated to the part of the natural world we inhabit.

In contrast, first peoples are spatially oriented. There are always new experiences and knowledge in the world, and verbal traditions can be adjusted to respond to changing conditions so that instructions for living are fit to the current ecological and historical context. Native knowledge and spirituality derive from the physical and biological environment that is part of daily life. As a result, Native attitudes and beliefs evolve as environmental conditions change, and the knowledge and experience gained through daily interaction with that environment. This is why it is important for Native people to state, "We have survived," because despite major changes in the environment resulting from encounters with Europeans and Western culture, we are still here.

If the environment continues to change to such a degree that the dominant culture cannot survive, Native people will continue to survive. We survived the Ice Age, which lasted longer and had at least as great an ecological impact as the arrival of Europeans. However, to survive we must not allow the Western way of thought, disconnected from nature as it is, to become the dominant way of thought among Native people.

Western spiritual knowledge and instruction is pedagogical and hierarchical, and its holy sites are removed from America in both time and space, relating to events that took place long ago in Europe and the Middle East. As a consequence, the sacred places of people of European descent are in those parts of the world. Europeans still go to visit and renew their spirits at places such as Stonehenge, the Dome of the Rock, the Wailing Wall, Chartres, Lourdes, and so forth. Because their sacred places are on another continent, Americans of European descent do not understand the sacred places of their new home, and treat the entire continent as a place only good for deriving wealth, or shaping to fit their own interests. They do not understand why the Black Hills are sacred to the Lakota people, who view these places as part of their home and their heritage. To Native people, mining or otherwise commercially exploiting the Paha Sapa is equivalent to tearing down Chartres Cathedral or Westminster Abbey.

Regardless of possible profit or reduced traffic congestion, the people of France or England would never tolerate such activities.

WOLF AND NATIVE PEOPLES

> From the dawn of our spiritual and psychological being our closest relative in the wild has been Makuyi. In English, Wolf. (Jack Gladstone, Blackfeet)

All of the predators were respected for their strength and their weapons, but one predator spoke particularly to humans. This was wolf, who lived in family groups and was not strong or swift enough to kill large prey alone. However, wolves working as a group could bring down even the largest plant eaters. As a hunter the wolf did not have the most strength or sharpest claw and teeth. His weapons were patience and perseverance; qualities the first peoples could develop in themselves. Even more important, however, was that if people were to emulate the wolf, they also had to exist to serve the environment and to accept the mutuality (connectedness) of life. As Joseph Marshall has written, "Understanding this reality made them truly of the earth, because every life ultimately gives itself back to the earth."

To the Comanche people, Wolf (Tutseena) was the original creator, who made a world where all things were good, and humans lived with other animals. In the early days of their existence, Wolf taught them how to hunt and to live in families in which each could depend upon all others.

Wolf's younger (little) brother Coyote (Kutseena) was always trying to outsmart others, and while making humans different from other animals (i.e., making culture), Coyote took the Comanche away from Wolf's perfect world. Coyote was different because he did not live closely with others but hunted alone and lived alone with his wife.

While this is an interesting story, it is also based upon careful observation and understanding of the nature of these two species of predator. In other words, it is good science. Wolves, especially on the plains where Comanche lived, lived in big family groups that hunted together, spent lots of time playing with each other, and were devoted parents who would give their lives to protect their children. In contrast, coyotes live alone or in pairs, are much less social, and are much less protective of their offspring. Coyotes do not make good companions for human beings, whereas wolves can be taught to live with people, make good companions for humans, and after several generations can become dogs.

Native people recognized that wolves and their relative, coyote, had relationships to many other creatures, and that these relationships were part of the connectedness of all things. In some cases these relationships were described as friendships, which implied that both participants benefited from the interaction. Western scientists belittled these stories since they failed to fit within the European ecological idea that different species had three possible interactions: (1) predator-prey, (2) competition for limited resources, or (3) indifference.

This is an area where Native knowledge was far ahead of European knowledge, since these stories have only recently been examined by Western science. Once examined, they revealed relationships either previously unknown or misunderstood. For example, a story often told by First Nations was that badger (*Taxidea taxus*) and coyote (*Canis latrans*) were "friends" and wandered about hunting together. Western ecological thought, driven by the idea that competition among species drives community dynamics, categorized the relationship between coyote and badger as competition between these two predators, or perhaps parasitism by coyote.

Recent study revealed that coyotes and badgers hunting ground squirrels each had significantly higher rates of capture when hunting together. Coyotes and badgers wander around together When they see a squirrel, coyote gives chase. If the squirrel goes into a burrow, badger will get it and have a meal. If the squirrel leaves by another burrow, coyote often gets it and has a meal. Both coyote and badger catch more squirrels (and probably more woodchucks, and prairie dogs as well) when they hunt together than when they hunt alone.

Similarly, stories of friendship between wolves (*Canis lupus*) and ravens (*Corvus corax*) have been supported by discoveries that these species may forage cooperatively, and even play games with each other. Ravens fly through the forest and look everywhere for animals that have died. In winter, if a raven spots a carcass that is frozen and too hard for the raven to peck open, it will call loudly, which attracts wolves or coyotes, which then chew open the carcass, making food available for the ravens as well as the wolves. Western scientists studying wolves have realized that Native people have far greater knowledge of the behavior and ecology of wolves than Western science, and have turned to Native people to help them in their study of these animals.

One startling revelation has been that Native people of North America typically considered wolves to be friendly, if cautious, animals that would never attack a human without provocation. This observance has been supported, since there has never been a reported fatal attack upon a human by a wild wolf in the history of North America. This is an apparent contrast to the relationship between wolves and humans in Europe, where there are numerous folktales involving wolves acting as predators upon humans or human analogues, for example, Little Red-Riding Hood, Peter and the Wolf, the Three Little Pigs, and so forth. In addition, Europe is the source of the legend of the werewolf, who was a human who turned into a wolf who preyed upon other humans.

The origins of these European stories are unclear. What is clear, however, is that Europeans hate and fear wolves, and brought this attitude with them to

America. What is distressing is that Europeans seem to be passing on their prejudices to young Native people. A recent study among Native people indicated that elders (over 60 years of age) did not fear wolves and viewed them as brothers; middle-aged people (30–60) did not like wolves but also did not really fear them; however, young people (15–30) feared wolves and stated that they would shoot wolves if they saw them. This is a classic case of Native people being poisoned by the perspective of European attitudes, and like Europeans revealing fear based upon ignorance, for of the people questioned, only the elders had actually seen wild wolves in their lifetimes. Even more ironic, among white people questioned, the results were just the opposite. That is, elders feared and would shoot wolves, and young people thought of them in a positive way.

2

Wars of the Peace Policy, 1869–1886

Robert M. Utley

The Peace Policy aimed at placing all Indians on reservations, where they could be kept away from the settlements and travel routes and where ultimately they could be civilized. The Indians often had other ideas—if not at first, then after they had sampled the reality of life on the reservation. Virtually every major war during the two decades after Appomattox was fought to force Indians onto newly created reservations or to make them go back to reservations from which they had fled. From such a perspective, it is not surprising that warfare characterized the Peace Policy.

As the years passed, moreover, the Peace Policy ceased to command the wide support it had at first. The army, in particular, grew more openly critical. Except for an occasional Lieutenant [Charles] Drew or Colonel [Benjamin] Grierson [known for their humane approaches to Indians], officers scoffed at the notion of conquest by kindness, and they had little use for the idealistic yet often corrupt people and purposes of the Indian Bureau. As General Sheridan remarked simplistically in 1869, "If a white man commits murder or robs, we hang him or send him to the penitentiary; if an Indian does the same, we have been in the habit of giving him more blankets." And as Lieutenant Schyler observed at the Camp Verde [Arizona] Reservation, the Indians "can be governed for the present only with a hand of iron, which is a manner of governing

Extracted and reprinted from Robert M. Utley, *The Indian Frontier of the American West, 1846–1890*, Albuquerque: University of New Mexico Press, 1984, pp. 164–201, by permission of the University of New Mexico Press.

totally unknown to the agents of the Indian Bureau, most of whom are afraid of the Indians and are willing to do anything to conciliate them." Western sentiment, always militant, encouraged the army in its view of the Peace Policy. "Let sniveling Quakers give place to bluff soldiers," ran a typical editorial comment.

Who is friendly and who is not? Military officers not unreasonably asked the civilian authorities. Those on the reservation were friendly and the exclusive responsibility of the Indian Bureau, came the answer; those off the reservation were hostile and the responsibility of the army. Superficially, it seemed a logical solution to a chronic dilemma. It drew a line that no one, including the Indians, could mistake. But as the record of the Fort Sill [Oklahoma] "city of refuge" demonstrated, a reservation could harbor a great many Indians of unfriendly disposition. Unfortunately, except for the rare Satanta [a Kiowa leader] who bragged of his exploits, their individual identities remained unknown or unprovable. Aggravating the army's frustration, garrisons on or near reservations had to watch helplessly while civilian corruption and mismanagement—or so it seemed to them—prodded Indians toward an armed hostility that would have to be suppressed at the risk of army lives. As General Sherman complained to a congressional committee in 1874: "The Indian Bureau keeps feeding and clothing the Indians, till they get fat and saucy, and then we are only notified that the Indians are troublesome, and are going to war, after it is too late to provide a remedy."

Except by government decree, moreover, Indians off the reservation were not necessarily belligerent. They might be out hunting, or headed for a visit with friends in another tribe, or simply wandering about seeing the country. Evan a whole band off the reservation did not automatically mean hostility. Indeed, few such could be clearly labeled friendly or hostile; ambiguity more accurately described their temper. Was Black Kettle's village on the Washita [River, in southern Colorado] friendly or hostile? No chief and no band more diligently pursued peace. Yet it was the trail of a party of Black Kettle's young men, their hands stained with the blood of Kansas settlers, that led Custer's cavalry to the luckless chief's winter lodges. The army never learned to discriminate between the guilty and the innocent, simply because a group of Indians was rarely unmistakably one or the other.

The army did not pursue its Indian-fighting mission very creatively. Occasionally a General Crook recognized his foes as superb guerrilla fighters who called for techniques quite different than had Robert E. Lee's gray legions. Crook fought Indians like Indians and usually, in fact, with Indians. But the army as an institution never evolved a doctrine of Indian warfare, never taught its aspiring officers at West Point the difference between conventional and unconventional war, and never issued official guidance for troops in the field.

Lacking a formal doctrine of unconventional war, the army waged conventional war. Heavy columns of infantry and cavalry, locked to slow-moving supply trains, crawled about the vast western distances in search of Indians, who could scatter and vanish almost instantly. The conventional tactics of the Scott, Casey, and Upton manuals sometimes worked—by routing an adversary that had foolishly decided to stand and fight on the white soldiers' terms, by smashing a village whose inhabitants had grown careless, or by wearing down a quarry through persistent campaigning that made surrender preferable to constant fatigue and insecurity. But most such offensives merely broke down the grain-fed cavalry horses and ended with the troops devoting as much effort to keeping themselves supplied as to chasing Indians.

But when they worked, these offensives worked with a vengeance. They were a forerunner of "total war" against entire populations, as pioneered by Sherman and Sheridan against the Confederacy. Under the guidance and inspiration of these two leaders—the one now general in chief of the army, the other heading the strategic Division of the Missouri, embracing all the Great Plains—the army set forth to find the enemy in their winter camps, to kill or drive them from their lodges, to destroy their ponies, food, and shelter, and to hound them mercilessly across a frigid landscape until they gave up. If women and children got hurt or killed, it was lamentable but justified because it resolved the issue quickly and decisively, and thus more humanely. Although prosecuted along conventional lines and often an exercise in logistical futility, this approach yielded an occasional victory, such as the Washita, that saved it from serious challenge.

No better than the army did the Indians adapt to new conditions. The westward surge of the white people after the Civil War confronted Indians with a crisis of apocalyptic implications, yet they met it, like the army, in the same old ways. Despite the common danger, tribal particularism and intertribal animosities remained as strong as ever. Sometimes tribes came together in alliance against an especially visible threat from the whites, but rarely did such an alliance hang together for very long. Even unity within a tribe proved elusive. Factions differed on how to deal with the white encroachment; some resisted, some accommodated, and some wavered and even oscillated between the two extremes. The highly individual character of tribal society inhibited the rise of leaders who could bring together diverse opinions, and, to make matters worse, the proliferation of "government chiefs" demoralized the traditional political organization. As one astute observer remarked, army officers, Indian superintendents and commissioners, and even agents had created so many chiefs that "Indian chiefs, like brevets in the army, are become so common they are not properly respected."*

Nor did fighting methods change. Indian culture still developed a superb fighting man. Warriors still practiced guerrilla tactics masterfully and made un-

---

*Brevets were soldiers who were temporarily granted higher rank without higher pay.

canny use of terrain, vegetation, and other natural conditions, all to the anguish of their military antagonists. But Indian culture also continued to emphasize the individual and withhold from any man the power of command, except through personal influence. Thus team discipline tended to collapse when opportunities for personal distinction or differing opinions on strategy or tactics arose. Man for man, the warrior far surpassed his blue-clad adversary in virtually every test of military proficiency, but unit for unit—however great the numbers—the Indians could not come close to matching the discipline and organization of the army. When Indians made the mistake of standing and fighting on the army's terms, they usually lost.

In the end, however, the relative fighting qualities of the opponents made little difference. Despite all the wars of the Peace Policy, the Indians did not succumb to military conquest. The army contributed to the final collapse, of course, with "war houses" scattered all through the Indian Country and with campaigns that hastened an outcome ordained by more significant forces. More than the army, railroads, settlements, and all the numbers, technology, and other trappings of an aggressive and highly organized society brought defeat to the Indians. Every white advance came at the expense of resources, especially wild game, essential to the Indian way of life. As the open land and its natural bounty shrank, the reservation offered the only alternative to extinction. For the Indians, General Sherman's jest held deadly portent: "I think it would be wise," he said of the Sioux insistence on hunting on the Republican River, "to invite all the sportsmen of England and America there this fall for a Grand Buffalo hunt, and make one grand sweep of them all."

Yet the Indians' armed resistance to the westward movement, and the army's armed response, form dramatic and significant chapters in the history of both peoples and of the frontiers across which they faced each other. In the Trans-Mississippi West, the final and most intense phase coincided with the final phase of the westward migration and settlement of the whites and was a direct consequence of the Peace Policy's imperative to confine all Indians to reservations.

Kintpuash had tried the reservation and did not like it. An able, ambitious young man, he and other Modoc leaders had signed a treaty in 1864 ceding their homeland among the lake-dotted, lava-scored plateaus of southern Oregon and northern California and had agreed to live on a reservation with Klamaths and Snakes. Homesick, bullied by the more numerous Klamaths, some sixty to seventy families followed Kintpuash back to their old homes on Lost River, just south of the Oregon-California boundary. As more and more whites took up homesteads on the ceded lands, tensions rose. Officials of the Indian Bureau pressed Kintpuash—with other whites, they knew him as Captain Jack—to go back to the reservation. Persuasion failing, they asked the army to use force. That move provoked the Modoc War of 1872–73.

At dawn on November 29, 1872, cavalry attacked the village of Kintpuash. After an exchange of fire, the Indians fled, later crossing Tule Lake in boats. Another party of Modocs, under a leader the whites called Hooker Jim, rode around the east side of the lake, killing settlers along the way. On the lake's southern shore they united in a wild expanse of black lava that nature had piled into a gigantic fortress. They knew its every fissure, cavern, and passageway. Patches of grass subsisted their cattle. Sagebrush and greasewood yielded fuel. Water came from Tule Lake. As the big army that quickly assembled discovered, it could not be penetrated by assault, reduced by artillery bombardment, or taken by siege. It swiftly drew national attention as "Captain Jack's Stronghold."

Kintpuash conducted the defense with great skill. For four months, with only about sixty fighting men, he held off an army whose numbers ultimately approached a thousand. Again the government decided to try diplomacy. A peace commission arrived and erected a lone tent on the plain outside the lava beds. Negotiations commenced. So did Kintpuash's troubles. Factionalism accomplished what an army could not. Hooker Jim and others challenged Kintpuash's course and taunted him for refusing to kill the peace commissioners in a bold stroke aimed at winning a reservation on Lost River. Ridiculed and humiliated, he finally agreed. On Good Friday, April 11, 1873, the Modoc leaders suddenly interrupted the peace talks, drew hidden weapons, and fell on the white negotiators. One escaped, but three were left on the ground shot, stabbed, and stripped. (Miraculously, one later recovered.)

The deed sealed the fate of the Modocs, for the head of the commission was none other than the commander of the military department, Edward R.S. Canby, who thus gained dubious distinction as the only regular army general slain by Indians in the entire history of the Indian Wars. (Others called general, such as Custer, held the rank by brevet or volunteer, not regular, commissions.) Foolishly, the Modocs had called down upon themselves the wrath of an outraged nation. The army responded with more troops and better leadership at the same time that quarrels among the Modoc leadership intensified. Finally the Indians scattered from the lava beds and were run down, group by small group, by pursuing columns of soldiers. On June 1st a detachment found Kintpuash and his family hiding in a cave. His "legs had given out," he explained.

Against people who had treacherously murdered a popular war hero, the precepts of the Peace Policy could not be expected to govern. Kintpuash and three others involved in Canby's death died on the gallows; their heads were cut off and shipped to the Army Medical Museum in Washington. A furious General Sherman demanded that Kintpuash's followers, who had compiled such an extraordinary record of skill and courage in holding the lava beds, be scattered among other tribes, "so that the name of Modoc should cease." In October 1873, 155 in number, they were resettled fifteen hundred miles to the east, in Indian Territory. The name did not cease, but their demand to live in their homeland ceased to be heard.

The Modoc War—more accurately, the slaying of General Canby—badly crippled the Peace Policy. Newspapers everywhere saw it as dramatic evidence that Indians could not be trusted or reasoned with. Whether favoring extermination or civilization, editors judged Canby's death a grievous blow to the Peace Policy. As always, however, events on the Great Plains more profoundly influenced public opinion and shaped policy than those elsewhere in the West. Throughout the 1870s, warfare with the Plains Indians rose to a thunderous finale on the Little Bighorn in 1876 that was almost universally regarded as marking the demise of the Peace Policy. Like the Modoc War, the Plains wars centered chiefly on the issue of whether or not tribes were to live on reservations as demanded by the Peace Policy.

On the southern Plains, the big nomadic tribes had agreed to reservations in the Medicine Lodge treaties. They actually lived there—Kiowas and Comanches at Fort Sill, Cheyennes and Arapahos at Darlington—because General Sheridan's winter operations of 1868–69, especially Custer's persistent and wide-ranging marches, had made fugitive life tiring and insecure. But reservation life proved confining. Clothing and ration issues were scant, of poor quality, and badly selected for Indian wants, and the encroachments of white cattlemen, whiskey peddlers, horse thieves, and other opportunists were unnerving, if not demoralizing. Particularly ominous to Indians, white hunters slaughtered the buffalo for their hides alone, leaving carcasses by the hundreds of thousands to rot on the prairies. Kiowas and Comanches regularly raided in Texas and Mexico, as they always had, while Cheyennes and Arapahos raided less often in Kansas. Discontent and mutual aggression finally boiled over in the Red River War of 1874–75.

For a time, while Satanta and Big Tree languished in the Texas penitentiary and the government held 124 women and children seized in an attack on a fugitive Comanche village, reservation-based raiders had restrained themselves. But the release of these captives, in exchange for promises of good behavior, had removed the restraint. The spring and summer of 1874 found Indians raiding in Texas and Kansas with new ferocity. In particular, Comanches and Cheyennes attacked a camp of white hide-hunters at Adobe Walls in the Texas Panhandle, where Kit Carson had fought the Kiowas in 1864, and Kiowas under Lone Wolf ambushed a detachment of Texas Rangers near the site of the Salt Creek Massacre of 1871. These aggressions provoked the government to lift the ban against military operations on Indian reservations. Suddenly army officers at the Fort Sill and Darlington agencies were compiling lists of "friendly" Indians. Everyone else, sure to be classed as "hostiles," headed west, beyond the reservation boundaries. Some eighteen hundred Cheyennes, two thousand Comanches, and one thousand Kiowas moved in large encampments among the breaks surrounding the headwaters of the Washita River and the various forks of the Red, in the Texas Panhandle—hence the designation "Red River War."

Suddenly this country, hitherto so remote and secure, swarmed with soldiers. From north, east, south, and west, five columns converged. One routed the Indians at the base of the caprock near the mouth of Palo Duro Canyon. Another fell on a Comanche village nestled deep in the canyon itself. August sun parched the land and dried the water holes. September brought days of rain, bank-full streams, prairies of mud, and an ordeal the Indians remembered as "the wrinkled-hand chase." Winter loosed blizzards and numbing cold. Through it all, the soldiers kept after the Indians. There were few clashes and little bloodshed, but gradually the exhaustion of the chase, the discomforts of weather and hunger, and, above all, the constant gnawing fear of soldiers storming into their camps at dawn wore them down. As early as October, some had tired and drifted back to the reservation. By the spring of 1875, all had returned.

At the agencies the Indians discovered white officials behaving with a sternness uncharacteristic of the Peace Policy. Throughout the winter, as parties straggled in from the West, army officers confined leaders who were somewhat capriciously judged guilty of particular "crimes" or simply of functioning as "ringleaders." Satanta found no disposition toward leniency; back he went to the Texas penitentiary, where three years later, in despair, he threw himself from an upper window to his death. As spring came to Fort Sill, soldiers herded seventy-four Indians, shackled and chained, aboard eight wagons. Among them were such noted chiefs as Gray Bear, Minimic, and Medicine Water of the Cheyennes; Lone Wolf, Woman's Heart, and White Horse of the Kiowas; and Black Horse of the Comanches. With women wailing their grief, the caravan moved out and headed for the railroad. After days of travel the Indians, so recently at large on the Staked Plains, found themselves enclosed by the thick walls and bastions of an ancient Spanish fortress on the Florida coast.

The army had gained a clear victory, not only over the Indians but over the more extreme proponents of the Peace Policy. From his Chicago headquarters General Sheridan had directed the strategy of convergence. Generals John Pope and Christopher C. Augur had overseen its execution. At least two field officers, Colonels Nelson A. Miles and Ranald S. Mackenzie, had won great distinction in carrying it out. Both had gained battlefield victories, Miles in the caprock fight, and Mackenzie in the celebrated charge into Palo Duro Canyon. But in the end it was not combat success but convergence, unremittingly prosecuted, that had won the war. Confinement of the "ringleaders" far from their homes and families helped ensure that another war would not occur. Never again did Kiowas, Comanches, Cheyennes, or Arapahos revolt against their reservation overlords. Never again did Texas and Kansas settlers suffer aggression from these tribes. Nor did Generals Sherman and Sheridan forget the lessons of the Red River War as they turned their attention to the northern Plains.

Here, Sioux, Northern Cheyenne, and Northern Arapaho had yet to be finally brought within the reservation system. Oglalas and Brulés drew rations at the Red Cloud and Spotted Tail agencies in northwestern Nebraska, where these two chiefs maneuvered tortuously between the opposing forces of white officialdom and their own people. Other Sioux formed tenuous connections with agencies along the Missouri River, the eastern border of the Great Sioux Reservation—Hunkpapas and Blackfeet at Grand River, Miniconjous and Sans Arc at Cheyenne River, and still others at Crow Creek and Lower Brulé. Cheyennes and Arapahos mingled with Sioux at Red Cloud. In all, these agencies counted perhaps twenty-five thousand adherents.

But the strength of the adherence wavered with the seasons and the competing influence of rival chiefs, for off to the west roamed a hard core of kinsmen who had no intention of abandoning the free life of the chase for the dubious attractions of the reservation. They looked for leadership to a chief of surpassing influence. Of compelling countenance and commanding demeanor, quick of thought and emphatic of judgment, Sitting Bull held power not only as war and political chief but also as religious functionary. "He had a big brain and a good one," recalled an old warrior, "a strong heart and a generous one." At the agency Indians he hurled a taunt: "You are fools to make yourselves slaves to a piece of fat bacon, some hard-tack, and a little sugar and coffee." And in fact, many did not. Nothing prevented them from sampling the old hunting life in the summer and the hardtack and coffee in winter. Back and forth they shuttled between the agencies and the camps of Sitting Bull and other "nontreaty" chiefs.

These "northern Indians" stirred up constant trouble. While on the reservation, they kept the agencies in turmoil, for they were ungovernable, a danger to white officials, and a bad influence on the agency Indians. While off the reservation, they did not always keep to the unceded hunting grounds guaranteed by the Treaty of 1868, but sometimes raided along the Platte and among the Montana settlements at the head of the Missouri and Yellowstone rivers.

That the whites called them hostiles and accused them of breaking the treaty while also enjoying its bounty did not bother these hunting bands. They could point to some treaty violations by the other side as well. For one thing, in 1873 surveyors laid out a route for the Northern Pacific Railroad along the northern margins of the unceded territory. For another, and most infuriating, in 1874 "Long Hair" Custer led his soldiers into the Black Hills, part of the Great

Sioux Reservation itself, and there found gold. Miners swarmed into the Indian country, and the government, making only a token effort to keep them out, hesitatingly broached the subject of buying the part of the reservation that contained the Black Hills. Then, later in 1875, runners arrived in the winter camps of the hunting bands with a stern message from the Great Father: Come to the agencies at once or be considered hostiles against whom the army would make war.

They ignored the summons, and as spring turned to summer in 1876 they discovered blue columns converging on their hunting grounds. In March, one attacked an Oglala camp on Powder River but bungled the follow-up and retreated under assaults of bitter cold and deep snow. As the snow melted, the fugitive camps swelled. Worsening conditions at the agencies, the Black Hills issue, and the attempt to take away the freedom to roam the unceded territory set off an unusually large spring migration of agency Indians to the camps of the hunting bands. June found them coming together in a village that steadily expanded as it moved slowly westward across the streams flowing northward into the Yellowstone. These Indians were not looking for a fight, but, as never before, they were proud, confident, and at the height of their power. Chiefs of ability fortified the leadership of Sitting Bull—Black Moon, Gall, Hump, Lame Deer, Dirty Moccasins, Lame White Man, and the incomparable Crazy Horse. Since his triumph as head of the party that decoyed Captain Fetterman out of Fort Phil Kearny ten years earlier, Crazy Horse had emerged as a splendid war leader and uncompromising foe of reservations.

By mid-June the Indians camped on a creek that ran into a river they knew as the Greasy Grass. Earlier, on the Rosebud, they had staged their annual Sun Dance. Sitting Bull had experienced a vision, in which he saw many dead soldiers "falling right into our camp." The people had thrilled to the image and the promise. Now scouts brought word of soldiers marching down the Rosebud. Crazy Horse led a large force to do battle. For six hours they fought, and after the Indians called off the fight the soldiers retreated.

But this was not the triumph foretold by Sitting Bull. Soldiers had not fallen into their camp. Down to the Greasy Grass the village moved, and here the largest number yet of agency Indians joined the alliance. Six separate tribal circles—Hunkpapa, Oglala, Miniconjou, Sans Arc, Blackfoot, Northern Cheyenne—extended for three miles along the banks of the Greasy Grass. The village probably counted twelve hundred lodges and mustered almost two thousand fighting men.

True to Sitting Bull's prophecy, many soldiers were in fact about to fall into this village. As in the Red River War, General Sheridan had plotted a strategy of convergence. Advancing from the south, General Crook had struck the camp on Powder River on March 17 but had been driven back at the Battle of the

Rosebud on June 17. Meantime, General Alfred H. Terry approached from the east, and Colonel John Gibbon from the west. They joined on the Yellowstone at the mouth of the Rosebud. From here Terry launched a striking force of some six hundred cavalry, under the same Long Hair Custer who had invaded the Black Hills two years earlier. Custer followed the Indian trail up the Rosebud, across the Wolf Mountains, and down to the Greasy Grass, which his map labeled the Little Bighorn. The village there, because of the recent arrivals of agency Indians, contained about three times as many warriors as he had expected. On the scorching Sunday of June 25, 1876, his soldiers fell into it.

George Armstrong Custer presided over one of the most complete disasters in American military annals. A century later it still commanded public fascination and fueled heated controversy. More immediately, the Sioux and Cheyennes discovered what the Modocs had so painfully learned; the slaying of a big white chief could spell the doom of a people. Custer's Last Stand shocked and outraged Americans, shook the Peace Policy to the verge of collapse, brought a flood of soldiers to the Indian Country, and afforded rationalization for forcing the agency chiefs, hitherto held back by the militant opposition of the northern Indians, to sell the Black Hills. An "agreement"— it resembled a treaty in all but name—legitimized the sale. For the Sioux and Cheyennes, final defeat lurked unseen in their soaring victory amid the brown hills overlooking the Greasy Grass.

Once again, winter combined with soldiers who could brave its blasts destroyed Indian resistance. Until the first snows the Sioux and Cheyennes, now fragmented in bands, easily eluded the big armies that ponderously gave chase. But winter, as usual, made them vulnerable. In the frigid, misty dawn of November 25, 1876, eleven hundred cavalrymen under Colonel Ranald S. Mackenzie burst into the Cheyenne village of Dull Knife and Little Wolf in a canyon of the Bighorn Mountains. Forty Cheyennes died, and the rest watched helplessly from the bluffs as the soldiers burned their tipis, clothing, and winter food supply. That night the temperature plunged to thirty below zero. Eleven babies froze to death at their mothers' breasts.

The suffering Cheyennes took refuge with Crazy Horse, but the soldiers tracked down these people too. In January 1877, on Tongue River, Sioux and Cheyenne warriors clashed with "walk-a-heap" bluecoats in a fight that petered out in a blinding blizzard. These soldiers had built a rude fort at the mouth of the Tongue, and they kept to the field all winter. Tired and discouraged, the Indians opened talks with the soldier chief at this fort. He wore a huge overcoat, and they called him "Bear's Coat." He was the same Colonel Nelson A. Miles who had so resolutely pursued the southern Plains tribes in the Red River War.

Bear's Coat's combination of fight and talk, together with peace feelers put out from Red Cloud Agency through the agency chiefs, gradually strengthened the peace elements in the hostile camps. Spring saw the surrender of almost all the fugitives. On May 6, 1877, Crazy Horse led his Oglalas into the Red Cloud Agency and threw his weapons on the ground in token of surrender. Four months later, amid circumstances that are still confusing, he died in a guardhouse scuffle, stabbed by either a soldier's bayonet or another Indian's knife. "It is good," said a fellow chief sadly, "he has looked for death and it has come."

The previous October, in a tense meeting between the lines, Sitting Bull told Bear's Coat that the Great Spirit had made him an Indian, and not an agency Indian. Rather than go to the reservation, he had led his people northward to the land of the "Great Mother." He got along well with her redcoats [Royal Canadian Mounted Police], but he and his people could not find enough food. Bear's Coat watched the boundary line like a hawk and prevented them from riding into Montana to hunt buffalo. Year after year, as they grew hungrier and hungrier, families and groups slipped away to surrender and go to the reservation. At last, in July 1881, Sitting Bull and about fifty families presented themselves at Fort Buford, Montana, the last vestige of the mighty alliance that had overwhelmed Long Hair Custer five years earlier. Sitting Bull handed his rifle to his eight-year-old son and told him to give it to the soldier chief. "I wish it to be remembered," he said, "that I was the last man of my tribe to surrender my rifle, and this day have given it to you."

By 1881, when the surrender of Sitting Bull marked the close of the Plains wars, all tribes of the American West save one had been compelled by military force to go to, or return to, their reservations. Of them all, only the Apaches had not yet been made to face the truth that the reservation represented their only possible destiny. At one place or another in the Southwest, Apache warfare had been virtually continuous since Spanish colonial times. In the early 1870s General Crook had seemed to be on the verge of ending it permanently. His masterful Tonto Basin campaign of 1872–73 had brought about the collapse of the most troublesome Apache groups and their confinement on the reservations set up earlier by Vincent Colyer and General Howard. But Crook went north in 1875, to do less than brilliantly against the Sioux, and the iron military regime relaxed. At the same time the Indian Bureau decided to do away with the multiplicity of small reservations and to concentrate all Apaches west of the Rio Grande on a single reservation. A hot, barren, malarial flat along Arizona's Gila River, San Carlos was a terrible place to live. The final phases of Indian warfare in the United States grew out of the refusal of two powerful Apache leaders and their followers to settle permanently on the San Carlos Reservation.

These leaders were Victorio and Geronimo. Victorio, of the Mimbres, had learned his skills from the great Mangas Coloradas, whom he equaled in courage, stamina, cunning, and leadership. He wanted peace with the whites, and for a time, with Loco, he had pursued it. But soon he saw that few whites were as trustworthy as the good Lieutenant Drew, and the command to settle at San Carlos banished all such notions. Geronimo, of the Chiricahuas, emerged as a leader shortly after the death of Cochise in 1874. Short, thick, scowling, and ill-tempered, he exhibited few appealing traits, even to his own people. But of all Apache leaders, his cousin later remembered, "Geronimo seemed to be the most intelligent and resourceful as well as the most vigorous and farsighted. In times of danger he was a man to be relied upon." No less than Victorio did Geronimo find the order to move to San Carlos in 1876 offensive.

For two years, 1877–79, Victorio tried to find a solution to the dilemma that the government's concentration program had thrust upon him. He even attempted to live at San Carlos. "That horrible summer!" recalled one of his followers. "There was nothing but cactus, rattlesnakes, heat, rocks, and insects. No game; no edible plants. Many, many of our people died of starvation." Victorio also tried to live on his old reservation at Ojo Caliente, but the government had decided to close that place down. He tried to settle with the Mescaleros on the Fort Stanton Reservation, east of the Rio Grande, but that did not work. In fact, nothing worked, and on September 4, 1879, he and sixty warriors attacked a contingent of black cavalrymen near Ojo Caliente in the opening clash of the Victorio War.

In Texas, New Mexico, and Chihuahua, Victorio exacted a terrible price for the government's attempt to put him at San Carlos. With fresh numbers from the Mescalero Reservation, he counted between 125 and 150 warriors. Here and there they darted with lightning speed, cutting down isolated sheepherders and waylaying hapless travelers. Time and again they eluded the soldiers, both American and Mexican, who combed the mountains and deserts in an exhausting and mostly vain effort to destroy the marauders. In July 1880, in the hot, barren wastes of western Texas, Victorio found himself, for a change, thwarted by hard-riding units of black troopers who expertly kept him from the few waterholes and ultimately forced him into Mexico. Hungry, destitute, and low on ammunition, the raiders began to tire. Eastward they drifted, into the parched deserts of Chihuahua, seemingly without plan or purpose. By October 1880 they camped amid three low peaks rising from the vast desert plain—Tres Castillos, the Mexicans called them.

At dawn on October 15 the Apaches awoke to the crash of gunfire and the shouts of Mexican soldiers and Tarahumara Indian allies. Their horse herd lost, the Indians scrambled up the boulder-strewn slope of one of the hills, and there they fought back. All day and into the night the two sides exchanged fire.

In the dark the Indians tried to slip away, but failed. Singing the death chant, they turned to throwing up rock fortifications for a fight to the last. At daybreak they watched as the Mexicans began filtering upward among the boulders. The struggle was desperate and bloody and, in its final stages, hand-to-hand. When the smoke and dust cleared, seventy-eight Apaches lay dead among the rocks and another sixty-eight were herded together as captives. Among the dead was Victorio.

At the time of Victorio's death, Geronimo was living, none too contentedly, at San Carlos. Besides its repugnant natural conditions, the reservation festered with intrigue, intertribal rivalries, incompetent and corrupt agents, and conflict between civil and military officials. White settlers pressed in on the reservation boundaries. Almost any spark could touch off an explosion. It came in August 1881. A medicine man had been preaching a new religion that whites regarded as incendiary. In an attempt to arrest him, the army got into a fight with his followers, shot and killed the prophet, and had to quell a mutiny among the Apache scouts. Frightened by the resulting military activity, Geronimo and other leaders, with seventy-four people, broke out and headed for Mexico.

An especially daring raid in the following spring drew attention to the deteriorating state of affairs in Arizona. Geronimo and others swooped down on San Carlos, killed the police chief, and forced old Loco and several hundred people to return to Mexico with them. That event prodded the government to decisive action. Early in September 1882 a familiar figure reappeared in Arizona—the "Gray Fox," General Crook. At once he clamped military rule on San Carlos. To keep the peace here and later to go after the "renegades" in Mexico, he recruited five companies of Apache scouts—"the wildest I could get"—and placed them under his brightest, most energetic young officers. Skilled packers organized efficient and sturdy mule trains. No cumbersome wagons would limit mobility.

The Sierra Madre of Mexico had always afforded Apaches an impregnable fortress. Its steep ridges, piled one on another toward towering peaks and perpetually shadowing plunging gorges and canyons walled in vertical rock, sheltered and protected these Indians and provided secure bases for raiding in all directions, on both sides of the international border. One Chiricahua group, the Nednhis, had made this wilderness their home for generations. Their chief, Juh, surpassed all others in power. Geronimo, Nachez (son of Cochise), Chata, Chihuahua, Loco, Bonito, battle-scarred old Nana (who had ridden with Victorio but had escaped Tres Castillos), and others deferred to Juh. But one day Juh fell from a cliffside trail to his death, and increasingly the captains of the Apaches in the Sierra Madre looked to Geronimo for guidance. From their mountain lairs they continued to raid. In a foray of special ferocity, in March

1883 Chato and twenty-five warriors slashed across Arizona and New Mexico, and then faded back into Mexico. In response, Crook marched.

A surprise attack by Apache scouts on Chato's camp high in the Sierra Madre gave notice to all the fugitives that their fortress had been breached. Where Mexican troops had never ventured, Americans had penetrated, and at the head of other Apaches. It came as enough of a shock that one by one the band leaders drifted in to talk with the Gray Fox. Geronimo, who had been raiding in Chihuahua, came last. Squatting around smoky campfires, the Indians listened to the harsh words of this general who so uncharacteristically wore a canvas suit and rode a mule. Surrender, he told them in a threat that he and all his listeners knew he could not carry out, or he would kill them all. At night, in long arguments among themselves, the chiefs debated what to do. Crook's success in reaching them in previously inaccessible refuges, combined with his ability to enlist their own people against them, tipped the balance. "We give ourselves up," Geronimo at last announced, "do with us as you please."

The surrender turned out to be only temporary. Back at San Carlos, tensions began building almost at once. A people accustomed to freedom found military rule irksome; the men especially bridled at the ban on beating their wives and on brewing the volatile intoxicant *tiswin*. In May 1885 off they went again, some 134 people, including Geronimo, Nachez, Chihuahua, and Nana. Once again they hid themselves deep in the Sierra Madre. Once again they discovered white officers leading their own people against them. And once again they quickly tired of keeping always on the run, always apprehensive of a sudden surprise attack. They sent word to the officer in charge of one of the scout units, Captain Emmet Crawford, that they wanted to talk. But before a meeting could be arranged, Mexican militia attacked the scouts, and the captain fell with a bullet in his brain. Later Geronimo and others met with Crawford's lieutenant, Marion P. Maus, and told him they wanted to talk with General Crook.

The meeting took place at Canyon de los Embudos, twelve miles south of the border, on March 25, 1886. Seated on the sides of a pleasantly shaded ravine, the general and the Apaches parleyed. As he had done two years earlier, Crook spoke sternly. Now the terms were harsher. The men with families must go to a place of confinement in the East for two years, and only then could they return to San Carlos. Otherwise, Crook vowed, "I'll keep after you and kill the last one, if it takes fifty years." After two days of argument among themselves, the Apache chiefs accepted Crook's terms. While the general hastened north to telegraph the good news to his superiors, the Indians moved slowly toward the border. Along the way they found a whiskey peddler. In the midst of a drinking bout Geronimo and Nachez had second thoughts. With twenty men and thirteen women, they stampeded back to the Sierra Madre.

This development profoundly discouraged General Crook. Worse, it brought him into conflict with General Sheridan, who had succeeded Sherman as head of the army. Sheridan had never trusted the Apache scouts, and he thought Crook should use regulars instead. Now he issued orders that not only implicitly criticized Crook's methods but required him to break his word to the Indians who had not fled with Geronimo and Nachez. Rather than carry out such orders, Crook asked to be relieved. Sheridan lost no time in dispatching a replacement, Nelson A. Miles, now a brigadier general. It was a hard blow to the Gray Fox, for he and Miles had long been bitter rivals, personally as well as professionally. Bear's Coat welcomed the chance to succeed where Crook had failed.

Astutely, Miles made a great show of employing regular soldiers against the Apaches, but in the end he quietly adopted Crook's methods. Apache scouts combed the Sierra Madre, keeping the quarry on the run. As a special peace emissary, Miles sent Lieutenant Charles B. Gatewood, whom the Indians knew as a friend, to see if he could find and persuade them to give up. Ironically, Gatewood was a Crook protégé.

As in the past, the little band of fugitives soon tired of running. On August 24, 1886, they admitted Gatewood and two Indian companions to their camp. At considerable peril to his life, Gatewood stated the new terms: The Apaches must go to Florida and wait for the President to decide their ultimate fate. Geronimo said he and Nachez would give up, but only if they could return to San Carlos. Then Gatewood played his high card. At San Carlos Geronimo would find none of his kinsmen, only rival tribes. All the Chiricahuas, even those who had loyally served Crook as scouts, had been herded aboard railway cars and deported to Florida. Stunned, the Indians debated for a long time, but at last they told Gatewood that they would give up to General Miles personally. In Skeleton Canyon, just north of the border, Geronimo faced Miles and handed over his rifle.

A trainload of Apaches rattling across the Arizona desert toward far-off Florida signaled the end of armed resistance to the reservation system. Every important Indian war since 1870 had been essentially a war not of concentration but of rebellion—of Indians rebelling against reservations they had already accepted in theory if not in fact. Geronimo and his tiny band of followers were the last holdouts, and they only because the wilds of Mexico offered them a haven denied to most other tribes. Thus the wars of the peace policy, and indeed the Indian wars of the United States, came to a close in Skeleton Canyon, Arizona, on September 4, 1886.

For Further Reading

ON AMERICAN INDIANS AND THE NATURAL ENVIRONMENT

Bol, Marsha C., ed. *Stars Above, Earth Below: American Indians and Nature.* Niwot, CO: Robert Rinehart Publishers, 1998.

Cornell, George. "Native Perceptions of the Environment." *Northeast Quarterly* 7, 1990.

Cronon, William and Richard White. "Indians in the Land." *American Heritage* 37, 1986.

Deloria, Vine, Jr. *Red Earth, White Lies: Native Americans and the Myth of Scientific Fact.* Golden, CO: Fulcrum Publishing, 1997.

Hughes, Donald J. *American Indian Ecology.* El Paso: Texas Western Press, 1983.

Interpress Columnists Service, ed. *Story Earth: Native Voices on the Environment.* San Francisco: Mercury House, 1993.

Jacobs, Wilbur R. "Indians as Ecologists and Other Environmental Themes in American Frontier History." In Christopher Vecsey and Robert W. Venables, eds., *American Indian Environments: Ecological Issues in Native American History.* Syracuse, NY: Syracuse University Press, 1980.

Krech, Shepard, III. *The Ecological Indian: Myth and History.* New York: W.W. Norton & Co., 1999.

Lewis, David Rich. *Neither Wolf nor Dog: American Indians, Environment, and Agrarian Change.* New York: Oxford University Press, 1994.

Marshall, Joseph, III. *On Behalf of the Wolf and the First Peoples.* Santa Fe, NM: Red Crane Books, 1995.

Martin, Calvin. "The Indian and the Ecological Movement." Epilogue to *Keepers of the Game: Indian and Animal Relations and the Fur Trade.* Berkeley: University of California Press, 1979.

Overholt, Thomas W. "American Indians as 'Natural Ecologists.' " *American Indian Journal* 5, 1979.

Powell, Bernard. "Were These America's First Ecologists?" *Journal of the West* 26, 1987.

Regan, Tom. "Environmental Ethics and the Ambiguity of the Native Americans' Relationship with Nature." In Tom Regan, ed., *All That Dwells Therein: Animal Rights and Environmental Ethics.* Berkeley: University of California Press, 1982.

Ross, Thomas E. and Tyrel G. Moore, eds. *A Cultural Geography of North American Indians.* Boulder, CO: Westview Press, 1987.

Turner, Allen C. *The Kaibab Paiute Indians: An Ecological History.* New Haven, CT: Human Relations Area Files, 1985.

Vecsey, Christopher and Robert W. Venables, eds. *American Indian Environments: Ecological Issues in Native American History.* Syracuse, NY: Syracuse University Press, 1980.

Waller, David. "Friendly Fire: When Environmentalists Dehumanize American Indians." *American Indian Culture and Research Journal* 20, 1996.

White, Richard. "Indian Peoples and the Natural World: Asking the Right Questions." In Donald L. Fixico, ed., *Rethinking American Indian History.* Albuquerque: University of New Mexico Press, 1997.

———, guest ed. "American Indian Environmental History." Special edition of *Environmental Review* 9, 1985.

——— and William Cronon. "Ecological Changes and Indian-White Relations." In William C. Sturtevant, ed., *Handbook of North American Indians,* vol. 4. Washington, D.C.: Smithsonian Institution, 1988.

ON THE MILITARY CAMPAIGNS AND THE INDIAN WARS

Bender, Norman. *New Hope for the Indians: The Grant Peace Policy and the Navajos in the 1870s.* Albuquerque: University of New Mexico Press, 1989.

Billington, Monroe Lee. *New Mexico's Buffalo Soldiers, 1866–1900.* Boulder: University Press of Colorado, 1991.

Brown, Dee. *Bury My Heart at Wounded Knee: An Indian History of the American West.* New York: Holt, Rinehart, and Winston, 1970.

Dobak, William H. *Ft. Riley and Its Neighbors: Military Money and Economic Growth, 1853–1895.* Norman: University of Oklahoma Press, 1998.

Greene, Jerome A. *Yellowstone Command: Colonel Nelson A. Miles and the Great Sioux War, 1876–1877.* Lincoln: University of Nebraska Press, 1991.

Hagan, William T. "How the West Was Lost." In Frederick E. Hoxie and Peter Iverson, eds., *Indians in American History: An Introduction.* Wheeling, IL: Harlan Davidson, 1998.

Hardorff, Richard G. *Hokahey! A Good Day to Die!: The Indian Casualties of the Custer Fight.* Lincoln: University of Nebraska Press, 1999.

———, ed. *Cheyenne Memories of the Custer Fight.* Spokane, WA: Arthur H. Clark, 1995.

———, ed. *Lakota Recollections of the Custer Fight: New Sources of Indian-Military History.* Spokane, WA: Arthur H. Clarke, 1991.

Jackson, Helen Hunt. *A Century of Dishonor: A Sketch of the United States Government's Dealings with Some of the Indian Tribes*. New York: Harpers Brothers, 1881.

Kenner, Charles L. *Buffalo Soldiers and Officers of the Ninth Cavalry, 1867–1898: Black and White Together*. Norman: University of Oklahoma Press, 1999.

Knight, Oliver and Sherry L. Smith. *Following the Indian Wars: The Story of the Newspaper Correspondents among the Indian Campaigns*. Norman: University of Oklahoma Press, 1993.

Leckie, William H. *The Buffalo Soldiers: A Narrative of the Negro Cavalry in the West*. Norman: University of Oklahoma Press, 1967.

Leiker, James N. *Racial Borders: Black Soldiers along the Rio Grande*. College Station: Texas A&M University Press, 2002.

Powers, Ramon and James N. Leiker. "Cholera among the Plains Indians: Perceptions, Causes, Consequences." *Western Historical Quarterly* 29, 1998.

Robinson, Charles M. *A Good Year to Die: The Story of the Great Sioux War*. New York: Random House, 1995.

Schubert, Frank N. *Black Valor: Buffalo Soldiers and the Medal of Honor, 1870–1898*. Wilmington, DE: Scholarly Resources, 1997.

———. *Buffalo Soldiers, Braves, and the Brass: The Story of Ft. Robinson, Nebraska*. Shippensburg, PA: White Mane Publishing, 1993.

Smith, Sherry L. *Sagebrush Soldiers: Private William Earl Smith's View of the Sioux War of 1876*. Norman: University of Oklahoma Press, 1989.

———. *The View from Officers' Row: Army Perceptions of Western Indians*. Tucson: University of Arizona Press, 1990.

Utley, Robert M. *Cavalier in Buckskin: George Armstrong Custer and the Western Military Front*. Norman: University of Oklahoma Press, 1988.

———. *A Clash of Cultures: Ft. Bowie and the Chiracahua Apaches*. Washington, D.C.: U.S. Department of the Interior, National Park Service, 1977.

———. *Custer Battlefield: A History and Guide to the Battle of the Little Big Horn*. Washington, D.C.: U.S. Department of the Interior, National Park Service, 1988.

———. *Frontier Regulars: The United States Army and the Indian, 1866–1891*. New York: Macmillan, 1973.

———. *Frontiersmen in Blue: The United States Army and the Indian, 1848–1865*. New York: Macmillan, 1967.

———. *The Indian Frontier of the American West, 1846–1890*. Albuquerque: University of New Mexico Press, 1984.

——— and Wilcomb E. Washburn. *The American Heritage History of the Indian Wars*. New York: American Heritage, 1977.

II

The 1890s and Early 1900s: Assimilation and Its Implications

The end of the nineteenth century and the first few decades of the twentieth century were years in which American Indians had to confront an overt attempt to be assimilated into mainstream society. The acculturation started soon after the end of the Indian wars, when American Indians were trying to adjust to reservation life. In 1887 Congress passed the General Allotment Act (or the Dawes Act), which authorized the president of the United States to allot lands on reservations to individual Indians. The idea was to break traditional tribalism by making Indians into independent land-owning farmers, even though the U.S. government would hold the land in severalty (as a trust title). The policy was irrespective of any past agricultural methods Indians engaged in, including a division of labor in which women were the primary agriculturists in most indigenous societies. In the next fifty years Indians lost nearly 90 million of their 138 million acres of reservation land to allotment. And while there has been much written on the Dawes Act, Elizabeth James-Stern offers a noteworthy case study here on how the Nez Perces of Idaho confronted it in their own unique way of "disinterest or outright resistance."

Another method used with the goal of assimilating American Indians was to try to indoctrinate their children with a European-American–style education. "Reform"-minded Americans, believing that education could provide a "civilizing effect" on Indians, established both on- and off-reservation boarding schools and industrial training schools. Conformity was key at these places; Indian children were not allowed to wear native dress, speak their tribal languages, or practice their own customs. Indian boys were not allowed to wear their hair long or in braids. Brutal punishment was used to enforce the rules. Many children ran away from the schools, but if caught, were treated harshly upon their return. Margaret Connell Szasz explores the history of this federal Indian education in her chapter on the topic. Both private churches and the Bureau of Indian Affairs* were involved with the various schools for Indians around the country, but as Dr. Szasz concludes, the education policy was "a notorious example of bureaucratic inefficiency and ineffectiveness."

In response to the suffering and distress of so many American Indians during these years, a movement arose that provided a sense of hope. It was started in Nevada by a Paiute Indian named Wovoka and spread very quickly from the Great Basin to the Great Plains. Wovoka became a prophet for many Native Americans by offering a vision of "revitalization"—a return to the life Indians knew before colonization by Anglo-Americans. The movement was characterized by the Ghost Dance, the history of which is detailed in a chapter here by L.G. Moses.

All of these policies and responses occurred during what is often referred to as the Progressive Era. Federal Indian policy during those years, however, is rarely examined in U.S. history textbooks or in works on American Indian history. Thus, the final chapter in this section fills in these gaps. Here, Russel Barsh examines federal Indian policy during the days of presidents Theodore Roosevelt, William Howard Taft, and Woodrow Wilson by looking at the philosophies that fueled the decision making, the bureaucracy involved, and the historical context in which the policies were enacted. He concludes by arguing that Indian policy then was a harbinger for policies to come.

Space constraints prevent discussion of other vital aspects of American Indian history (e.g., the role of Native Americans in World War I) during this time period. For those interested in such topics, please refer to the list of additional reading at the end of Part II.

---

*The Bureau of Indian Affairs (BIA) was established in 1824 as part of the War Department. It was shifted to the Department of the Interior in 1849, where it remains today.

3

Becoming a Community: The Nez Perces Confront the Dawes Act

Elizabeth James-Stern

In November 1892, a man from Lewiston, Idaho, reported a terrifying experience on the Nez Perce reservation in north Idaho. Traveling across the reservation, he had stopped in a picturesque valley to camp overnight. In the middle of the night, he awoke to find his camp the site of a spectral battle—ghosts, he reported, of Nez Perce warriors engaged "in deadly conflict." The apparitions seemed to pay no attention to the traveler as they engaged their battle, but the intensity of their combat frightened him so badly he fled into the darkness. When he related his experience to Nez Perce elders, they told the man he had witnessed a prophecy—this appearance always preceded disaster for the tribe, whether pestilence, famine, or war.

At that moment, the Nez Perce tribe stood on the brink of significant change. The reservation had just undergone allotment, and negotiations to open the reservation to non-Indian settlers were about to begin. At the end of the nineteenth century, Nez Perce life had already undergone profound transformations. Missionaries, treaties, and military conflict all brought changes to Northwest Indians long before this 1892 portent. But for the Nez Perces, the surrender of 500,000 acres of their reservation and the manner in which it was done would begin to reshape their community.

Prior to contact, the Nez Perces lived in scattered autonomous villages along the Snake, Clearwater, Salmon, and Wallowa rivers of the interior

This chapter was originally a paper presented at the 40th Annual Conference of the Western History Association, San Antonio, TX, October 11–14, 2000.

Northwest. They frequently gathered for a variety of social, economic, and political purposes, but beyond the local community, adhered to little in the way of formal or compulsory organization. Throughout the nineteenth century, European Americans introduced centralized institutions to the Nez Perces, including a head chief system and Protestant religious hierarchies. These structures have been charged with creating dissension and tribal factionalism that may not have otherwise existed. This allegation has been overemphasized, but the development of centralized institutions did alter social and political life for the Nez Perces.

Missionary Henry Spalding and subagent for Oregon Indian Affairs Elijah White created the position of head chief among the Nez Perces in 1842. Within five years, Lawyer, a relatively minor leader from the Kamiah area, became head chief and held the position until his death thirty years later. In that period, he oversaw two major treaties with the United States, the second of which ceded the Wallowa Valley and eventually led the Wallowa and Salmon River Nez Perces to war against the U.S. army.

Presbyterian missionary sisters Sue and Kate McBeth proselytized and pursued an assimilationist program among the Nez Perces beginning in the 1870s. They focused their efforts on preparing young men for seminary training and teaching women European American housekeeping. They helped create an elite among Presbyterian Nez Perces by venerating their students and vilifying the unconverted. These two institutions, the head chief system and the Presbyterian power structure, worked in tandem. They attempted to break down traditional systems, but the beneficiaries and heirs of centralized authority used the new structure to the tribe's advantage when they needed to respond to pressure for land cessions in 1892.

Missionaries and government agents tried to advance the assimilation program with a consolidated tribal political structure, but the new leaders in this system sacrificed their individual authority in favor of acting as tribal representatives. They faced a formidable challenge in the form of the Dawes Act. The legislation passed Congress in 1887 and provided for the allotment of reservation land into individually owned tracts. A second provision of the Dawes Act permitted the federal government to purchase nonallotted land specifically for the purpose of opening it to non-Indian settlement. By approaching the situation as a tribal problem, the committees provided the foundations of twentieth-century tribal government forms.

Nez Perce reactions to the Dawes Act reveal a clear pattern of either disinterest or outright resistance. Severalty caught the tribe unprepared, but when negotiators arrived on the reservation to ask the tribe to cede nonallotted lands, the Nez Perces met the challenge. Although ultimately unsuccessful in resisting demands for their land, these experiences formed the basis by which the Nez Perces would, in the future, attempt to meet external threats. The experience of negotiating demonstrated that collective interests were best approached in that way—collectively. In the process, the reservation as a whole became a new constituent category on the reservation. The reservation merged, on a political level, into one larger community rather than several disparate settlements, churches, or social groups. The structures and methods used by missionaries and the government thus served to create the means by which the Nez Perces reasserted political autonomy in the twentieth century.

Allotment began in the summer of 1889. Allotting agent Alice Fletcher arrived and announced her intention to divide the reservation into individually owned parcels. She quickly discerned that the Nez Perces knew nothing about the Dawes Act. Almost immediately, James Reuben, a Presbyterian and prominent leader, journeyed to Washington, D.C., to verify the plan. During his absence, no one registered for an allotment. Fletcher did not even see any Indians upon whom to force an allotment. One allotting party member mused that had they not known better, they might have believed the Nez Perce tribe existed only in myth. Fletcher finally called public meetings in which she tried to convince them of the efficacy of allotment. She impressed almost no one. Few Nez Perces spoke, but those who did indicated quiet but firm opposition. One commented, for example, "We are content to be as we are." Another bluntly stated, "We do not want our land cut up in little pieces; we have not told you to do it." Someone else suggested the Nez Perces confer among themselves to decide whether or not they wished to accept allotment. But there would be no debate: the reservation would undergo severalty, whether they approved it or not.

Reuben's journey to Washington, D.C., demonstrated that the tribe would not accept government policy unquestioningly. The Nez Perces may have had little input in the formation of policy, but they did not quietly acquiesce to it. Only when Reuben finally sent affirmation did Fletcher finally begin the process of allotting the Nez Perce Reservation. The Nez Perces had delayed the inevitable for two months. But still they did not passively resign themselves. Rather, in effort to mediate between Fletcher and allottees, the Nez Perces formed an allotment committee. The committee held no specific duties and disbanded with the completion of allotment. But its very existence anticipated future methods of addressing reservation issues. Each of the nine committee members were affiliated with a Christian church from different areas of the reservation. No non-Christians served, and in fact, five men were Protestant ministers. Although the exact purpose and function of this committee remain unclear, these men volunteered to intercede on behalf of any tribal member who needed advice, reassurance, or assistance with regard to their allotments. Attempting to alleviate some of the confusion surrounding the issue, they served the entire reservation. Afterwards, all but James Stuart, the official allotment interpreter, served on the committee to negotiate the cession of surplus lands.

The Nez Perces remained unenthusiastic about allotment. Despite little or no organized resistance, several incidents illustrate their indifference. People sometimes failed to meet the allotting agent at appointed places and times. In one instance, several allottees agreed to meet her, but instead traveled north to trade with miners. Another year, large groups of Nez Perces departed on their annual hunting, fishing, and berrying expeditions, events that usually lasted for several weeks. Even when the commissioner of Indian affairs issued an order to prohibit such activities until the Nez Perces received allotments, few heeded the command.

After four years of surveying and recording, Nez Perce allotment was complete. Almost immediately, three commissioners arrived on the reservation to negotiate the sale of unallotted land. It was during this interim the Lewiston traveller reported his experience with phantom Nez Perces.

A large group of Nez Perces gathered at the Lapwai agency to meet the commissioners and in anticipation of the proceedings had selected a committee, chaired by Presbyterian minister Archie Lawyer, the son of former head chief Lawyer. Twelve others, almost all of them Christians, served on the committee, representing each district on the reservation. Nine had served on the earlier allotment committee as delegates or alternates. The negotiating committee was larger than the allotment committee but still represented primarily the Christian, assimilated population. But that did not mean they were accommodationists. Ten members distinctly opposed any sale of surplus lands. Only James Reuben and Eddie Connor spoke publicly in favor of a cession.

For ten days, the Nez Perce committee met with the commissioners and recounted their reasons for wanting to keep reservation land in tribal possession. As a group, the Nez Perce committee proved adamant and never surrendered their opposition. Even before permitting formal negotiations to begin, they insisted on a stenographer to record the proceedings so as to avoid any later misunderstanding. Once the discussions began, the Nez Perce committee showed no signs of giving in. Selling the land seemed to many simply a bad idea. Several emphasized the need to preserve land for the next generation. George Moses offered no specific reason but frankly stated, "I consider that the land which we have left after the allotment is made belongs to us and our stock that runs on that land." Others refused to consent to the sale because of problems related to allotment: some people had been inadvertently overlooked and others were unsure of their assigned tracts or boundaries.

Feeling unsettled about surrendering title, they also worried about the people who might come to live on the reservation. Even James Reuben, one of the two men on the committee who supported the sale, recognized the need for fee patents. A lack of documented title would put the Nez Perces at a distinct disadvantage. Previous treaties had restricted non-Indian use of reservation land, but unethical entrepreneurs often disregarded the law. Cattle ranchers, rustlers, and squatters had long caused conflicts. These people, Reuben pointed out, would be quite unlikely to respect new boundaries. William Wheeler clearly did not want non-Indians on the reservation, stating, "I could not live right mixed up with the whites." The Nez Perces could not have made it any plainer they were not interested in selling surplus lands. The commissioners, however, refused to take no for an answer.

Disregarding the adversity before them, the commissioners drew up a draft proposal offering the tribe $2.50 per acre. Reuben and Connor again favored the sale, but the rest of the committee maintained their opposition. The government commissioners responded angrily, questioning the methods and motives of the committee members. Only Reuben and Connor, in the words of one commissioner, displayed "the courage and unselfishness to speak in behalf of the common people." Another assailed the remaining committee: Every Nez Perce should have a chance to speak, he said, not just a select few.

The Nez Perces assumed their rejection of the proposal would end the matter, but the commissioners absolutely insisted on meeting again. As far as they were concerned, negotiations remained open. On the eighth council day, they increased their offer to three dollars per acre, but the Nez Perces still resisted. The deadlock continued without a break for the next two days. A story appeared in the newspapers that rich Nez Perce stock owners obstructed negotiations so they might enjoy the free use of unallotted lands for grazing. The commissioners specifically blamed the negotiating committee. Yet no one questioned James Reuben when he claimed during a council meeting that "most of those that are here seated in council are in the same fix as I am, not having many cattle or horses."

The commissioners were finally forced to abandon the council meetings. They adopted a divide and conquer strategy, traveling door to door to convince people individually. It worked. Whereas the Nez Perce committee resisted the commissioners, home visits undermined any solidarity they might have depended on. Even Archie Lawyer, the committee chair, relinquished his position and publicly supported the agreement. Over the next three months, the commissioners collected the signatures of a majority of adult men (236 total, 204 needed).

What changed their minds? Archie Lawyer and his brother James Lawyer opposed the sale during the initial meetings, but both signed the agreement. Few other committee members, however, actually changed their minds. George Moses, William Wheeler, James Hines, Enoch Pond, and Harrison Kip-kip-pal-e-kan all served on the committee and spoke against selling the surplus land. None of their names append the treaty. Entrusted to represent their districts, they perceived the potential disadvantages of land loss, recognized it meant an uncertain future, and refused to consent.

The commissioners simply bypassed the Nez Perce committee when it failed to yield to government demands. Some signers presumably supported the land cession in the first place, as did Reuben and Connor. But the commissioners finally won by enticing particular interest groups on the reservation. People in more immediate need of money were vulnerable to the agreement's provision for per capita payments. Other articles promised to investigate outstanding payments for scouts, messengers, and couriers who served the U.S. army during the Nez Perce War. Several of them signed the agreement. The commissioners also inserted a provision to settle the Langford Claim, a contentious land issue that interfered with allotment claims of several families. Other provisions appealed to church congregations by promising land grants or purchase options for various churches on the reservation. Finally, the agreement also banned alcohol from the reservation for twenty-five years, an attractive idea to the many prohibition supporters among the tribe.

An even more insidious force may have been at work. Local press coverage followed the negotiations intently, having long agitated for access to Indian land. George Moses questioned an article in the *Lewiston Teller* promising the reservation would be opened to settlement whether or not the Nez Perces consented. In the ensuing discussions, commissioner Cyrus Beede deliberately misled the Nez Perces, according to legal scholar Dennis Colson. Quoting from the newspaper, which stated "If the matter can not be adjusted the Government will take action at once," Beede may have omitted the word "not" while reading it out loud. The commissioners also sometimes spoke in war metaphors, which Colson interprets as veiled threats against the Nez Perces. The Nez Perces had reason to believe that if they did not agree to the price offered, they would still lose their land and get nothing in return.

In the end, the negotiations appear a mere formality. The Nez Perce Reservation was going to open to non-Indian ranchers and farmers despite anything the Nez Perces said or did. A good deal of protest followed the agreement of 1893; signers asked to have their names removed, and others challenged the procedures. But to no avail. In November 1895, thousands of white settlers flooded the reservation, almost immediately outnumbering the 1400 Nez Perces living there.

The implementation of the Dawes Act on the Nez Perce reservation demonstrated the advantage of a tribal approach versus independent response. The two committees formed during the implementation of the Dawes Act were among the first political bodies specifically formed to represent the interests of the whole reservation. The core membership on both were the same: primarily

Christian men who continued in secular leadership positions for years. Ironically, they were heirs of the head chief system and Christian elite, both created by non-Indian institutions. While the first committee was ill defined and the second ultimately unsuccessful in resisting the sale of surplus land, the two demonstrated a potential strength in meeting external threats. They served as models for future committees and political organizations, and gave participants important experience in government–tribal relations.

Subsequent bodies frequently changed and modified, but they were "tribal" organizations, ensuring representation from Nez Perce communities across the reservation. As these organizations evolved into a federally recognized tribal government, the reservation had become on a political level, a single community. Social, political, and religious divisions within the tribe remained, but to the outside, they now knew the value of a united front. The ghosts of Nez Perce warriors fighting an unseen enemy predicted disaster in 1892, but from the devastation of the Dawes Act, the tribe drew a lesson of how the divide and conquer method worked. Their struggle remained in the temporal world, but the disaster also provided an opportunity to develop a newer approach.

4

Federal Indian Education

Margaret Connell Szasz

In the fifty years before the publication of the Meriam Report, the federal government pursued a policy of total assimilation of the American Indian into the mainstream society. Recognizing the vast difficulties in achieving this goal, Congress and the Indian Bureau adopted a plan to remold the Indian's conception of life, or what came to be known as his "system of values." If this could be changed, assimilationists reasoned, the Indian would then become like the white man. The Indian's system of values was expressed in the education of his children and in his attitude toward the land. Consequently, the assimilationists chose to attack these two concepts as the major targets of their campaign.

The land issue was easily resolved. If the Indian owned his own land, they reasoned, he would assume a responsibility for taking care of it and would thus become a good citizen. Land allotment was secured through the passage of the Dawes Act (more commonly known as the Allotment Act) of 1887, which provided for the allotment of lands in severalty of Indians on the various reservations. The remolding of Indian education to conform to white cultural values could not be achieved by a single piece of legislation, but during this same decade the federal government began to assume responsibility for Indian education and provided the first significant federal funding for Indian schools.

Reprinted from Margaret Connell Szasz, *Education and the American Indian: The Road to Self-Determination Since 1928*, Albuquerque: University of New Mexico Press, 1999, pp. 8–15, by permission of the University of New Mexico Press.

Federal Indian Education

During the first century of U.S. Indian policy, the federal government made provision for Indian education through legislation and treaties. In 1819, Congress established the "civilization fund," which provided for a small annual sum for instruction. Between 1783 and 1871, when the treaty period ended, a number of Indian treaties set aside portions of tribal annuity payments for education, or included specific provisions for schooling. Although the federal government funded these efforts, missionary groups administered most of the schools. Among the southeastern Indians, however, several tribes developed their own highly successful education systems.

Although there had always been a small number of people who were convinced that the Indian could be civilized, the public generally believed that he was incapable of progress. This negative view was reinforced by attitudes on the frontier. Many frontiersmen were inveterate Indian haters, and as the frontier shrank in physical size this attitude seemed to intensify. Those who encountered the Indian under the often brutal frontier conditions had little respect for the humanitarian viewpoint of the easterner.

In the post-Civil War decades the public attitude began to shift, and within the space of a few years, in spite of the antagonism of westerners, assimilation became the popular approach. The impetus for this change of opinion was provided by reformers who responded to a national outcry against publicized incidents of white injustice. Events like the Nez Perce retreat, the Ponca removal, and the flight of the Northern Cheyenne, as well as the intrusion of white settlers into Indian Territory and the exposure of graft within the Indian Bureau, increased congressional concern and aided the reformers in their efforts to secure legislation to change the national Indian policy.

In this era of individual fortunes and economic dreams, the presence of idealistic reformers may seem somewhat strange. On the other hand, the American system had yet to be shaken by internal doubts. Consequently, these reformers, like many other Americans, held their society in such high esteem that they developed an almost imperialistic attitude toward cultures that responded to other values. Armed with this type of evangelistic fervor, the reformers stood a good chance of succeeding. By the late 1870s they had begun their campaign.

The first extensive federal funding of Indian education was stimulated by the efforts of Richard Henry Pratt, the U.S. Army captain who founded Carlisle School in 1879. Captain Pratt's most important contribution was to convince the public that the Indian was educable. The success of Carlisle, which was acknowledged by a large congressional appropriation in 1882, led to a sudden expansion of off-reservation industrial boarding schools. Those that were to have the longest life spans included schools at Forest Grove, Oregon, established in 1880 (later known as Chemawa), Albuquerque (1884),

Chilocco (1884), Santa Fe (1890—renamed the Institute of American Indian Arts in 1962), Haskell (1884—renamed Haskell Indian Junior College in 1965), Carson (1890—later known as Stewart), Phoenix (1890), Pierre (1891), and Flandreau (1893). By the turn of the century twenty-five off-reservation industrial boarding schools had been opened.

In spite of the rapid expansion, reformers were by no means unanimous in their enthusiasm for this type of school. Although critics recognized the merits of Captain Pratt's "acculturation policy," they soon began to question whether the negative features of the industrial training schools did not outweigh the positive. They argued that such schools trained too few Indian youths at too great expense. However, the most convincing criticism was that many Indians who attended the schools "returned to the blanket."

The problems faced by this minority of educated Indian youth did not lend themselves to an easy solution. When the pupils returned to the reservation, they often became the objects of ridicule. This situation was complicated by the fact that the training they had received had little or no application to reservation life. Thus these pupils became the first victims of the "either/or" policy of assimilation. Their education forced them to choose either the culture of the white man or the culture of the Indian; there was no compromise.

Despite these drawbacks, the off-reservation industrial boarding school became an entrenched form of federal Indian schooling during the assimilation period. Shortly before the turn of the century, however, other forms of education were introduced. The main alternatives were reservation boarding or day schools. Critics of off-reservation education supported this type of schooling because it offered several distinct advantages. In the first place, reservation schools were less expensive. Day schools required little transportation or boarding, and transportation to reservation boarding schools was much cheaper than to off-reservation schools. Second, reservation schools were more acceptable to parents, who were generally hostile to the idea of having their children taken any distance from home. Incidents of enforced seizure of children to fill the quotas of off-reservation schools during this period have been reported too frequently to be considered mere exaggeration. Although many parents objected to off-reservation schooling, opposition to education itself was by no means a universal phenomenon among Indians. However, as historian Robert M. Utley has written, those parents who did object may have "understood . . . that it represented the most dangerous of all attacks on basic Indian values, the one most likely to succeed in the end because it aimed at the children, who had known little if any of the old life."

As an adjunct, then, to the off-reservation industrial boarding schools, the reservation schools were the second type of federal Indian education. Day schools in particular increased after the turn of the century. Many of those who promoted Indian assimilation, however, predicted that public schools would prove to be the best solution to the problems of Indian education. Early observers of the effects of public schooling on the Indian child concluded that separate Indian schools supported by the federal government would eventually become an anachronism.

With the exception of eastern Indians not under the jurisdiction of the federal government, the first tribes subject to public schooling were those whose reservations were allotted. As whites responded eagerly to the newly available leases and surplus lands of these reservations, they brought with them demands for public schools for their children. By 1902 Agent Jay Lynch wrote from the Yakima Reservation that there were "so many white people renting land on the reservation . . . it was found necessary to have schools for white people renting Indian lands." On reservations that were not allotted (including most reservations in the Southwest), public schooling did not become an issue. Where it existed, it encouraged assimilation. As Agent Lynch wrote, "Indian children progress much faster when thus thrown in contact with white children than they do when they are all kept together with whites excluded."

By the turn of the century these three major forms of Indian education had become firmly established. A fourth form that should be mentioned was the mission school, the forerunner of both federal and public Indian education, which retained its foothold during this period. Although mission schools did not educate a significant proportion of Indian children, they were responsible for a consistently small percentage, with considerable variation from reservation to reservation. One of the reasons for their continued existence was simply that not enough schools were built to take their place. However, mission schools continued to exist even after the Indian Bureau was able to report that the majority of Indian children were enrolled in some other type of schooling. Another reason for their tenacity may have been that they had become established institutions.

It appears more likely, however, that the hold of mission schools on Indian education was due to the persistence of both the churches and the Indians themselves. Dedicated educators within the churches fought hard to maintain their schools. They believed that Indian children who were unable to attend public school would receive a better education in a mission school than in a federal school. William M. Chapman, who was director of St. Elizabeth's School (Episcopal) on the Standing Rock Reservation for a short period, maintained that even though conditions at his school were by no means ideal, they were "better than in the big government boarding schools which sometimes housed five hundred Indian children." Chapman also suggested that the "church training" offered by the school "meant a great deal" to the children because they were "naturally devout." A large portion of the budget for these schools came from tribal funds, and Indians were vehement defenders of sectarian schools threatened by closure.

At the beginning of the twentieth century the status of the Indian was not only bleak, it was hovering on the edge of disaster. The dual inheritance of the assimilation policies of education and the land allotment had already given some indication of their potential ability to damage if not destroy a majority of the Indian people. During the next three decades (1900–1930) the unchecked pursuit of these policies led the Indian to a point of no return. By the end of World War I he was suffering increasingly from disease and a short life expectancy, malnutrition and starvation, a diminishing land base, and a stagnant, unrealistic school system. In the early 1920s federal Indian policy was a notorious example of bureaucratic inefficiency and ineffectiveness, and the possibility of change from within appeared to be hopeless. The time was ripe for reform.

The decade of the 1920s witnessed the movement for reform; the decade of the 1930s saw the rhetoric of reform transformed into action. Reformers of the 1920s uncovered extensive mismanagement within the Bureau, which gave them ready ammunition for their attack on the administrative walls of the structure. Failures of the education system provided some of the most lethal ammunition. The reformers dwelt on the "plight" of Indian children through a direct, emotional appeal that drew immediate response from an increasingly irate public.

Reform in the 1920s followed a pattern not uncommon to other reform movements in the United States. It was triggered by a *cause célèbre*, an incident that occurred when the climate of opinion was ready for reform. The Bursum Bill of 1922, "an act to quiet title to lands within Pueblo Indian land grants," proposed to give potential legal rights to white men who had settled on Pueblo lands and force the Pueblo Indians to prove ownership of their lands. Establishing such proof would have been difficult if not impossible, for the Pueblos would have had to clarify ownership through three periods of occupation—Spanish, Mexican, and American. The Bursum Bill and the Dawes, or Allotment, Act bore witness to the land hunger of those who lived near reservations. Although the Dawes Act had been encouraged in 1887 by reformers who were anxious for Indians to become independent, self-supporting citizens, it had also received a hearty push from westerners who were eager to acquire Indian land. However, in 1922 the Bursum Bill served as a catalyst for change because it was proposed at a time when the increasingly disastrous effects of the Dawes Act had become apparent to advocates of Indian rights.

Serving as a target for these sympathizers, the controversial bill provided a focal point of discontent and thus led the reform movement to its second phase—development of dynamic leadership among the reformers themselves. During the 1920s a number of leaders emerged from Congress and from the new organizations formed to fight the Bursum Bill. One man overshadowed all the rest. This was John Collier, the outspoken idealist whose life became intertwined with the fortunes and futures of the Indians. Collier went on to become commissioner of Indian Affairs from 1933 to 1945 under Franklin D. Roosevelt, holding that position longer than anyone else before or since.

Collier's interest in Indians dated from 1920, when he and his family came to Taos at the invitation of Mabel Dodge Luhan, a friend from New York City, where she had been best known for her salon. Like many other members of the "Lost Generation," Mabel Dodge Luhan had been depressed and dissatisfied with America after the war. Unlike her contemporaries who fled to Europe, she sought her new life in the American Southwest. For Collier, also, it was dissatisfaction that initially led him to the West, first to California and then to New Mexico. Among the Taos Indians he found a perfect example of the communal life he valued so highly. From these Indians his interest spread, first to the other Pueblos, then to tribes across the continent. The fight against the Bursum Bill propelled him into the forefront of the reform movement.

As the principal spokesman for the reformers, Collier was pushed into the limelight when he became executive secretary of the American Indian Defense Association. This organization, formed in direct response to the Bursum Bill, became the strongest and most outspoken of the Indian reform groups of the 1920s. Although its directives (many of them Collier's) came from the main office in New York, California claimed four of the seven chapters that formed between 1922 and 1927. Many of the California reformers were also active in the Division of Indian Welfare of the General Federation of Women's Clubs. The goals of the two organizations were complementary.

The American Indian Defense Association was determined to reach the public. It published its own bulletin, *American Indian Life*, in the muckraking tradition established at the turn of the century by men like Lincoln Steffens, and it also had ready access to the press. Liberal magazines like *The Nation*, *Survey Graphic*, and *The New Republic* turned a sympathetic ear to the popular topic of Indian reform, but the issue was also covered in prestigious journals like *Current History* and *The Forum*. The magazine that became the primary voice for the reformers, however, was *Sunset*, a popular California publication edited by Walter V. Wohlke. A prominent crusader, Wohlke wrote many of the articles that criticized the Bureau.

Through this publicity the reformers launched the third phase of the reform movement—public response and encouragement. The level of the appeal was emotional; the crusaders often contrasted the appalling extent of Indian poverty with the general prosperity of the 1920s. Reader reaction to this approach indicated its effectiveness. One *Sunset* reader wrote, "I have been shocked and pained at the revelations brought out by these articles. I feel that in the name of humanity and to keep our great country from blackening its fair name any further, something should be done and that right soon. . . . I want to know what I can do to help."

Public response led the reform movement into its final and most significant phase—action. In the 1920s, however, the action taken failed to satisfy the demands of the reformers, for it came primarily in the form of independent, private studies commissioned by the federal government. The twentieth-century reformer already had begun to learn that the results of such studies often lie neglected. This was what happened to the first study made in the 1920s, a report compiled by the Committee of One Hundred, a group of citizens who met in Washington, D.C., on December 12 and 13, 1923, to discuss the direction of Indian affairs and to make suggestions for their improvement. The recommendations of this committee, particularly in the area of education, were noteworthy, but they had little effect on the Bureau. Although the Indian Service began to encourage public-school enrollment and to reorganize its own schools in order to offer more advanced instruction, these steps did not radically alter its total education system. Few federal boarding schools had a high-school curriculum, and none of those that did compared favorably in quality to the public schools. Vocational training in Bureau schools remained inferior, and other courses continued to be unrelated to the reservation life that the pupil generally returned to when he left school. Although the Bureau recognized the existence of the report, its overall effect was negligible and it served only to point out that the work of the reformers was far from finished.

5

"The Father Tells Me So!" Wovoka: The Ghost Dance Prophet

L.G. Moses

The Hebrew Prophet Joel, in a time of great distress, warned the Israelites to turn away from sin. A plague of locusts was ravaging the land; the day of the Lord's wrath was approaching. If the people gathered, repented, and renewed their covenant with the Almighty, however, Joel assured them that bounty would again reign in Zion. God, speaking through his early surrogate, warranted that for the chosen people, having returned to righteousness, "I will pour out my spirit upon all flesh; and your sons and your daughters shall prophesy, your old men shall dream dreams, and your young men shall see visions." Prophets, dreams, and visions were very much a part of the Judeo-Christian tradition, and both Old and New Testaments are replete with direct divine guidance to mortals. The same was true among American Indians, who, like the Israelites, suffered from great distress. Prophets emerged among many Indian groups, and by far one of the most important was Wovoka, the "Ghost Dance" Prophet.

The Ghost Dance, one of the largest social and religious movements among American Indians during the nineteenth century, developed as a result of many factors. The tribes had been defeated militarily, concentrated onto reservations, removed from their homelands, and forced to accept new laws directed by the government of the United States. Broken treaties, land encroachment,

Reprinted from the *American Indian Quarterly*, volume 9, number 3 (summer 1985) by permission of the University of Nebraska Press. Copyright © 1985 by the University of Nebraska Press.

depletion of game, and assimilationist programs of the Bureau of Indian Affairs had demoralized the tribes to such an extent that they awaited deliverance from their depression and sorrow. Indeed, by 1880 Indians in the American West retained small hope of ever challenging the white man's government. Consigned either through persuasion or force to reservations, Indians were subjected to government-sponsored programs of assimilation, believing that the "Indians must conform to the white man's ways." Government agents encouraged Indians to abandon their tribal affiliation, to accept allotments of land, and to lead, in the opinion of Indian-policy reformers, productive lives as citizen-farmers. "This civilization may not be the best possible," wrote Commissioner of Indian Affairs Thomas Jefferson Morgan, "but it is the best the Indians can get." Their children were forced to attend reservation day or boarding schools, or distant boarding schools such as the Carlisle Indian Industrial Training School in Pennsylvania. They were to become educated and white-like, abandoning forever their "Indianness." It was the hope of white reformers that, within a generation, Indians would cease to be Indians, and, for the allotted tribes, that individual freeholds would have provided them with the means of livelihood, independence, and a respect for private property.

Indians had difficulty adjusting to the new order created by the reservation system, and many Indians turned inward toward their religions in search of divine help in their demoralized state. Throughout the ages frightened and oppressed humans have longed for deliverance, and Wovoka's message of renewal, rebirth, and "revitalization" offered hope for many Indian people. Like many prophets, Wovoka "died" and was reborn, returning from heaven with divine messages about how to live and worship. Furthermore, God gave Wovoka specific instructions about a sacred dance and ceremony, which the Prophet was told to bring back to the Indians. The ritual and dance became known by many names but is best remembered as the "Ghost Dance." Wovoka believed that all Indians—living and dead—would be reunited in a world paradise, where Indians would be eternally free from poverty, disease, and death. Wovoka prophesied a great cataclysm whereby whites and their ways would be swept away, inaugurating an Indian millennium. All of this would be hastened by the continual performance of the "Ghost Dance," a religious movement that spread rapidly among numerous western tribes.

The leader of the Ghost Dance was born around 1858 near the Walker River in Mason Valley, Nevada. Wovoka (the Cutter) was a full-blood Paiute Indian who was born during an era of radical change for the Paiutes and other Indians in the West. Little is known about Wovoka's mother, but his father, Tavivo (White Man), helped shape the life of the future Prophet. Tavivo followed the teachings of a spritual leader named Wodziwob who was part of the first Ghost Dance movement of the 1870s and taught that the world would soon end and whites would be destroyed. Tavivo himself was a " 'dreamer' with supernatural powers," and both he and Wodziwob shaped the beliefs and values of young Wovoka. As a boy of twelve or fourteen, Wovoka learned about the great cataclysm prophesied by Wodziwob and others, and of the new religious wave that was rolling across the plains, mountains, and deserts of the West. "The prophetic claims and teachings of the father," wrote James Mooney, the renowned anthropologist who studied Wovoka's religion, "the reverence with which he was regarded by the people, and the mysterious ceremonies which were doubtless of frequent performance in the little tule wikiup at home must have made early and deep impressions on the mind of the boy, who seems to have been by nature of a solitary and contemplative disposition, one of those born to see visions and hear still voices." But Wovoka is equally remembered as Jack Wilson, "stepson" of David Wilson.

As a youth Wovoka worked at the ranch of David Wilson who in 1863, with his brothers William and George, had preempted table lands along the southern rim of Mason Valley, land wooded in juniper and scrub pine but otherwise ideal for running cattle. David Wilson, a devout Presbyterian, and his sons gave Wovoka his anglicized name, provided him with steady work, and introduced him to Christianity. So it appears that Tavivo, Wodziwob, the Wilsons, and their seemingly incompatible religions shaped the youth of a man who would become one of the most significant of the Indian prophets.

In the twenty years that separated the Ghost Dances of the 1870s with those of the 1890s, Wovoka grew to adulthood. Those twenty years also marked the military conquest of the Plains and Great Basin tribes. Apparently, at the age of eighteen Wovoka ended his association with the Wilsons, gravitating to his father and the ritual life of the Paiutes. "For two years," wrote Wovoka's only biographer, Paul Bailey, Wovoka "shunned his white brothers, and wrestled with a hate for the whole white race that all but consumed him." The documentary evidence upon which the author bases the remark is nonexistent, but the biblical allusion is inescapable. The seeker, prophet, the "messiah," withdraws into the wilderness—of his own making in this instance—to search his soul for answers to questions that throb in his brain. At the end of his exile, he beholds his vision and begins his public ministry.

By the time Wovoka was twenty, he stood nearly six feet tall. He married a Paiute woman to whom he gave the name Mary, in honor of David Wilson's wife, a fact that belies some of the self-consuming hatred for whites alluded to by Wovoka's biographer Paul Bailey. Wovoka may also have visited the states of the Pacific Coast. Bailey, using the reminiscences of E.A. Dyer, for many years a friend of Wovoka and a storekeeper in Yerington, Nevada, claims that the Prophet traveled extensively in California, Oregon, and Washington. Dyer, in the transcription of his memoir edited by his son, stated simply that not much "is known of his activities as a young man, except that he did considerable wandering about this state and neighboring California." Regarding his travels he was never "loquacious." Paiutes were hired as pickers in the hop fields of Sonoma and Mendocino counties in northern California. But elsewhere in his account, Dyer equivocates that probably "young Jack Wilson also traveled to the California hop fields." Bailey inferred that Wovoka traveled widely and therefore came into contact with other Indian messianic or millennial religions, particularly the Washani or "Dreamer" religion and the Indian Shakers of John Slocum. Given certain similarities in beliefs, James Mooney also wondered if these Indian religions of world renewal had influenced Wovoka.

In 1892 Mooney learned that two Indian Shaker missionaries had traveled throughout the Willamette Valley and other parts of Oregon. "It is said among the northern Indians that on this journey those apostles met," Mooney wrote, "a young man to whom they taught their mysteries, in which he became such an apt pupil that he soon outstripped his teachers, and is now working even greater wonders among his own people. This man can be no other than Wovoka." The only question that troubled the anthropologist was whether the story told among the Columbia tribes was a legend based on vague rumors of a great prophet to the south or whether Wovoka actually derived his knowledge from these northern apostles. Mooney knew from his survey of correspondence in the files of the commissioner of Indian affairs that Indians occasionally visited Mason Valley and the nearby Walker River Reservation. But, as Wovoka had told Mooney and even earlier, Arthur Chapman, Wovoka had never wandered far from his home. Thus, we may accept that Wovoka knew about Wodziwob, John Slocum, Smohalla, Jesus of Nazareth, and perhaps even the revelations of Joseph Smith, whose followers labored among the "Lamanite" descendants in Nevada.

Wovoka probably began his public ministry as weather prophet and healer in the mid-1880s, but it was not until January 1, 1889, according to Mooney's calculations, that Wovoka experienced his major revelation. Wovoka had been hearing "voices" for about two years, when on New Years Day, 1889, he lay ill in his wikiup with a high fever. The day was marked by an eclipse of the sun, and on this day Wovoka "died" and journeyed to heaven. According to Mooney,

He saw God, with all the people who had died long ago engaged in their oldtime sports and occupations, all happy and forever young. It was a pleasant land and full of game. After showing him all, God told him he must go back and tell his people they must be good and love one another, have no quarreling, and live in peace with the whites; that they must work, and not lie or steal; that they must put away all the old practices that savored of war; that if they faithfully obeyed his instructions they would at last be reunited with their friends in this other world, where there would be no more death or sickness or old age. He was then given the dance which he was commanded to bring back to his people. By performing this dance at intervals for five consecutive days each time, they would secure this happiness to themselves and hasten the event. Finally God gave him control over the elements so he could make it rain or snow or be dry at will, and appointed him his deputy to take charge of affairs in the west. . . . He then returned to earth and began to preach as he was directed, convincing the people by exercising the wonderful powers that had been given him.

Wovoka had already introduced a dance two years before, but it was apparently nothing more than his version of the Paiute Round Dance. Following his revelation, however, the ceremony, staged at the appropriate intervals as commanded by God, became the Ghost Dance where, in their exhaustion and delirium, the participants communicated with the dead.

There has been a tendency among certain authors who write about Wovoka to interpret his revelation as entirely self-serving. Many have relied on Bailey's account wherein Wovoka, seeing so many of his people defer to him, is swept up in the masque. But it may be simpler to explain. Wovoka believed himself to be a prophet ordained by Providence with a special mission to the American Indians. So intense was his conviction that he elicited the assistance of the farmer-in-charge at Walker River Reservation. In February 1890, James O. Gregory wrote to the Indian superintendent of Nevada S.S. Sears stationed at the Pyramid Lake Reservation, admitting that "You will doubtless be amazed at the letter you will have received from Jack Wilson the prophet." Gregory confided that Wovoka "has got the Indians all wild at his wonderful command of the Elements," because the Prophet had apparently convinced the people "that he alone is responsible for the storms of this season." Wovoka had written Sears to learn if the government believed "in him and will acknowledge him as a prophet." Gregory reported that well over two hundred men, women, and children had turned out to see and hear the Prophet, despite a driving snow storm. Indeed, the crowd talked "of nothing but Jack Wilson and the miracles he performs" and they took up a collection of $25, which they presented to the holy man. According to Gregory, Wovoka wanted "to come on the reservation to farm and guarantees the Indians that if the government gives him permission to come he will cause lots of rain to fall and they will never lose a crop again." Wovoka and the other Indians expected the government to answer the letter, but Sears never forwarded the correspondence. There is no reason to suspect that he would have, once confronted with the fantastic claims of, as far as he was concerned, an "ignorant" and superstitious people. The letter is only remarkable in retrospect and takes on added significance when one considers the response of the government to the Ghost Dance. It is part of the tragedy that the first information received by the Bureau of Indian Affairs about the religion spoke not about an apocalyptic religion of peace and fraternity, but rather of a possible rebellion among disaffected Sioux. Gregory's letter is equally noteworthy because it supports the implication that Wovoka took his mission seriously. In addition, corroborating testimony appears in the correspondence of the commissioner of Indian Affairs. From the Indian Territory seven months later, Cheyenne and Arapaho agent Charles F. Ashley wrote that a letter had recently arrived from the Wind River Reservation in Wyoming which told that the "messiah" had written to the "Great Father in Washington" to ask that he remove within two years all whites from the western United States lest they be destroyed.

Following his New Year's revelation, Wovoka's renown increased throughout 1889, first among Paiutes and later among western and southwestern tribes who heard the good news of the Prophet. In March of the year Sarah Winnemucca, daughter of a Paiute headman, reported to the editor of the *Daily Silver State* that "a prophet has risen among the ignorant and more credulous Piutes [*sic*]. He says the spirits of all the Piute [*sic*] warriors who have died . . . are to return to earth and resume their old forms. They have condemned the whites and the Indians who write and speak their language or adopt their customs, and will exterminate them from the earth." By summer, news about Wovoka had reached distant Plains tribes who learned, not about a prophet who foretold wondrous things, but instead about the "Indian Messiah" himself. Elaine Goodale, teacher at the White River Industrial School on the Great Sioux Reservation, reported that while camping with a hunting party on the evening of July 23, she met Chasing Crane, a Sioux just returned from the Rosebud agency. He had a wonderful story to tell. "God," he explained, had "appeared to the Crows across the Stony Mountains." The appearance of "Christ" among the Crows, as Goodale described him, suggests both the rapidity with which Wovoka's doctrine had spread and his transformation from prophet to Messiah, as the rumors flew from reservation to reservation growing more fantastic with each retelling.

Although Wovoka would have disavowed the honor of being the Indian Messiah, his identity underwent a metamorphosis in the minds of the faithful from the Paiute Prophet to the Indian Messiah, and finally to the inviolate Christ. By the time the Plains tribes began their investigations of the new religion, Wovoka had ascended to such spiritual heights that his visitors, by some accounts, approached him with averted eyes. Wovoka, however, never said he was the Messiah, claiming only to be a prophet of God. Indeed, this fact was recorded by John S. Mayhugh, former agent at the Western Shoshone Reservation in Nevada and the allotment officer of the Nevada tribes. Mayhugh, who knew Wovoka, wrote that the Prophet foretold the coming of a Messiah who would appear on Mount Grant near the Walker River Agency. Mayhugh's accurate message never became the prevailing view, and even today Wovoka is usually referred to as the "Indian Messiah."

Wovoka's message spread quickly from the Paiute wikiups huddled around Walker Lake, southward to the Hualapais and eastward to the Bannocks, Shoshones, Arapahos, Crows, Cheyennes, Caddos, Pawnees, Kiowas, Comanches, and Sioux. To learn more about the doctrine, tribal delegates traveled westward to Mason Valley to sit at the Prophet's feet. They then returned to their tribes with written instructions. Engaged in research among the Southern Cheyennes, James Mooney obtained what he called a "Messiah Letter." His free rendering appears here in its entirety.

When you get home you must make a dance to continue for five days. Dance four successive nights, and the last night keep up the dance until the morning of the fifth day, when all must bathe in the river and then disperse to their homes. You must all do in the same way.

I Jack Wilson, love you all, and my heart is full of gladness for the gifts you have brought me. When you get home I shall give you a good cloud which will make you feel good. I give you a good spirit and give you all good paint. I want you to come again in three months, some from each tribe there in Indian Territory.

There will be a good deal of snow this year and some rain. In the fall there will be such a rain as I have never given you before.

Grandfather says, when your friends die you must not cry. You must not fight. Do right always. It will give you satisfaction in life.

Do not tell the white people about this. Jesus is now upon the earth. He appears like a cloud. The dead are all alive again. I do not know when they will be here; maybe this fall or in the spring. When the time comes there will be no more sickness and everyone will be young again.

Do not refuse to work for the whites and do not make any trouble with them until you leave them. When the earth shakes do not be afraid. It will not hurt you.

I want you to dance every six weeks. Make a feast at the dance and have food that everybody may eat. Then bathe in the water. That is all. You will receive good words again from me some time. Do not tell lies.

Wovoka gave this message, or one very much like it, to all the delegations that visited him. The first Sioux delegates, for example, left their reservations in the fall of 1889 and after many adventures, returned in the early spring of 1890. By summer Ghost Dances had been organized at a number of reservations scattered throughout the west. The government's response was premised, however, on the hostility of a religion as practiced among the Sioux that promised the destruction of whites through whatever means.

When the western Sioux, then among the most populous tribes in the United States and popularly recognized as the most warlike and recalcitrant Indians, embraced the religion, the Ghost Dance conjured images of half-crazed "savages" ready to follow lives of rapine and slaughter. During the fall and early winter of 1890, newspaper accounts from the Dakotas sustained the prevalent image of the Indian as erstwhile predator. For all the years the Sioux had huddled around the agency—lulled into submission by rations and gimcracks—they were now portrayed as demonic killers. Mythical stories about treacherous Sioux, joined by other "hostiles" in a grand Indian conspiracy, overshadowed the actual story of Wovoka and his religion of peace and love. Dancing, peaceful Indians awaiting their divine redemption did not sell newspapers, so journalists surfeited the country with stories about Indians dancing themselves into frenzies as they awaited reinforcements from the risen dead. No journalist and no official of the Indian service ever traveled to Mason Valley to hear the Prophet's unadorned message. Instead, misunderstanding of Wovoka's religion significantly contributed to the Dakota disaster that ended at Wounded Knee, South Dakota.

On the cold morning of December 29, 1890, Big Foot's band of Miniconjou Sioux were attacked by troopers of the famed Seventh Cavalry. The Indians were encamped at Wounded Knee, and most of them were followers of the Ghost Dance, a religion that had been banned by agents on the Sioux Reservations. Fighting had erupted after the soldiers decided to search the camp and some of the Sioux had refused to submit. The camp of tipis was raked by the bullets of Hotchkiss guns, and at least 150 Indians—men, women, and children—were killed while many others were wounded. Wovoka's vision of an Indian world filled with peace, restoration, and brotherly love crumbled that bleak December day. Three days after the tragedy at Wounded Knee, a burial party interred in a mass grave the frozen corpses of the Sioux, and it buried something else as well. In the words of Black Elk, an Oglala Sioux holy man who had witnessed part of the slaughter, a dream was buried with the slain Sioux. That dream was of a redeemer who would "drive out the usurper and win back for his people what they had lost." For a few short seasons Wovoka's dream had flourished, but his religion of hope died with the Sioux on the snow-swept plains surrounding Wounded Knee.

When Wovoka learned about Wounded Knee, he understandably feared that he would be blamed. He counseled delegates, whose ardor still sent them to Nevada seeking news of the millennium, that they should return to their respective tribes and stop the dances. The Indian resurrection had been postponed. For the nation, the Ghost Dance soon retreated into memory as the "Last Indian War." As one historian has noted, the Sioux died at Wounded Knee at the end of the same year in which the superintendent of the census announced the closure of the frontier. Thus, Wovoka, his religion, and Wounded Knee have become a metaphor for a nation in transition from the wilderness to a modern industrial state.

Transition was equally an appropriate element of Wovoka's life, especially during that period after Wounded Knee. Although his promise of an Indian millenium was not fulfilled, he still inspired devotion among followers beyond his own Paiutes. That devotion represented, in part, a continuing desire for a better life. Burdened by the present and discomfitted by a future that offered little hope, many Indians sought succor in a restored past. For his followers, Wovoka served as a last link in a chain that bound them to individual ways of life, separate and distinct from mainstream American society, which stood poised on the threshold of a new century. Through relentless government programs, Indian societies had been undermined, their leaders had been dishonored—sometimes imprisoned or killed for their recalcitrance—their traditional means of subsistence had been destroyed, their lands had been expropriated or considerably reduced, their religions had been harassed, and their children in many instances had been taken from them and sent to the white man's schools. The government, with the assistance of a legion of well-intentioned reformers, had decreed that Indians should be like other Americans. They should lead useful and productive lives. For some tribes, the Dawes Act divided tribal lands into 160-acre parcels upon which Indians would farm and grow independent. Once independent, the reformers and government agents believed anachronistic tribalism would retreat, giving way to "civilization." The favorite aphorism of Richard Henry Pratt, a contemporary of Wovoka and a proponent of Indian education, was "kill the Indian and save the man." It is little wonder that for thousands of Indians Wovoka offered solace and a sense of continuity with the past in an alien world. Although Wovoka did not preach his religion as extensively after 1891, he continued to serve the Paiutes as a holy man and healer, and for erstwhile ghost dancers, as an object of continued veneration. Wovoka has been most criticized for the latter capacity. Charges were made that the Prophet personally gained from his celebrity. Indeed, some claimed that Wovoka connived with a local storekeeper, E.A. Dyer, to create a lucrative business in Ghost Dance memorabilia.

For years after the demise of the Ghost Dance, Wovoka received letters of supplication from the faithful. Many asked for sacred objects such as the red clay paint used in the dance. Very few of these letters have been preserved, but Dyer reported that Indians asked for Wovoka's "garments, particularly shirts," which they believed held "miraculous powers." In fact, anything "he had worn, owned, touched, looked upon or simply just thought about" reportedly had powers. "In time a great many requests were for hats, specifically for those which he had personally worn. I was very often called upon to send them his hat, which he would remove forthwith from his head on hearing the nature of the request in a letter." In return Wovoka reportedly expected, and got, $20 for such a gift. Dyer and others criticized Wovoka for conducting "a steady and somewhat profitable business in hats." Wovoka also sold "magpie tail feathers and red ochre" but his critics remarked that the prices were "on a par with those asked for similar 'war paint' and geegaws in our modern salons." That Wovoka "sold" objects or received money for services is only significant if one disregards the traditions of Paiute shamanism and "gift giving" among most Indian peoples. Objects such as feathers, hats, or paint were signs of individual power—analogous in a broad sense to the use of sacramentals, such as holy water or blessed medals by Roman Catholics. Wovoka transmitted signs of his power and occasionally their efficacy, by giving them to his followers, who returned the favor with a gift or offering.

Yet Wovoka could also demur. Johnson Sides, a Paiute who liked to call himself the "peace maker" and who was for years Wovoka's enemy, reported that the Prophet refused a gift of forty silver dollars dumped at his feet by a Pawnee delegate who happened to be in the service of the Indian Bureau. The money represented a collection taken by the tribe for the Prophet. Sides explained that Wovoka feared the money was tainted and that he might be killed through witchcraft. Sides may have been telling the truth, but if Wovoka were as grasping and as calculated as is often suggested, why should he refuse such a handsome gift? A charlatan with his eye on a chance to gain would never have refused. Clearly, not all Paiutes were enamored with Wovoka, but for many he was held in respect, his advice sought on matters pertaining to the people at Walker River, and his powers over the weather and disease invoked. On communal rabbit hunts, for example, his position was always one of honor; he rode in a wagon. He had no need to shoot his own game. Every member of the hunt shared his prizes with him.

According to one account, Wovoka remained on the Wilson ranch until 1920, whereas another holds that between 1912 and 1932 he lived in the Paiute colony at Yerington, Nevada. Sometime before 1920 he traveled to Idaho, Wyoming, and twice to Oklahoma where his former followers feted and presented him with many gifts that he treasured for the remainder of his life. In the spring of 1919, Grace Dangberg, an aspiring ethnologist and historian, learned that Wovoka's sight and hearing were failing. At the invitation of Carrie Willis Wilson, wife of James Wilson, Wovoka's boyhood companion, Dangberg retrieved some letters from the basement of the ranch house in Nordyke, Nevada, where Wovoka once lived. These twenty-one letters and fragments, deposited at the Nevada State Historical Society, were written between 1908 and 1911 and indicate the esteem people held for Wovoka. The letters are all that remain of the many hundreds the Prophet received. Dangberg hoped to interview Wovoka, but at the last moment, he refused. She did not press the issue.

Later in the 1920s Wovoka agreed to speak to Colonel Tim McCoy, the only non-Indian, except James Mooney, to speak to the Prophet specifically about his religion. In the winter of 1924 the actor and showman was serving as technical director for the filming of *The Thundering Herd*, on location in Bishop, California. McCoy had been a long-time friend of former ghost dancers among the Northern Arapahos. He hired a few of them as "extras" for the film. McCoy knew that he was within easy distance of the Ghost Dance Prophet, and decided to go on a "fool's errand" in search of him. McCoy recorded that he drove to Yerington where he found Wovoka and persuaded him to visit Bishop the following day. Three decades after the end of the Ghost Dance, Wovoka found the Arapahos deferential. But McCoy commented: "Whatever he was to the Arapahoes, Wovoka was still a Paiute Medicine Man to me and I would not put out of my head the story that some years before, after prophesying an early winter, he had directed a flunky to dump blocks of ice into the river near his home. The story of the floating ice, repeated in numerous accounts of the Prophet, may have been that "miracle" witnessed by E.A. Dyer on the banks of the Walker River. Wovoka had told a group of Paiutes that he would make ice fall from the heavens despite the mid-July heat. According to Dyer, Wovoka probably secreted a block of ice high in the limbs of a cottonwood tree whereupon, after sufficient melting, it dropped to the ground, shattering and thereby amazing a hundred Paiutes gathered around their holy man.

Another story, the one alluded to by McCoy, tells of Wovoka having caused ice to float down the river in mid-July. The "flunky" that McCoy refers to was actually two people, the Wilson boys, who served as the Prophet's confederates in a ruse to awaken credulity among the Paiute congregation. This story is repeated by Bailey, who used as his source Beth Wilson Ellis, daughter of William Wilson. That McCoy knew of this episode at the time he met Wovoka is doubtful. He probably learned about it from Bailey who had interviewed him for the biography of Wovoka. Dyer himself had heard this story a number of years after he witnessed the ice "miracle." But of the ice-in-the-river incident he wrote: "Whether that was a distortion of what I witnessed or a separate affair I can't state." McCoy also told Bailey during the author's research that the Prophet "appeared to have the impression that he would never die." In his memoirs, however, McCoy writes that, just before leaving the movie set at Bishop, Wovoka turned to him and said, "I will never die." What had been an impression became a declaration, but it is doubtful that Wovoka truly believed himself to be immortal. The difference in the accounts, on the surface quite trivial, nevertheless account for some of the misperceptions about Wovoka.

The last years of Wovoka's life were relatively uneventful, but he lived for nine years after his visit with McCoy. Wovoka, the great Ghost Dance Prophet, died on September 20, 1932 and was buried in the heart of the Paiute country.

Joseph McDonald of the *Reno Evening Gazette* wrote an obituary about Wovoka, explaining that after the Prophet's death in Yerington, his body was taken to the Paiute cemetery at Shurtz. As family and friends shoveled dirt into his grave, a Christian missionary, the Reverend E.H. Emig, recited prayers. "Whether a special marker will be placed over the grave," McDonald wondered, "has not been decided. It is in the family plot in the Indian burying ground, but Indians at Shurtz and vicinity have indicated that it will represent no special shrine of worship for them . . . though Wovoka once was the Powerful Paiute of the tribe. Of late years he has acted as a medicine man, but failing health caused him to become very inactive recently." Ironically, the same newspaper reported the following month that "Indians were staging a ghost dance at Pine Grove under the direction of Jack Wilson, the Indian Messiah."

The most comprehensive study of Wovoka was made by James Mooney, an anthropologist of the Smithsonian Institute's Bureau of American Ethnography. Between 1890 and 1894, Mooney studied the Prophet and his religion, documenting a good deal of his information directly from Wovoka. Mooney left an extensive work on Wovoka, a classic memoir entitled "The Ghost Dance Religion and the Sioux Outbreak of 1890." Aside from this study, Wovoka's life and religion evoked little interest until 1957 when Paul Bailey published the first and only biography of the Prophet. Like Mooney's study, Bailey's book is sympathetic to Wovoka but intimates that the Prophet trifled with fate and reaped the whirlwind. According to Bailey, Wovoka's religion "came at a time when the Indian was a beaten, frustrated, starved creature, without hope." And Wovoka, "whether divinely inspired prophet, or opportunist and faker," provided hope for numerous Indians. The inference drawn by Bailey is that chance, in all its perversity and irony, intervened and swept along the Prophet and his vision of a restored Indian world toward an unimagined destiny.

Although Wovoka was one of the foremost Indian prophets of his time, no one has erected a monument in his honor at his gravesite at Schurtz, Nevada. However, in 1975, at a cost of $900, the Yerington Paiute tribe placed a marker as its bicentennial project in the town where Wovoka spent the last twenty years of his life. In the windswept cemetery at Schurtz, the wood grave marker first placed there in 1932 still stands and records the birth and death, not of Wovoka, the Ghost Dance Prophet, but of Jack Wilson. The mound of sand, well-tended, bears the weathered gifts and offerings—mostly sprigs of sage, flags made of ribbon, and now desiccated flowers in dry mason jars—left there periodically by those who still honor his memory. Anthropologists, historians, and buffs have written thousands of words about Wovoka, trying unsuccessfully to unravel the mysteries that conceal the character of the man. In all the speculation, use of imagination, and other methods of their art, no person has written a more fitting epitaph than that of Edward A. Dyer, Jr., son of

Wovoka's trusted friend. "Despite the narrow opinion of some of Jack's white contemporaries in Mason Valley," Dyer wrote, "I submit that he was a very great man who without help, tools, or understanding tried to better the lot of his people who were hit by a cataclysm with which they were unable to cope."

Like Joel, Paul, and countless other prophets and religious leaders, Wovoka had dreamed a dream and had seen a vision. That his vision was unshared by the majority of his countrymen should not diminish his contributions to the rich religious heritage of the American people. Rather than dismiss Wovoka as an opportunist whose doctrine unwittingly inflamed a large number of American Indians who longed for a deliverer, one might also envision a sincere prophet who misdiagnosed the end of the world. In this regard he was far from unique. He was probably as surprised and disappointed as his coreligionists when his dream failed and the glory of the Indian millennium failed to unfold.

The Ghost Dance religion, identified as a "revitalization movement" more than a half-century after its dissolution, was only one of many such Indian movements. Like the others, it sought to return the world to a happier time. However, none of the Indian movements, up until 1890, were as widespread or as popular as the Ghost Dance. Wovoka, the Ghost Dance Prophet, offered American Indians surcease through the intervention of the supernatural to their tragic confrontation with the dominant society. As Joel had promised the Israelites, if they rededicated themselves to the religion of their fathers, God would pour out his blessings. Wovoka told his followers to lay aside their differences, celebrate their heritage, and await the blessings of the Creator. By any standard, Wovoka, the Ghost Dance Prophet, was one of the most significant holy men ever to emerge among the Indians of North America.

6

Progressive-Era Bureaucrats and the Unity of Twentieth-Century Indian Policy

Russel Lawrence Barsh

The history of American Indian policy has been described as a series of policy reversals driven by a dialectic of separation and assimilation. The attention given to John Collier, credited with the renunciation of assimilation in the 1930s, strengthens the image of an heroic, Manichean struggle. A strong case can be made that Indian policy has been marked by a diversity of forms, but a continuity of effect, at least as far as land and resources are concerned. Continuity is inconsistent with heroes and struggles. It points to the steady, guiding hand of bureaucracy.

Progressive-era bureaucrats viewed the subdivision of Indian lands, establishment of tribal governments and corporations, and transfer of federal responsibilities to the states as successive stages of a *single* policy of gradual integration and assimilation of Indians. In 1912 New York activist Arthur C. Ludington, a former colleague of Woodrow Wilson at Princeton University, was employed to prepare a reassessment of Indian policy. Ludington's long-term plan, while never formally endorsed by the Indian Office, accurately anticipated events of the next fifty years. This suggests that Ludington crystallized the thinking of the generation of bureaucrats who were still in control when John Collier purportedly "reversed" direction in 1934.

Before examining the details of Ludington's plan, it will be useful to place him and his work in the context of the social and economic forces that were shaping national politics in the years just prior to the First World War.

Reprinted from the *American Indian Quarterly*, volume 15, number 1 (winter 1991) by permission of the University of Nebraska Press. Copyright © 1991 by the University of Nebraska Press.

WILSON AND THE "NEW FREEDOM"

The first fifteen years of the twentieth century witnessed profound changes in the way Americans conceived themselves and their destiny. The domestic frontier had vanished, replaced by a germinal transoceanic empire as a result of the 1898 war with Spain. Domestic social and industrial conditions were attacked by "muckrakers," and growing labor unrest led to the emergence of the "Wobblies." Immigration increased so alarmingly, in the eyes of native-born citizens, that a special Congressional commission was created to study its causes and control. Public confidence in traditional institutions was eroding rapidly.

The immense popularity of Theodore Roosevelt was buoyed by his forceful advocacy of government intervention in the cause of social justice. "The people had come to regard him as a Moses to lead us into the Promised land of justice for the common man," James Truslow Adams caustically observed, "but Roosevelt himself had no map of the way into that land." Disappointment with his successor and protégé, William Taft, led Roosevelt to reclaim his Presidential throne in 1912 and, when he was unable to secure the Republican nomination, to take the Progressive wing out of the party. Although this virtually assured victory for Woodrow Wilson, the Democratic candidate, the race produced a rich debate on the prospects and methods of social change.

The need for fundamental reform was readily accepted by both presidential candidates. Where they differed was with respect to the *form* government intervention should take. Roosevelt believed in the necessity of strict government regulation of economy, while Wilson abhorred paternalism and placed his faith instead in promoting equal opportunity and stimulating competition. He was a liberal in the classic mold who preferred "the structural steel of law, so that no man can doubt what his rights are," to social bureaucracies engaged in "tutelage and supervision." Although a scholar by profession, he was emphatic in denouncing "scientific" government as antidemocratic. "What I fear, therefore, is a government of experts. God forbid that in a democratic country we should resign the task and give the government over to experts. What are we for if we are to be scientifically taken care of by a small number of gentlemen who are the only men who understand the job?" The cornerstone of Wilsonian reform, then, was individualism sustained by law rather than what he disparaged as "benevolence." "Benevolence never developed a man or a nation," Wilson explained during the presidential campaign. "We do not want a benevolent government."

SOCIAL CHANGE AND EVOLUTION

During the 1880s, American scholars promoted an evolutionary model of social development that influenced the design of Indian policy, immigrant programs and colonial policy in the Pacific. According to this view, each race was destined to pass gradually through the same structural stages of economic, intellectual, and social organization. Anthropologists described a progression from savagery (hunting) to barbarism (pastoralism) and civilization (agriculture), while political scientists elaborated on the transformation of simple monarchies into aristocracy and various forms of individualistic democracy.

One of Roosevelt's professors at Columbia, John Burgess, had been a champion of evolutionism, and in his opus, *The Winning of the West*, Roosevelt expounded at length on Anglo-Saxon racial superiority. He maintained this perspective as president.

On the one hand I very firmly believe in granting to Negroes and to all other races the largest amount of self-government which they can exercise. On the other hand, I have the impatient contempt that I suppose all practical men must have for the ridiculous theorists who decline to face facts and who wish to give even to the most utterly undeveloped races of mankind a degree of self-government which only the very highest races have been able to exercise with any advantage.

Roosevelt did not doubt the capacity of other races to learn self-government, but only as the result of a gradual achievement. To a class at Tuskegee Institute, he explained:

The race cannot expect to get everything at once. It must learn to wait and bide its time; to prove itself worthy by showing its possession of perseverance, of thrift, of self-control. The destiny of the race is chiefly in its own hands, and must be worked out patiently and persistently along these lines.

If anything, Wilson was even more committed, intellectually, to the evolutionist viewpoint. As a political scientist he had ascribed to the notion of a "law of coherence and continuity in political development," in which forms of political organization evolve inexorably in every society, in the direction of liberal democracy. By the same reasoning, "revolutions" were bound to fail. "Political growth refuses to be forced; and institutions have grown with the slow growth of social relationships; have changed in response, not to new theories, but to new circumstances. The evolutions of politics have been scarcely less orderly and coherent than those of the physical world." The practical significance of this was plain to reformers of the Progressive era. Backward social classes, nationalities, and races were capable of gradual improvement, but only by means of leading them through the proper sequence of developmental stages. Any other course would naturally fail.

IMMIGRATION AND ASSIMILATION

Assimilating the waves of "new" immigrants from southern and eastern Europe was a more pressing issue than the assimilation of American Indians.

More than a million immigrants arrived in 1910 alone, a quarter of them from Austria-Hungary, compared with the total Indian population of fewer than 300,000. It was popularly believed that Indians were "vanishing," moreover, while the rising tide of immigration showed no sign of abatement.

Progressive-era policy reflected President Roosevelt's own outspoken aversion to "hyphenated Americans," and his commitment to complete assimilation.

We are a nation, and not a hodge-podge of foreign nationalities. We are a people, and not a polyglot boardinghouse. We must insist on a unified nationality, with one flag, one language, one set of national ideals. We must shun as we would shun the plague all efforts to make us separate nationalities. We must all of us be Americans, and nothing but Americans.

In this America there was little room for distinct cultures, European or indigenous. The "Dillingham Commission," created by Congress in 1907 to study the immigration problem, concluded on rather dubious statistical grounds that the "new" immigrants were racially inferior to those of Anglo-Nordic stock who had arrived previously. In opposition to this assessment, the "settlement" movement based in New York City argued that immigrants' miserable social conditions were not due to any inherent inferiority, but to the absence of programs to prepare them for the competitive, democratic American lifestyle. Settlement work was a nursery for reformers and political activists, including Indian Commissioner Robert Valentine, Arthur Ludington, and John Collier.

Accompanying this advocacy of the educability of immigrants was a larger concern with social adjustment to an increasingly industrial economy, for which even native-born workers were unprepared. "Industrial training" became fashionable as teachers sought ways of using schools as instruments of social change and development. As W.B. Hunter wrote in the *School Review* in 1910, "Can the public schools of our country be so vitalized in purpose and methods that their graduates may be of immediate service to businessmen and to manufacturers, instead of necessitating two or three more years of special training in order properly to perform their duties?"

The Progressive Era was likewise characterized by an abiding faith in the value of extending democracy to all spheres of life, from schools to factories. Student participation in decision-making was extolled for teaching "the spirit of democracy in school life," resulting in "growth in self-control and personal responsibility." Industrial co-management was the best means of avoiding the evils of confrontative unionism and socialism. Democracy was not so much a matter of right as a means to an end, the end being full citizenship in a liberal society.

Woodrow Wilson was not immune to the prejudices of his time. His *History of the American People*, written at Princeton, refers disparagingly to the "new" immigrants, a fact that was to cause him intense embarrassment during his presidential campaign, and at Princeton he had opposed the admission of blacks. He could not regard backwardness as hereditary, however, and was even accused of naivete for advocating self-government for colonized peoples abroad. Wilson likewise endorsed an "expedition" for American Indian citizenship organized by a number of private businessmen, and recorded a message of brotherhood to be played to each tribe on a phonograph lent for this purpose by Thomas Edison.

INDIAN ALLOTMENT AND CITIZENSHIP

The idea of individualizing Indian land ownership to promote civilization had roots in the early nineteenth century. By the 1850s, Indian treaties authorized the president to subdivide and allot reservation lands, and the 1887 General Allotment Act extended this authority to most Indian reservations, irrespective of treaties. For Theodore Roosevelt, allotment was the "great pulverizing engine" needed to break down Indians' collective economic and social institutions.

The original program provided for an initial 25-year "trust" period, during which the individual allottee would remain under federal supervision before receiving legal title and citizenship. In 1906 the Burke Act gave the Indian Office discretionary authority to grant fee title on individual applications. In 1910, Congress authorized "forced fees," that is, granting title with or without the consent of the Indian allottee. From 1906 to 1915, the pace of subdivision and fee-patents accelerated, resulting in a considerable reduction of the Indian land base. During the same period, government Indian schools were restructured along the "industrial" model, and for the first time children were permitted to enroll in other public or private schools "according to the wishes of the parents."

Indian adaptation was rapid and often successful. The aims of agrarian self-sufficiency and individualized citizenship were moreover supported by the growing ranks of Indian professionals, speaking through the Society of American Indians and other newly formed Indian organizations. Some thirty thousand Indians were already registered to vote. This was, nonetheless, also a time of growing romanticism among Americans as a whole, for the cultures they had destroyed. J.P. Morgan invested $1.5 million in the ethnographic work of Edward Curtis, and Congress set aside land on Staten Island for a "memorial to the memory of the American Indian." An ambivalent combination of nostalgia and assimilation was directed equally at immigrants.

Traditional culture was tolerable if it was trivial or could be used as an instrument of social change. A 1907 Indian Office circular exemplified this attitude:

I am glad to have the simple songs which the Indians have learned at home in their childhood preserved by their young people, just as among the children of the Caucasian race the nursery songs and lullabies are among the sweetest memories they carry into later life. Although I would use every means to encourage the children to learn English, that being one of the objects for which they are brought to school, I do not consider that their singing their little songs in their native tongue does anybody any harm, and it helps to make easier the perilous and difficult bridge which they are crossing at this stage of their race development.

PROGRESSIVES' INDIAN POLICY

Robert Valentine was the ideal Progressive commissioner of Indian Affairs. A Harvard graduate, he had done settlement work in New York City before coming to Washington, D.C. His career with the Indian office began as secretary to Commissioner Francis Leupp, a Roosevelt appointee who was occupied with civil service reform and management efficiency. Valentine continued this course when he became commissioner in 1909. After the 1912 Progressive presidential defeat, Valentine left government service to work as a business consultant, and was credited with "the introduction of objective standards into collective bargaining." He was also a leading figure in the movement for industrial democracy.

Valentine's prescription to make the Indian "first, a solid, healthy human being, and second, a good laborer or other workman" was based on providing real incentives. "They often are lazy just as you or I would be lazy if we had no great worry as to where our means were coming from." For this reason he supported selling "surplus" tribal land, and issuing rations only in cases of demonstrated need. At the same time, he opposed the wholesale opening of reservations, or the automatic granting of patents and citizenship to Indians, preferring to take citizenship decisions in individual cases. He believed in the possibility of planned assimilation, employing the most modern methods. "The whole Indian Service is one great citizenship school for Indians, and all the lands and forests and rivers, all the funds, tribal and individual, are but textbooks and laboratories in this school wherein teach over five thousand men and women, the employees of the Indian service." This included instituting representative democracy at the earliest possible stage. In an address to Indian students at the Sherman Institute, he stressed, "The day has come when the Indian Bureau at Washington makes a mistake if it seeks to take a single forward step in connection with your affairs without consulting you Indians yourselves about it." It was "humiliating," he observed for a bureaucrat to do things that "Indians could have told him more about than he knew himself."

Valentine once described his job as "a steady, daily case of listening to persons with doubtful standards and not losing one's own; of meeting people who mean well but do little, and not being made a mere idealist." He hoped to rebuild the Indian agency with a carefully screened staff of "practical sociologists with more or less actual experience of business and in meeting human problems," who were imbued with the "true missionary spirit" and might be found in settlement work and in colonial administration. The Indian office would pursue "experiments" such as organizing a tribal council to manage the Hoopa Reservation, and recruiting an expert from the American administration in Cuba to promote student democracy in Indian schools.

At the same time there was growing pressure from Congress to complete Indians' assimilation and wind up the costly operations of the Indian Office. The process of subdividing and patenting Indian reservation lands was barely half completed by 1912, and impatient legislators threatened to dismantle the Indian Office by 1922. Interior Department officials agreed with "giving the Indians every opportunity to become independent, self-sufficing citizens." To succeed, however, "the guiding principle in this effort must be to place on every Indian as fast as possible the greatest burden he can bear, but not to overwhelm him with burdens."

A "definite plan" was nevertheless being prepared, Congress was assured, for completing all allotments by 1925, and preparing all Indians to be citizen-freeholders by 1950. "What the federal Government has not accomplished by that year, it had better leave to the Indians themselves."

ARTHUR LUDINGTON'S TASK

Independently wealthy, Ludington attended Yale, Heidelberg, and Columbia, but never received a degree beyond his bachelor's. At age 26, he left a Wall Street brokerage house to serve as Woodrow Wilson's personal assistant at Princeton, then in 1908 returned to New York to pursue "political reform work" as a Progressive. His chief interest appears to have been ballot reform, an exceedingly technical aspect of the contemporary movement for more representative democracy, and on this topic he published a number of didactic articles in the journal of the fledgling American Political Science Association, in which he was active. After his sudden death at the age of 35, colleagues described him as "intensely useful and rarely conspicuous." He was, then, a consummate *eminence grise* in the political reform circles of his day when asked to prepare the "definite plan" for Indian assimilation.

Ludington approached the task methodically. He distributed a standardized survey to all Indian reservation superintendents, asking whether citizenship had been effective as a means of either "stimulating an Indian to greater effort" or of "educating the Indian." He read published works on European colonial policy, and studied the past policies and practices of the United States in detail. By April 1912, he had drafted an assessment of the allotment program, followed by "a tentative outline of Indian policy," which laid out his proposal for the next 25 years of Indian programs.

Ludington observed that the United States "had always followed the policy of allowing immigrants to vote as soon as possible," which had "proved an effective means of assimilating aliens rapidly." But immigrants "have come from countries living under a more or less civilized government, and where property has been privately owned for centuries." Even with that advantage, experts "pretty well agreed that far more should be done for them." This led him to focus his reading on the "nature-nurture" question. His notes on one book ask:

How far are the backward races educable? Is there a point at which their physical make-up prevents further mental development? Or is their backwardness merely the result of an environment different from ours—and can we gradually bring them up to our level by changing their environment?

"Native races must develop, without a complete break with their past," Ludington learned from one treatise. "Some institutions, however, must be deliberately undermined and eventually attacked openly," to be replaced by more "helpful" ones. In any case, a study on South Africa warned, "We should not be in too much of a hurry to make progress with them, but should give them time to let the results of what they have learned sink in."

From these comparative studies, Ludington hit upon the idea that limited self-government might constitute one element of the "new environment." He wrote this "suggestion" to himself:

Indian communities may need for some time to come, even after all their members are citizens, some form of discipline and control over their members in minor matters (such as is exercised on reservations by the superintendent). If so some way should be devised by which the authority exercising this supplementary control should be constituted by the Indians themselves.

Emphasize the importance of local self-government as a means of training the Indian during the preliminary—as well a during the trust period.

The original idea of allotment, Ludington reasoned in his first report to the commissioner, was to use the 25-year period of limited citizenship as "a training school for the eventual grant of complete and unrestricted citizenship." The Burke Act had undermined this by perpetuating federal supervision over the allottees. "Citizenship is not regarded as in any sense *something which educates*," as a result, "but solely as *something which one must be educated for*." The exercise of citizenship can only be learned through "practice," however. "In practice paying taxes, being sued for debt in a local court, being prosecuted for offences against state laws, being solicited for his vote, being freed from agency control—these things will teach the Indian in a year more as to the meaning of citizenship than all the other forms of training put together."

Allotment failed to teach citizenship because "the citizen Indian [is] treated in exactly the same way as the non-citizen Indian." Both were subjected to "arbitrary restraint by the agent of their personal liberty," and both were indulged in the provision of free rations and farm supplies. It was essential to replace this with a "clearly marked" distinction between citizen and noncitizen status.

THE PLAN FOR INDIAN REFORM

In a second paper, Ludington moved from policy analysis to a long-range "program of action." He first reassured the Indian Office that there could be no retreat from the goal to "train them [Indians] for the unrestricted exercise of citizenship, with a view to their complete assimilation eventually into the mass of the white population."

The alternative policy of maintaining the separate tribal organizations as semi-independent bodies-politic, keeping them permanently segregated on closed reservations and encouraging them to preserve their inherited institutions, customs and religion, while still theoretically conceivable, has long been practically out of the question.

"Most of the methods and activities proposed are those which are now being employed," Ludington added. They were "merely grouped, summarized and presented in such a way as to be readily grasped in their proper relation to the program as a whole," although he admitted suggesting a number of "totally new lines of activity" as well.

The allotment policy involved "training for full citizenship by means of a preliminary period of citizenship under the tutelage of the federal government," that is, "a period of training for complete control of property by means of restricted control of property; a period of training for unaided citizenship by means of guided and assisted citizenship." This was a sensible principle, but it had never been implemented properly. Citizenship had been granted all at once, not in graduated stages. The program had moreover placed too much of an emphasis on property, as opposed to the political aspects of citizenship. The remedy was a phased approach, including "some system of local self-government on the reservation" to serve as "preparation" for participation in state government.

Ludington suggested a "*period of preliminary training*," to be completed by 1925; a "*period of final training*, or trust period," to end by 1950; then "unrestricted citizenship." This "steady, orderly progression" avoided "too large and abrupt an increase in responsibilities." Nonetheless "the Indian should be made conscious of a real and well-marked change in the conditions of his daily life" at each stage, else "the educational value of our training process is lost."

In the first stage, Indians would continue to maintain their tribal organizations, live on closed reservations, and hold land in common. Tribal institutions would be modified gradually, however, to train Indians for the exercise of political rights. "This could be done by establishing some form of local self-government on each reservation modelled, so far as possible, on the local government of neighboring communities. School republics in the schools would also be useful for this purpose." Indian courts would also be strengthened, and required to follow procedures more like those applied in state courts to give them a "greater educative value."

By 1925, all Indians would be living on their individually allotted lands, intermingled with whites. "This is important if citizenship is to have any education value," Ludington noted. "Citizenship where there are no white men, and no organized local government, is a rather meaningless term." They would continue to be subject to certain restrictions as to their property, but not in their civil rights. Since "the only real training in the exercise of these rights is experience," Indians would be "urged" to vote, serve on juries, and pay taxes. They would have to look to lawyers and state courts, rather than the Indian Office, for the protection of their rights.

For this "final training" to be effective, however, Indians would not be completely dispersed or individualized. Allotments should be clustered "to produce compact, organic communities" of Indians, who might continue to manage nonagricultural property jointly through incorporation.

Certain kinds of property, not susceptible of physical division to advantage—such as timber, coal, oil, gas and mineral lands—as well as tribal industries requiring any sort of common plant—such as a saw-mill—to be divided up by means of a share-holding plan under which the Federal government will retain the legal, and the shareholders the equitable title.

After 1950, Indians would enjoy "complete and unrestricted citizenship." Social needs, such as education and public health, would be transferred to state control. Any remaining tribally owned enterprises would simply self-destruct: "It is probable that the ownership of most of the shares would, in time, fall into the hands of whites; and it is provided in the plan that such a majority of white shareholders can at any time terminate the trusteeship of the Federal government."

Ludington cautioned against applying this scheme uniformly to all parts of the country without regard for actual conditions. It would have to be "elastic." It was also a two-way process. The states needed time to "gain as much experience as possible in dealing with the Indians" before 1950, and during the interim the Indian Office would have to be prepared to resume responsibility if state programs proved "ineffective," or failed to "treat the Indians fairly."

BUREAUCRACY AND CONTINUITY

After Ludington's departure from the Indian Office in 1913, there was no further official reference to him. The pace of the allotment program accelerated, however. Congress conferred citizenship on all Indians in 1924, close to Ludington's target, and in the restricted form he had recommended. Congress also took steps to settle remaining land claims and thus, it was hoped, to cut away any residual attachment Indians may have had to their tribes.

John Collier took command of the Indian Office in 1933, just as Congress was considering legislation to fix a target date for completing the citizenship process. His plans for Indian self-government were politically appealing precisely beccause they were consistent with the goal of assimilation, and he used Ludington's arguments to underscore this point. Self-government would offer Indians "experience in civic and business responsibility and the opportunity to manage property and money," which would educate them for "real assimilation." That Congress viewed Indian self-government in these terms, rather than as a matter of right, is clear from the fact that it authorized the Indian Office to begin transferring programs to the states during the same session. Indeed, Congress demanded to know whether self-government was *still necessary* as early as 1943, and began dismantling tribes in earnest ten years later. Even the Supreme Court was Ludingtonian in its interpretation of the Indian New Deal. While states were obliged to respect the "right of reservation Indians to make their own laws and be ruled by them" lacking federal legislation to the contrary, the real aim was to transfer responsibility to the states "as soon as the educational and economic status of the Indians permits the change without disadvantage to them."

It is probably no coincidence that the rhetoric of "Indian self-determination" emerged in the 1970s during another period of fiscal strain, or that its strongest advocates were Republican presidents. Stripped of its symbolism, the practical result of post-1970 Indian policy has been to shift responsibility from federal to state and tribal authorities, and to integrate tribes into the overall national administrative and political framework. If tribal, state, and federal institutions continue to converge, is this not very effective assimilation?

Through all of this, the Bureau of Indian Affairs survived by repeatedly persuading Congress to prolong the "period of final training," and to try different techniques of assimilation. When Congress considered winding it up in 1912, the agency countered with a "definite plan" that would take 50 years to implement. The next time Congress considered sunset legislation was in 1931, and the agency suggested that reorganizing tribal society would be more effective than continuing allotment. When Congress rumbled again in 1947, the bureau argued that some tribes were not ready for state control, and produced a list. The bureau's adoption of the rhetoric of tribal sovereignty in the 1980s is no less defensive and does not reflect a genuine change in U.S. policy objectives.

The 1971 Alaska Native Claims Settlement Act is arguably the exception that proves the rule. Just a year after President Nixon renounced "termination" in a message to Congress, Alaskan tribes were terminated. The bureau cooperated with Congress in designing the act, and has fought it ever since.

Bureaucrats outlast elected officials, and believe they know their job better. Because they control implementation, they can deflect any effort to change policy direction. In the 1880s the Indian bureau responded to reformers by seizing upon the idea of a "civilizing mission" to justify increasing its own staff and resources, and perpetuating its existence. Since then, efforts to emancipate Indians as individuals or as tribes have met with arguments for extending the "weaning period" from trusteeship. Gradualism is always effective because it confounds self-interest with apparent sympathy for Indians.

Bureaucracies also have long memories. Their organizational culture spans the lives of the oldest bureaucrats. The use of self-government as an instrument of assimilation was not entirely novel, even in 1912. Indian tribal police, courts, and councils were used for "educational" purposes in many parts of the country as early as the 1870s. Ludington's work simply underscores the consistency of this reasoning, from the mid-nineteenth century to the Indian New Deal.

CONCLUSIONS

Arthur Ludington's plan was a product of its time, an era of confidently nationalistic and self-consciously scientific social instrumentalism. Societies could be reshaped at will to fit new industrial and political conditions, and society itself was but a tool for social change. The assimilation of Indians ceased to be a religious mission or a business proposition; it was a job for professionals. Ludington made sense to bureaucrats because his was a consummately bureaucratic vision. What is more important, it saved the company. Congress went away for another 19 years.

There is no need to reassess the nature of the assimilation-separation dialectic. It is not chronological but institutional, between Congress and the bureaucracy, in which the latter plans to put off the date by which assimilation must be completed. As long as there are any distinct tribal entities, they will be easy targets for budget-cutters, so "assimilation in earnest" will be characteristic of every recession. Thus far, the bureaucracy has succeeded in co-opting these periodic Congressional encroachments, however, by agreeing with the ultimate assimilation goal, but offering to do the job better and more thoroughly, if given more time and new tools.

For Further Reading

ON THE DAWES ACT AND ASSIMILATION

Benson, Todd. "The Consequences of Reservation Life: Native Californians on the Round Valley Reservation, 1871–1884." *Pacific Review* 60, 1991.

Berthrong, Donald. *The Cheyenne and Arapaho Ordeal: Reservation and Agency Life in the Indian Territory, 1875–1907.* Norman: University of Oklahoma Press, 1976.

———. "Legacies of the Dawes Act: Bureaucrats and Land Thieves at the Cheyenne-Arapaho Agencies in Oklahoma." In Peter Iverson, ed., *Plains Indians in the Twentieth Century.* Norman: University of Oklahoma Press, 1985.

Black Elk. *Black Elk Speaks* (orig.). New York: Morrow, 1932.

Carlson, Leonard A. *Indians, Bureaucrats and the Land: The Dawes Act and the Decline of Indian Farming.* Westport, CT: Greenwood Press, 1981.

Farr, William E. *The Reservation Blackfeet, 1882–1915: A Photographic History of Cultural Survival.* Seattle: University of Washington Press, 1984.

Fritz, Henry F. *The Movement for Indian Assimilation, 1860–1890.* Philadelphia: University of Pennsylvania Press, 1963.

Hinckley, Ted C. "'We Are More Truly Heathen Than the Natives': John G. Brady and the Assimilation of Alaska's Tlingit Indians." *Western Historical Quarterly* 11, 1980.

Holford, David M. "The Subversion of the Indian Land Allotment System, 1887–1934." *The Indian Historian* 8, 1975.

Hoxie, Frederick E. *A Final Promise: The Campaign to Assimilate the Indians, 1880–1920.* Lincoln: University of Nebraska Press, 1984.

Keller, Robert. *American Protestantism and United States Indian Policy, 1869–82.* Lincoln: University of Nebraska Press, 1983.

Meyer, Melissa L. "'We Can Not Get a Living as We Used to': Dispossession of the White Earth Anishinaabeg, 1899–1920." *American Historical Review* 96, 1991.

Milner, Clyde. *With Good Intentions: Quaker Work Among the Pawnee, Otos, and Omahas in the 1870s.* Lincoln: University of Nebraska Press, 1982.

Nespor, Robert Paschal. "From War Lance to Plow Share: The Cheyenne Dog Soldiers as Farmers, 1879–1930s." *Chronicles of Oklahoma* 65, 1987.

Prucha, Francis Paul, ed. *Americanizing the American Indian: Writings by the "Friends of the Indians," 1880–1900.* Cambridge, MA: Harvard University Press, 1973.

Standing Bear, Luther. *My People, the Sioux.* Boston: Houghton Mifflin, 1928.

Trennert, Robert A. *White Men's Medicine: Government Doctors and the Navajos, 1863–1955.* Albuquerque: University of New Mexico Press, 1998.

Washburn, Wilcomb E. *The Assault on Indian Tribalism: The General Allotment Law (Dawes Act) of 1887.* Philadelphia: Lippincott, 1975.

ON BOARDING SCHOOLS AND INDIAN EDUCATION

Adams, David Wallace. *Education for Extinction: American Indians and the Boarding School Experience.* Lawrence: University Press of Kansas, 1997.

Archuleta, Margaret L., et al., eds. *Away from Home: American Indian Boarding School Experiences.* Phoenix: Heard Museum, 2000.

Barker, Debra K.S. "Kill the Indian, Save the Child: Cultural Genocide and the Boarding School." In Dean Morrison, ed., *American Indian Studies: An Interdisciplinary Approach to Contemporary Issues.* New York: Peter Lang, 1997.

Bloom, John. *To Show What an Indian Can Do: Sports at Native American Boarding Schools.* Minneapolis: University of Minnesota Press, 2000.

Carroll, James T. *Seeds of Faith: Catholic Indian Boarding Schools.* New York: Garland Publishing, 2000.

Child, Brenda J. *Boarding School Sessions: American Indian Families, 1900–1948.* Lincoln: University of Nebraska Press, 1998.

Churchill, W., N.S. Hill, and M.J. Barlow, "Twentieth Century Native American Athletics." *The Indian Historian* 12, 1979.

Coleman, Michael C. *American Indian Children at School, 1850–1930.* Jackson: University of Mississippi Press, 1993.

Cooper, Michael L. *Indian School: Teaching the White Man's Way.* Boston: Houghton Mifflin, 1999.

Fuchs, Estelle and Robert Havighurst. *To Live on This Earth: American Indian Education.* Garden City, NY: Doubleday, 1972.

Kickingbird, Kirke and Lynn Kickingbird. "A Short History of Indian Education." *American Indian Journal* 5, 1979.

Lomawaima, K. Tsianina. *They Called It Prairie Light: The Story of Chilocco Indian School.* Lincoln: University of Nebraska Press, 1995.

McBeth, Sally J. "Indian Boarding Schools and Ethnic Identity: An Example from the Southern Plains Tribes of Oklahoma." *Plains Anthropologist* 28, 1983.

Mihesuah, Devon. *Cultivating the Rosebuds: The Education of Women at the Cherokee Female Seminary, 1851–1909.* Urbana: University of Illinois Press, 1997.

Pratt, Richard Henry. *Battlefield and Classroom: Four Decades with the American Indians, 1867–1904.* New Haven: Yale University Press, 1964.

———. *The Indian Industrial School, Carlisle, Pennsylvania: Its Origins, Purposes, Progress, and the Difficulties Surmounted.* Carlisle, PA: Cumberland County Historical Society, 1979.

Prucha, Francis Paul. *The Churches and the Indian Schools, 1888–1912.* Lincoln: University of Nebraska Press, 1979.

Riney, Scott. *The Rapid City Indian School, 1898–1933.* Norman: University of Oklahoma Press, 1999.

Stein, Wayne J. "American Indian Education." In Dean Morrison, ed., *American Indian Studies: An Interdisciplinary Approach to Contemporary Issues.* New York: Peter Lang, 1997.

Szasz, Margaret Connell. *Education and the American Indian: The Road to Self-Sufficiency Since 1928.* Albuquerque: University of New Mexico Press, 1999.

Trennert, Robert A. "Educating Indian Girls at Nonreservation Boarding Schools, 1878–1920." *Western Historical Quarterly* 13, 1982.

———. *The Phoenix Indian School: Forced Assimilation in Arizona.* Norman: University of Oklahoma Press, 1988.

Wood, Jeremy. "Non-Indian High School Has Serious Flaws." *American Indian Journal* 6, 1980.

ON THE GHOST DANCE MOVEMENT

Hittman, Michael. *Wovoka and the Ghost Dance.* Lincoln: University of Nebraska Press, 1997.

Kehoe, Alice Beck. *The Ghost Dance: Ethnohistory and Revitalization.* New York: Holt, Rinehart, and Winston, 1989.

Lame Deer, John (Fire) with Richard Erdoes. *Lame Deer: Seeker of Visions.* New York: Simon and Schuster, 1972.

Miller, David Humphreys. *Ghost Dance.* New York: Duell, Sloan, and Pierce, 1959.

Mooney, James. *The Ghost Dance Religion and the Sioux Outbreak of 1890* (reprint of 1896 report). Lincoln: University of Nebraska Press, 1991.

Moses, L.G. "Jack Wilson and the Indian Service: The Response of the BIA to the Ghost Dance Prophet." *American Indian Quarterly* 5, 1979.

Thornton, Russell. *We Shall Live Again: The 1870 and 1890 Ghost Dance Movements as Demographic Revitalization.* New York: Cambridge University Press, 1986.

Utley, Robert M. *Last Days of the Sioux Nation.* New Haven: Yale University Press, 1963.

ON WORLD WAR I AND PROGRESSIVE ERA POLICIES

American Indian Quarterly 15:1, Winter 1991 (edition on "Progressive-Era Bureaucrats").

Britten, Thomas A. *American Indians in World War I: At Home and at War.* Albuquerque: University of New Mexico, 1999.

Finger, John R. "Conscription, Citizenship, and Civilization: World War I and the Eastern Band of Cherokees." *North Carolina Historical Review* 63, 1986.

For Further Reading

Henriksson, Markku. *The Indian on Capitol Hill: Indian Legislation and the United States Congress, 1862–1907*. Helsinki: Studia Historica, 1988.

Hoxie, Frederick E., ed. *Talking Back to Civilization: Indian Voices from the Progressive Era*. New York: Bedford/St. Martin's, 2001.

Miner, Craig. *The Corporation and the Indian: Tribal Sovereignty and Industrial Civilization in Indian Territory, 1865–1907*. Columbia: University of Missouri Press, 1976.

Prucha, Francis Paul. *American Indian Policy in Crisis: Christian Reformers and the Indian, 1865–1900*. Norman: University of Oklahoma Press, 1976.

Roberts, Charles. "The Cushman Indian Trade School and World War I." *American Indian Quarterly* 11, 1987.

Spence, Mark David. *Dispossessing the Wilderness: Indian Removal and the Making of the National Parks*. New York: Oxford University Press, 1999.

Tate, Michael L. "From Scout to Doughboy: The National Debate over Integrating Indians into the Military, 1891–1918." *Western Historical Quarterly* 17, 1986.

III

The 1930s–1945: American Indians during Depression and War

The changes that affected American society so drastically in the 1930s and early 1940s also had a significant impact on American Indians. The economic hard times of the Great Depression were intensified in Indian Country, where starvation conditions already existed on many reservations. Worse, the harsh blizzards, abnormally cold winters, and the severe drought and Dust Bowl conditions of the "dirty thirties" were painfully felt by Native Americans, especially those in the Great Plains and the Southwest.

These were the years of the Franklin Roosevelt administrations and the New Deal. Roosevelt's choice for Commissioner of Indian Affairs was John Collier, who brought a new vision and spirit to his office. Collier, who had lived in New Mexico and studied Pueblo society, hoped to restore vitality to American Indian communities. He also believed in "no interference" with tribal sovereignty and labored to end the allotment policies of the Dawes Act. He also worked to form an Indian New Deal in which thousands of unemployed Native Americans joined an Indian Civilian Conservation Corp to work on public works projects. Collier's greatest contribution, however, was in engineering the Indian Reorganization Act (IRA), which advocated self-government and communal enterprises on reservations. It passed in 1934 and then went to the Indian tribes themselves for approval. One hundred eighty-one tribes accepted it, 77 rejected it (primarily because of distrust in any federal policies, and most notably by the Navajos, who feared federally mandated stock reductions on their already overgrazed lands), and fourteen tribes came under the IRA because they did not vote at all. D'Arcy McNickle's chapter on the subject places these events in their historical context. He makes a strong case that the overall failure of the IRA in the 1930s reflected the bureaucratic stagnation of the Progressive Era and served as a "mirror of the future" concerning the direction Indian policy would soon be going.

The IRA failed when America's entrance into World War II redirected all government attention away from domestic policies. The BIA offices were even moved from Washington, D.C., to Chicago to make more room for the war effort. American Indians were actively involved in all facets of the war. They served in the various branches of the armed forces, were instrumental as "code-talkers," and worked in war-related industries at home. The war created a space for more contact between Indians and Anglo-Americans than had previously existed, and, as Tom Holm points out in his chapter here, helped blend the two distinct cultures. This triggered calls for "termination," which came in the 1950s.

7

The Indian New Deal as a Mirror of the Future

D'Arcy McNickle

We are moving far enough away from the 1930s and the reform movement commonly termed "the Indian New Deal" to view it dispassionately, without any sense of involvement. Strong lines were drawn up in those partisan days, each side charging its opposite with unworthy motives, each side dressing up its own purposes in seemly rhetoric. Now that the dust of combat has settled, one can begin to see what the true issues were, what the gains and what the losses.

First, a brief description of the social, economic, and political conditions that gave rise to programs of reform. One general set of circumstances prevailed during the period. It was a time of deep, seemingly inescapable depression—a time of long soup lines in the cities, of rioting farmers in the countryside, of bank closings, of unemployed businessmen selling apples at street corners. One does not always see behind the headlines and news broadcasts the reality of economic disaster. I walked to work in midtown Manhattan one morning just after a victim of the times had leaped from a tall apartment building and was spread all over the sidewalk. Even nature contrived to add to human misery, for that was a period of the dreadful duststorms, when the topsoil of the wheat-growing prairie states ascended into the jet streams and swirled out over the Atlantic. I saw that, too, standing in shock in a New York street. It was a time when men began to talk about ecological balance, and a documentary

This chapter originally appeared in Ernest Schusky, ed., *Political Organization of Native North Americans*, Lanham, MD: University Press of America, 1980, pp. 107–118, and is reprinted here by permission of Ernest Schusky.

film, "The Plow That Broke the Plains," was viewed by hushed audiences. Men came face to face with themselves in those days and questioned the very society they had created, and which had created them.

A time of doom, but it was also a time of opportunity. Under the lash of the desperate emergency, social reform made giant strides. Banking methods were overhauled, the marketing of securities was regulated, vast holding company cartels were broken up, and systems of social insurance and unemployment compensation were created. The management of national forests, grazing lands, wild life, water, and minerals was made responsive to the public interest. Vast public works projects were undertaken to repair some of the damage wrought through generations of heedless resource exploitation and abuse. Some of this concern for the environment, and some of the appropriated funds, managed to trickle down to the Indian community.

It is important to understand the conditions that prevailed in the Indian community. The older Indians of that period still lived with the defeats that many tribes experienced in the closing years of the nineteenth century. The tragedy of the first Wounded Knee affair was less than fifty years in the rear, a brief lifetime.

When Collier assumed the commissionership in 1933, the General Allotment Law had been operating for better than forty-five years, and in that interval some 90 million acres of land had passed out of Indian ownership; an estate of 138 million acres, all owned in common in 1887, had been reduced to 48 million acres. For the most part, the alienated lands were the best lands: the river bottoms, rich grasslands, prime forests. But land losses tell only part of the story. The allotment process, the individualizing of community-owned assets, created forces that had never before operated in Indian society. Families and individuals competed for choice lands, for water, or other advantages. Outsiders intruded as homesteaders on so-called surplus lands, and inevitably meddled in the internal affairs of the tribe. Social structure was disoriented in many ways, as non-Indians married into a group, and kin groups were scattered throughout the reservation area. In each allotted reservation a class of landless, homeless individuals came into existence who, having no resources of their own, doubled up with relatives and intensified the poverty of all.

That, too, tells only part of the story. Tribes had been moved about like livestock until, in some cases, the original homeland was no more than a legend in the minds of old men and women. Children had been forcefully removed from the family and kept in close custody until they lost their mother language and all knowledge of who they were, while the schooling to which they were subjected was conducted as an exercise in animal training. Tribal religious practices, when they were not proscribed outright, were treated as obscenities. The bureaucratic apparatus had penetrated the entire fabric of Indian life, usurping tribal decision-making, obtruding into the family, and demeaning local leadership. It was totally oblivious to its inadequacies and its inhumanity.

Part of John Collier's initial problem, as the incoming commissioner, was to remove some of the tar with which he himself had plastered the Bureau. He had been an outspoken and caustic critic of the Bureau, and suddenly he was in the position of asking Indians to have confidence in the institution. While he occupied the office for twelve years, he never entirely extricated himself from the awkward situation.

One of his first acts, intended to moderate the harsh image of the Bureau, was the issuance of an order (Office of Indian Affairs 1934) declaring: "No interference with Indian religious life will be hereafter tolerated. The cultural history of Indians is in all respects to be considered equal to that of any non-Indian group. And it is desirable that Indians be bilingual—fluent and literate in English, and fluent in their vital, beautiful, and efficient native languages."

In a further early effort to undo the past, he secured the repeal of twelve obsolete laws, some dating from as early as 1790, which collectively placed inordinate power over civil liberties in the hands of bureau officials. The repeal of these laws, needless to say, was not enough to change the authoritarian nature of the bureau.

Collier, of course, is associated with the Indian Reorganization Act (IRA), which in the context of the Roosevelt administration was known popularly as the Indian New Deal. The legislation had been adopted by a reluctant Congress in 1934, reluctant because the act by open declaration was a denunciation of the policies followed by Congress and national administrations through the previous half-century. The reluctance moreover went deeper than bruised feelings. Most legislation as it emerges from the Congressional mill bears small resemblance to the bright promise that was fed into the hopper. The Indian Reorganization Act was no exception. Congress wanted the "Indian business" cleaned up, but it was not ready or willing to transfer real power to the Indian tribes. This unwillingness was emphasized by the rejection of four critical features: (1) an orderly procedure for transferring services and functions from the bureau to an organized Indian community; (2) the creation of tribal corporations for the management of reservation resources, with power "to compel" the removal of any federal employee on grounds of inefficiency or "other causes"; (3) a training program to prepare Indians to take over and administer community services, including courses of study in Indian history and culture; and (4) the establishment of a tribal court system, with right of appeal to the federal appellate court and to the Supreme Court.

It was the first piece of major legislation dealing with Indian affairs ever taken into the Indian Country and discussed in open meetings. And here the long history of bureaucratic misrule loomed as a major challenge to Collier's reform program. At every one of the regional meetings called to consider the pending bill, the motives and the purposes of the Bureau were questioned, heatedly at times. The distrust and suspicion voiced at these meetings, and in subsequent meetings in Washington, were reflected in the tribal elections that followed. By its terms, the act was not to apply on any reservation where a majority rejected it. Out of 258 tribes, bands, and rancherias voting in these elections, 77 voted against application. The Navajo was one of the tribes voting in the negative.

The bill as introduced in Congress was a document of some fifty typewritten pages, but what emerged was a scant six pages of print. The reduction in bulk was not critical, but what was stricken in the course of debate practically guaranteed that the nature of the bureaucracy would not be altered. By eliminating the provision giving the Indians a deciding role in the selection and retention of reservation employees, colonial rule was left intact. By deleting the articles creating a federal Indian court system, the control over law and order was left in the hands of the secretary of the interior, and it encouraged the states, in later years, to seek to extend state law, and state taxation, to reservation lands. One other deletion deserves passing mention. If the article providing for courses of study in Indian history and culture and in administrative management had been retained, Indian studies programs might have been operating forty years ago.

The Indian Reorganization Act did retain two features central to Collier's reform program. The first of these was the prohibition against any future allotment of tribal lands; the other was a watered-down provision dealing with tribal government and property management. While the range of discretionary tribal action was greatly reduced from the original proposal, what remained was tacit recognition of the tribe as a surviving political entity with definable inherent powers. The act referred specifically to "all powers vested in an Indian tribe or tribal council by existing law"; and that, of course, included treaty stipulations and court decisions, as well as statute law. In addition it recognized the right of a tribe to embody in a written constitution the power to "prevent the sale, disposition, lease or encumbrance of tribal lands." Within this legal framework it became possible for an Indian tribe to function as a municipal body and to exert the common law rights of a property owner.

The legislation was not the emancipating instrument that had been hoped for, and within less than a decade of its enactment the nation was at war, with the moneys authorized for salvaging the Indian community going elsewhere. But the act did mark the way into the future—if there was to be an Indian future. In Collier's day that was not at all a certainty; indeed twenty years after the adoption of the Indian Reorganization Act, the Eisenhower administration almost closed out that possibility forever.

To go back a moment: The misgivings and outright opposition expressed by many Indians during the hearings on the Indian Reorganization Act were symptomatic of more basic trouble. Since the United States in 1871 renounced the policy of negotiating treaties with the tribes, a practice that had endured from colonial times, the Indians had not been consulted in any major decisions affecting their property, their family life, or the training of their children. All such matters came within the reach of a bureaucratic structure, which developed attitudes and formalities impervious to Indian participation. And as the bureaucracy hardened, the Indian community withdrew deeper into itself and set up its own barriers to communication.

But Collier's problem did not come entirely from the fact that for those sixty-odd years since the renunciation of treaty-making the government had barred Indians from assuming responsibility for their own lives. The unseen and, indeed, the larger problem had to do with the ethic of social intervention which, in the 1930s, still functioned as a tradition out of the nineteenth century—a heritage of colonial administration.

In a major crisis that developed early in his administration the reluctance or the inability of the bureaucracy to respond to human conditions had disastrous consequences. The occasion was the decision to reduce Navajo sheep herds, the principal subsistence base of the tribe, in order to bring the animal population into balance with deteriorating range lands. Studies carried out by professional agronomists demonstrated that top soil was blowing away, perennial grasses were being replaced by annual weeds of low nutrient value, summer rains were eroding deep gullies and carrying mountains of soil into newly constructed power and flood control reservoirs, threatening to fill them with silt.

In designing a control program, Collier directed that reduction would be on a "sliding scale," with the largest reduction on the larger herds and a lesser reduction on smaller herds, while herds of a minimum size would be left intact. The directive was later made specific in providing that herds of up to 100 head of sheep would not be reduced. Herds of that size were considered subsistence herds required to provide family support.

A report prepared soon after the reduction program was initiated in 1933 states that: "The larger owners flatly refused to make all the reduction from their herds. After an all-night session (at Tuba City, in November 1933) it was agreed . . . that every Navajo should sell 10 percent of his sheep. . . . The same agreement became widespread over the entire reservation, since the large owners consistently refused to make the total reduction from their flocks." In practice, the owners of small herds found themselves under greater economic pressure than the owners of large herds; they sold out their entire holdings and found themselves completely dependent on the emergency work programs financed by the government. When these programs ran out of funds, real hardship followed.

Other complications quickly arose. The government had offered to buy sheep at prices ranging from $1.00 for ewes to $2.25–$3.00 for wethers. Chee Dodge, the respected leader of the tribe, argued that the government should concentrate on the purchase of good breeding ewes, at better prices; otherwise, the Navajo livestock owners would offer only old ewes and other nonproductive stock, and reduction would not be achieved. These prices, however, had been established in Washington by the emergency relief administration, the source of the funds, and they could not be altered in the field. The disappointing results confirmed what Chee Dodge had predicted.

Perhaps the most serious oversight was the failure to recognize the fact that women were in many instances the principal owners of the family herds. Women were not members of the tribal council, however, and they were not consulted as negotiations went forward between the government and the tribal leaders. When the leaders returned to their families and found the women opposed to plans for reduction, any agreements with the government became meaningless.

What Collier did not discover until it was too late to intervene was that field employees sometimes resorted to coercive action. This interference occurred specifically in the eastern Navajo area, where it was expected that legislation, then pending in Congress, would be enacted and would result in extending the eastern boundary of the reservation to include an additional two million acres. In anticipation of the increased acreage, the Navajos of the area were induced to sell their goats, with the idea of eventually replacing them with sheep. By the fall of 1935 formidable opposition had developed against the legislation, making it unlikely that it would be adopted. Nevertheless the goat reduction program went forward. As Collier reported to the Senate subcommittee in the summer of 1936: "In my judgment, we should not have carried out the goat purchase program within the eastern area . . . because we were no longer assured of the enactment of the boundary bill. . . . Why we did proceed with the goat purchases in this area, frankly, I don't know. . . . At the time we did not, at Washington, have any information, or evidence that duress was being, or was to be, employed anywhere. It was not directed to be employed, but on the contrary, all the sales were to be voluntary. However, before the close of the goat purchase operation, I began to receive . . . information that overpersuasion, and even duress, had in fact been employed in this area."

Elsewhere in his statement to the subcommittee, he commented: "The purchase was an error and I cannot, and do not desire, to evade responsibility for that error. . . . I am the Commissioner."

Such episodes were possible because the bureaucracy was the instrument of an older view of the relationship with the Indian people. In that older view Indians were incompetent to make decisions, especially when questions of a technical nature were involved—and livestock management was considered to be of that nature, even though Navajos had been successful herdsmen for several centuries. Indeed, their very success in increasing their herds was in part responsible for their predicament. In a chain of command situation, such as characterizes bureaucratic structure, responsibility is diffused; one is never accountable for someone else's mistakes.

Collier's hope of restoring to the Indian community some measure of self-government was diminished by the same impersonal, insensate play of bureaucratic forces. Anyone who has worked in government knows that project financing is based on performance. If funds allocated to a field project are not expended within a time limit, usually the fiscal year, it is assumed by those who approve budget requests that the money was not needed. The amount approved for a subsequent operating period will likely be reduced. This leads to various stratagems to keep ahead of the finance wizards, the commonest of which is to pile on expenditures before the end of the fiscal period, thus demonstrating the accuracy of the original estimate and the soundness of the project.

The Indian Reorganization Act authorized federal funds to assist tribes in formulating and voting on written constitutions and charters of incorporation. Collier intended that the organization documents should reflect a tribe's traditional ways of arriving at decisions and selecting leaders. To carry out this purpose he recruited a staff of cultural anthropologists, who were to work with the field employees engaged in the program. This move would appear to be one of the first attempts, if not the first, to use anthropologists as technical assistants by a government agency.

The planning came to grief on two counts. When it was discovered in Congress that the commissioner was spending money on something called anthropology, the appropriation was promptly disallowed and the unit was abandoned, although some anthropologists continued working for the bureau under other titles. A more serious difficulty grew out of the fiscal year syndrome. To satisfy the budget watchers and the wardens of the treasury, it was necessary to show progress in bringing the tribes under written constitutions. This involved sitting down in meeting after meeting and conducting a tribal drafting committee through a maze of *Whereas* clauses and *Therefore, be it enacted* resolutions. Leaders, who often were non-English-speaking or who had only a primary grade education, were exposed to the full battery of Anglo-Saxon parliamentary syntax, and they had to act before the end of the fiscal year. The result was the hurried adoption of tribal constitutions prepared in Washington and based on conventional political instruments with no provision for action by consensus or for the role of ritual leaders. The tribes were given tools, such as majority rule, for which they had no accustomed usage, and these became devices for community disruption and for petty demagoguery.

One should not conclude from this analysis of the Navajo that no positive gains were registered during the Collier administration. The long record of diminishing land and other resource holdings was halted. The total land base was actually enlarged by some four million acres, the first time in history that Indians gained instead of losing land. Credit financing was begun on a modest scale and made possible resource development and utilization, where previously Indians had leased out tribal and individual lands for lack of capital. A start was made, again modestly, in providing low-cost housing. Day schools were built at a number of reservations as an alternative to the off-reservation boarding schools, and they were designed and operated as community centers, anticipating the movement of recent years to provide centers for recreation, adult education, and cultural activities.

These gains, modest as they were, were cut short by the crisis of war. When the shooting was over and Indian GIs and war industry workers came home, they found their reservations in ruins. Employment opportunities were gone, social services were severely curtailed (schools, hospitals, houses in disrepair or shut down entirely), and credit facilities denied. And presently, a hostile administration came to power committed to the ultimate extinguishment of tribal life.

What has come to the surface in tribal communities in recent years, notably at Wounded Knee and on the Pine Ridge reservation generally, is the anger that remained unuttered, but unappeased, for generations. It was an overwhelming anger growing out of the kinds of experiences suggested here; my account of these experiences has been mild and polite. Older Indians, still conscious of the defeats inflicted on their people in the closing years of the last century, withdrew from open challenge and tried passively to live with the white man's inscrutable ways. That former period seems to have come to a crashing end.

The generation of Indian leaders now emerging lacks that consciousness of defeat that inhibited their elders. More than that, as a consequence of international wars, the collapse of colonial empires, rioting and burning in urban ghettos, and an economy that destroys the environment, the white man seems not as invincible as he once seemed.

It was possible at Wounded Knee in 1890 for an army unit—Custer's own 7th Cavalry, indeed—to slaughter a Sioux camp of men, women, and children. At that same site in the winter of 1973, armored vehicles and troop detachments surrounded another Indian camp, but no slaughter occurred. Two reasons suggest themselves. The surrounded Indians had access to the world beyond their lines and they were able to verbalize their grievances to listeners who were sympathetic even though they might not understand what was going on. This access to public opinion was enough to discourage hasty action by gun-carrying troops. An even more compelling restraint was the changed circumstance behind that surrounding army. Men in power no longer had a mandate to kill Indians trying to protect their right to be themselves. Perhaps that is a measurable gain.

Where, then, have we come? One point certainly seems clear. Because Indians are discovering the uses of power in modern society, it is no longer possible to exclude them from the decision-making process in matters affecting their property, their families, the training of their children, or the nature of the accommodation they choose to make within the dominant society. John Collier helped to make these issues evident, but as a man of good will standing outside the Indian community, he was limited in what he could do. He could not substitute his will and vision for Indian will and vision. Nor can any man stand in the place of another.

That, too, is a discovery Indians have made in these very recent years. The simple demonstration of this discovery is the astonishing growth of news media operated by Indian groups reporting on conditions, and the equally remarkable growth of political and cultural organizations devoted to advancing Indian interests. The non-Indian "Friend of the Indian," that nineteenth-century image of altruistic involvement, is being told politely but firmly to stand aside.

Collier has been charged with turning the clock back on Indian advancement. The basis of this charge, of course, was his insistence on extending religious and cultural freedom to Indian groups and his commitment to the cause of revitalizing Indian society. A modern critic asserts that Collier mistakenly assumed, from his knowledge of Indians of the Southwest, "that Indians everywhere would wish to return to tribal, communal life, if given the opportunity."

What this writer fails to recognize, even in this late day, is that Indians "everywhere" have always been, and remain, more tribal, communal if you will, or conscious of ethnic boundaries, than observers from the outside generally realize. Already in Collier's day the studies of A. Irving Hallowell and others were offering evidence that culturally wrought personality persists even in circumstances where the outward forms of behavior have accommodated to the dominant society.

Other critics of Collier's effort to build upon the tribal past were people whose ideas had been formed largely in the nineteenth century, who saw Native society as incapable of development into modern forms. In this view, the Native American existed in a world devoid of logic, or sentiment, or dynamics. Indian life came from nowhere and went nowhere.

Collier challenged this view in many published statements and in his public career. He saw Indian society as "not fossilized, unadaptive, not sealed in the past, but plastic, adaptive, assimilative, while yet faithful to . . . ancient values." And again he wrote, "Societies are living things, sources of the power and values of their members; to be and to function in a consciously living, aspiring, striving society is to be a personality fulfilled."

Whether or not they are aware of John Collier's insight in this matter, Indians today have discovered the truth that lies in this vision. This discovery accounts, in part, for the Indian studies centers that have come into existence at major institutions across the country. The Navajo Community College springs from this vision. In a harsher mode, it accounts for the incidents at Wounded Knee.

Indians were not held back by Collier's efforts to build upon the tribal past. Instead, they have plunged affirmatively into the twentieth century, asserting their identity, and acquiring the skills that will enable them to survive as Indians and members of an Indian community.

8

Fighting a White Man's War: The Extent and Legacy of American Indian Participation in World War II

Tom Holm

In 1942, the *Saturday Evening Post* informed its many readers that a Nazi propaganda broadcast had "predicted an Indian uprising in the United States," should Americans be "asked to fight against the Axis." If quoted correctly, these German statements were not made without a degree of elementary logic. In the name of American progress, Indians had been slaughtered, dispossessed of lands, forcibly stripped of many aspects of their tribal cultures, and left the poorest of the nation's poor. "How could," Radio Berlin was reported to have asked, "the American Indians think of bearing arms for their exploiters?"

But in defiance of German logic and much to the satisfaction of white Americans, the *Post* also reported that Indians were flocking to join the armed forces in order to fight and possibly shed blood for the United States. American Indians flung themselves into the war effort. Indeed, Indian participation in World War II was so great that it later became part of American folklore and popular culture. It was a magnificent gesture worthy of a great people, yet one that would eventually provide little consolation. That the disastrous policy of termination followed so closely the Indian commitment to America's war effort was not a mere historical coincidence. Whites, who made Indian policies at the time, came out of the war with new, or at least different, images of Indian people. These changed views created an atmosphere in which men of varying

Reprinted from the *Journal of Ethnic Studies*, Volume 9, Number 2 (Summer 1981) by permission of Western Washington University.

motives and goals could institute the termination policy under the cloak of liberal rhetoric.

During World War II and for the first time ever, all American Indian males between the ages of 21 and 44 were eligible to be drafted. That they were subject to military conscription developed, ironically enough, out of the American Indian experience in World War I. Prior to 1917 not all Indians living in the country were citizens of the United States. Some Indians had obtained citizenship by taking allotments under the Dawes Act of 1887. At the same time others had been denied citizens' rights on the grounds that they had been judged by whites to be incompetent in the legal sense. A few refused to even request citizenship because they believed that it would deny tribal sovereignty and destroy the basis on which treaties could be recognized. Those persons not holding citizenship were exempted from selective service laws. When the United States plunged itself into the war during 1917, thousands of American Indians entered the armed services regardless of their individual legal positions at the time. Many took the military oath to defend the Constitution of the United States without possessing any rights under it, refusing to take advantage of their draft exemptions. By 1918 there were over 10,000 American Indians in the Army, Navy, and Marine Corps, eighty-five percent of whom, according to the Indian policy reform newsletter *Indian's Friend*, entered voluntarily. As the periodical reported, "Indians—men and women alike—are doing their bit to help make the world safe for democracy."

In that era, most government policies toward American Indians were based on the idea that Indians were wards of the government. To the average white American, wardship and citizenship—semibondage and freedom—were not compatible. One could not, through government, regulate citizens without infringing upon the individual liberties of the nation's citizenry. Most Americans in the early part of this century were steadfastly against many forms of government interference in the private lives of voting Americans. Indians, according to this line of thought, would have to remain wards, and therefore noncitizens, so that the government could carry out policies of acculturation, allotment of reservation lands, and education. It was not until after the government, or at least the country's lawmakers, became fully imbued with the idea that individual liberty could be subordinated to the public welfare or to national security and were able to place controls on the white population, that American Indian citizenship became justifiable to most whites.

World War I was met with a tremendous outburst of patriotism—patriotism that called for unswerving loyalty and devotion to the nation. As a result, the war also created a mindset within which the government could increasingly regulate individuals with only slight opposition. Congress, through sedition, espionage, and acts of subversion, could essentially remove the guarantees of the Bill of Rights. Regulation, and with it a kind of wardship, became less incompatible with freedom in the American mind. The government, in providing for the general welfare, could—indeed should—curb individual liberties if the rest of society were threatened. Given this notion, it was not difficult for many whites to ease their qualms about conferring citizenship on those Indian people who had fought so willingly and bravely in France. They could remain wards without apparent constitutional conflict.

Subsequently, Indian soldiers and sailors received citizenship in 1919, and in 1924 the United States offered certificates of citizenship to all American Indians not already holding them. Thus Indians, as a result of wartime ideologies, received very few of the actual freedoms of citizenship, but were expected to accept any and all of the responsibilities that went with it. Although many American Indians were denied the right to vote or even to wear tribal clothing or conduct religious ceremonies, they were not excluded from certain duties; when World War II broke out, they became subject to military conscription.

At the beginning of World War II, American Indians readily accepted these duties. They registered at selective service centers in the cities and at their agencies. There was little protest against the draft, and very few attempted to avoid service on grounds that it was a white man's war. In fact, many Indians refused to wait the prescribed time to enter the military and either requested early conscription or contacted a recruiter and volunteered. The Indian people, just as they had done in 1917, accepted their share of the burden of the war.

According to the then commissioner of Indian Affairs, John Collier, there were over 7500 American Indians in the armed forces as of June 1942, less than six months after the attack on Pearl Harbor. By October another observer reported that the number of American Indians in the military had swollen to well over 10,000. By 1944 almost 22,000 American Indians, not counting those who had become officers, were part of the United States armed forces. At the war's end there were over 25,000 Indians in the Army, Navy, Marine Corps, and Coast Guard. "While this seems a relatively small number," wrote Commissioner Collier, "it represents a larger proportion than any other element of our population."

Not only did Indians fight "in greater proportionate numbers than any other race" but they also seemed to draw some of the worst wartime assignments. Again, this experience matched that of the First World War. During World War I whites, as well as most Indians, had argued persuasively that American Indians should be integrated in all of the white regiments and treated like any other soldier. Yet, the *Indian's Friend* proudly reported that "Indians in the regiments are being used for scouting and patrol duty because of the natural instinct which fits them for this kind of work." This kind of racial stereotype, following as it did an attempt to argue against racism in the military, would have been laughable had it not forced Native Americans into precarious assignments.

For the most part these stereotypes were carried over to the Second World War. Indians were natural "scouts" and "warriors." Stanley Vestal, a leading authority on the tribes of the Plains, added to this image of American Indians. "The Indian, whose wars never ended, was a realistic soldier," Vestal wrote. "He never gave quarter nor expected it. His warfare was always offensive warfare." American Indians were never segregated into separate units as were blacks and Japanese-Americans; yet, they were always mentioned in the press as being quite different from whites. Secretary of the Interior Harold Ickes wrote about the "inherited talents" of American Indians that made them "uniquely valuable" to the war effort. According to Ickes, the Native American fighting man had "endurance, rhythm, a feeling for timing, coordination, sense perception, an uncanny ability to get over any sort of terrain at night, and, better than all else, an enthusiasm for fighting. He takes a rough job and makes a game of it. Rigors of combat hold no terrors for him; severe discipline and hard duties do not deter him."

American Indians for the most part accepted these attitudes toward them and often did their best to conform to such views. A month after the war began, the *New York Times* reported that Chief Kiutus Tecumseh, of Cashmere, Washington, was attempting to organize an Indian "Scouting force." One Sioux man, Kenneth Scission, of South Dakota, volunteered for a British-trained American commando unit and quickly managed to become the group's leading German-killer. On a single patrol, Scission was reported to have added "ten notches on his Gerand rifle." Another man, Robert Stabler, a member of the Omaha tribe, landed "alone under heavy fire" to mark the beaches for the infantry in advance of the assault at Licata, Sicily, in 1943. During the Normandy invasion of 1944 a group of thirteen American Indians were in the first wave of paratroops dropped with demolitions in advance of the Allied landings in France. Given these exploits, it was small wonder that American Indian servicemen garnered several Silver Stars, the Distinguished Service Cross, the Navy Cross, and numerous Purple Hearts, signs that one had not only engaged the enemy but had shed his own blood for the United States.

In 1944, Lieutenant Ernest Childers, a Creek tribal member from Broken Arrow, Oklahoma, was awarded the nation's highest decoration for bravery in battle—the Medal of Honor. He had earlier distinguished himself in the fighting in Sicily with the famed 45th "Thunderbird" Division. Indeed, it was in Sicily that Childers received his battlefield commission. In September, 1943, near Oliveto, Italy, Childers, singlehandedly and in spite of severe wounds, destroyed three German machine-gun emplacements, thus opening "the way for the advance of his battalion which had been in danger of annihilation." Childers' exploits implanted the "warrior" image in the American mind.

Perhaps the first American Indian to gain fame in the war was General Clarence L. Tinker. Tinker, on the Osage tribal rolls, had been the first person of Indian descent since the Civil War to become a general officer in the United States Army. After the attack on Pearl Harbor, Tinker was placed in charge of the all-but-destroyed air forces in Hawaii. One of America's pioneer bomber pilots, Tinker reorganized the remaining forces and before the battle of Midway was fought in June 1942 had turned them into a well-trained, highly disciplined unit. Tinker was killed at the battle of Midway. "Ignoring the dangers and refusing to assign anyone else the task," Tinker "personally led the squadrons of bombers which supplied the American spearhead of the attack." Cited for bravery, he was posthumously awarded the Distinguished Service Medal. In the words of John Collier, the Osage general "exemplified the modern Indian soldier."

Tinker was not the only high-ranking officer of Indian descent in the military service. Listed on the Dawes Commission rolls as one-eighth Cherokee, Joseph J. "Jocko" Clark was the first American Indian to have received an appointment to Annapolis. Clark became a rear admiral and was active in many parts of the Pacific during World War II.

But the deepest impressions on the American public were made by an American Indian unit and a single Pima man, "the outsider," Ira Hamilton Hayes. Hayes became a national hero in 1945 when he and some fellow marines were photographed raising the American flag on Mount Suribachi during the battle of Iwo Jima. The photograph seemed to capture the imagination of the public. It exemplified the courage, strength, and tenacity of America's struggle against the enemy. Hayes was returned to the United States to help promote the sale of war bonds and to bolster morale. He became an alcoholic and later died, a relatively young man, on the reservation of his birth. To many Americans, Hayes' life came to symbolize the American Indian participation in the war. He was a hero who fought to preserve the United States but was never given the opportunity to share in America's wealth or society. Although he survived the war, he was doomed to a life of poverty and prejudice. In the American mind he became, along with the hundreds of other Indian veterans, an "outsider." When a very poor motion picture was made in 1955 based on the life of Ira Hayes, its title, *The Outsider*, aptly expressed white images of American Indians. America had used them and then had cast them aside.

If Ira Hayes' life came to symbolize to whites what had happened to Indian veterans after the war, a group known as the Navajo code-talkers became the symbol of the great contribution Indians had made during the war. Early in 1942 the Marine Corps recruited an all-Indian platoon. When basic training ended in July of that year, the men were assigned to units overseas. In battle the Navajos acquitted themselves with much glory and later attracted widespread coverage in the national press. During the war their mission had been kept secret. Trained in communications, they had adopted the Navajo language as a code that helped in large part to foil the Japanese attempts to break the advance of American marines in the Pacific. In 1945, when it was revealed that the Navajo language had done so much to help the United States win the war against Japan, the "code-talkers" instantly became national heroes and part of American folklore. In the postwar years nearly every motion picture made about the fighting in the Pacific contained scenes of usually anonymous Indians speaking their native languages into field radios and leaving the enemy hopelessly confused and ready to be soundly defeated.

American Indians gave the United States more than heroes to glory in or to sympathize with. Indian people also contributed food and money to the war effort. The Crows of Montana offered their reservation's resources and tribal funds to the government for the duration of the war. The Navajo, Shoshone, and several other tribal governments authorized the secretary of the interior to purchase war bonds from tribal funds. In this manner alone the tribes contributed millions of dollars to the war effort. In 1944, Harold Ickes reported that at least $2 million worth of bonds had been purchased by Indians in one year. In that same year Indian Commissioner Collier estimated that the total Indian commitment to the war effort in monetary terms amounted to some $50 million.

Throughout the war Indian men and women not already in the armed forces left the reservations to find work in the cities. The war had, of course, expanded industry, and the war economy was booming. Jobs became easy to obtain and easy to keep. It was estimated that between the years 1941 and 1945 approximately 40,000 American Indians left their home areas to work in the factories of a wartime nation. John Collier called this movement "the greatest exodus of Indians" that had ever taken place. More important, it was looked upon as an inspiring commitment to the United States by people who previously had not been welcomed outside of their homelands.

On the reservations, which by 1944 were critically short of a male workforce, Indian women accounted for much of the production of food. They drove heavy equipment, repaired tractors, and herded cattle. Principally because of Native American women, the production of Indian livestock doubled in the ten years between 1933 and 1943. Agricultural output greatly increased as well, accounting for a significant rise in the standard of living on many reservations compared to the truly terrible conditions of the Depression years. By 1945 it was estimated that nearly 150,000 American Indians directly participated in the industrial, agricultural, and military aspects of the American war effort.

One reservation was even called upon to participate in the government's internment of Japanese-Americans. In 1942 the War Relocation Authority gave "the Indian Bureau the care of 20,000 unhappy Japanese." These people, forced from their homes on the Pacific Coast, were sent to the Colorado River Reservation's "20,000 acres of desert." According to one writer, the internment of the Japanese-Americans on an Indian reservation could become a "valuable piece of social experimentation."

There were a great number of other Indian contributions. In the press American Indians were used to boost morale. Newspapers and magazines projected images of Indians as being loyal, brave, trustworthy fighters, dedicated to the American cause. To most Americans the war was a duel to the death between democracy and fascist injustice. It was a war to free the people of the world from the clutches of Nazi totalitarianism. American Indians, in throwing themselves so unflinchingly and wholeheartedly into the war effort, seemed to validate the American sense of mission. Indians, after all, had been treated miserably; however, even they were totally committed to the crusade against the Axis. According to one young Columbia River tribal member who was quoted in a national magazine, even though his people had been treated badly by the United States, Hitler would be much worse: "We know that under Nazism we should have no rights at all; we should be used as slaves." If oppressed peoples sided with the United States, then logically the American crusade was a just cause.

The media's outlook on American Indians during the war years was decidedly ambiguous. The press generally viewed the Indian war effort as a great boost to the nation's morale. During the first years of the war, groups of American Indians adopted and made "chiefs" of Franklin D. Roosevelt, General Douglas MacArthur, Wendell Willkie, and even Joseph Stalin. Tribes, in efforts to maintain a semblance of autonomy, individually declared war on the Axis. The League of the Iroquois in New York had never ceased hostilities with Germany. The Grand Council of the League simply renewed their declaration of war made in 1917 and included Italy and Japan. Many tribal dancers and singers aided war-bond rallies, and elders posed in their warbonnets for pictures with young men in their new, crisp uniforms. The entire press coverage of American Indians in war was geared to give the impression that Indian people were not only aiding white Americans in the war effort but fervently hoping to share in the victory over fascism and become part of the American democratic way of life.

At the same time, the motion picture industry, perhaps the most powerful image-maker, continued to portray American Indians as savage barriers to the spread of American progress. Most "horse operas" tended to glorify the American past—a past that included western expansion and the theft of American

Indian lands. In a few westerns, however, there appeared more and more fre-quently the "Indian companion" character who, just as in the war, aided the white American in his crusade against injustice. In the war movies an American Indian was usually part of the beleaguered infantry platoon which, because it was made up of members of nearly every ethnic group in the United States, with the exception of blacks, projected a microcosm of America. The Ameri-can Indian member was presented as loyal, fearless, and capable of sacrifice in defense of the group.

Whites accepted these images with satisfaction. Not only did Indian contri-butions during the war years tend to endorse the greatness of America's cru-sade but they were also interpreted to mean that Indians were desperately trying to prove themselves worthy of the rest of society. Actual American Indi-ans' motives for willingly going to war, however, remained far less clear than media coverage led the whites to believe. Among some Indian people there was a strong urge to become accepted by the general population. Taking part in the war could possibly work favorably toward this end. "We want to win the war," an Indian rancher was reported to have said, "because victory will mean new hope for men and women who have no hope."

In their renewed declaration of war against the rulers of Germany, Japan, and Italy, the Six Nations of the Iroquois League not only demonstrated that Indian and white Americans shared a common belief in democracy but made a pronounced statement against the racist policies of Nazi Germany without mentioning the racism practiced at home. "It is the unanimous sentiment among the Indian people that the atrocities of the Axis nations," the league councilman wrote, "are violently repulsive to all sense of righteousness of our people." Moreover, "this merciless slaughter of mankind upon the part of these enemies of free peoples can no longer be tolerated."

Other Indian people saw the Axis as a threat to liberty. The Cheyennes con-demned the German, Japanese, and Italian alliance as an "unholy triangle whose purpose is to conquer and enslave the bodies, minds and souls of all free people." A number of California Indians representing some thirty reservations simply thought of themselves as loyal American citizens ready to aid the coun-try. This same group was, at the time, engaged in several lawsuits and claims against the United States government. When war came, they telegraphed President Roosevelt indicating their "readiness to serve our great Nation." In the same vein, the Navajo tribal council declared that "any un-American movement among our people will be resented and dealt with severely."

Among some tribes a strong warrior tradition actually still existed. The ide-ologies of most tribal groups, and nearly all of the tribes with the strongest war traditions, were based on ideals of continuity and order. In traditional societies there was a common belief that the Creator had placed the group on earth for specific reasons. Tradition and religion were intermixed so as to be insepara-ble. Tribal social, economic, and ecological order must be maintained or the entire system would be thrown out of balance and the "good life" destroyed. Although tribal societies were not static—there were adaptations and changes as in every other social group—certain obligations to tradition still had to be maintained. Much of Native American ceremonialism came out of the effort to preserve the social continuity of the tribe and to observe certain obligations to the retention of the traditional view of world order.

Within tribes with strong warrior traditions, such as the Sioux of the north-ern Plains and the Kiowa of western Oklahoma, the keepers of social philoso-phy and tribal ceremony were most often males who had *counted coup* on an enemy of the tribe and therefore on an enemy of tribal conceptions of order. After the wars with the whites and the time when the tribes were forced to leave off battling with traditional enemies, the numbers of these prestigious people who had performed acts of honor began to dwindle. The soldier societ-ies to which many of these men belonged were rapidly becoming devoid of members. Because there were no wars, the younger men could hardly *count coup* and thus become part of these groups. The ceremonies that were part of the warrior societies also began to die out.

The First and Second World Wars offered to many Indian people the oppor-tunity of becoming not just American servicemen but soldiers in the tribal meaning of the term. World War II, because it lasted longer and because more men became involved, gave some Indian men the chance to gain prestige among whites and, most important, obtain status within their own tribes. Ki-owa veterans of World War II, for instance, were able to revive the Tia-piah Gourd Dance society, where previously only a handful of men had status as a result of war to participate in the ceremonies of the group. The revival of the society, which has since splintered, meant that a ceremonial obligation to the cultural viability of the tribe could be retained, and with it the Kiowa ideals of order and social continuity would be carried forward. Victory dances were held after the war by several tribes. One, a Hunkpapa Sioux ceremony held at Little Eagle, South Dakota, gave a great deal of prestige to the returning veter-ans of World War II because they were then able to take part in the dance with Takes-his-gun, an elder, a veteran of the tribal wars, and a symbol of the conti-nuity of Hunkpapa society.

Whites vaguely understood the meaning of a warrior tradition within tribal societies. It became, however, a focus and an explanation for all Indian partici-pation in the war. John Collier reported that many Indian men, young and old alike, came to the agencies, rifles in hand, to sign up for the army and "proceed immediately to the scene of the fighting." A Blackfoot contemptuous of the selective service system was said to have stated: "Since when has it been necessary for Blackfeet to draw lots to fight?" Thousands of these kinds of quotes littered the nation's press. In many cases, Indians were made to appear ignorant of modern methods of war, yet they were willing to die for the United States. In all cases their effort demonstrated the "Indian people's faith in their country and their devotion to the cause of Democracy."

The upshot of Indian devotion to the country was a white movement to "amalgamate" Indians into American society. In 1944, Oswald Garrison Villard, writing for *Christian Century*, reaffirmed the American Indian contribution to the war effort and assured readers that the thousands of Indians fighting overseas and working in war industries were striving to become part of the American mainstream. "Their sole request is that they be awarded citizenship like other Americans," he wrote, "a citizenship unhampered by restrictions which do not apply to everybody." Reservations and federal guardianship, according to Villard, were restrictive and un-American. He was totally convinced that most Indian men and women no longer wanted "to stay at home and be confined within the reservations."

Although Villard sought "to break up no reservation," his entire discourse was directed toward that very goal. According to him, tribal cultures, arts, and ceremonies were unique and worthy of perpetuating but doomed to extinction. American Indians will, Villard asserted, "tire of being considered circus exhibits." Harking back to the arguments of the whites who in the 1880s sought to allot Indian lands and destroy tribal lifestyles in the name of assimilation, Villard thought, along with a pamphlet entitled *Indian Wardship*, that "imprisoning" the Indian "in his yesterday's culture is futility itself." It would mean, he said, "halting his modern adaptation." Ominously, Villard quoted and obviously felt kinship with a California Indian agent whose own personal goal in Indian policy was "to liquidate the U.S. Indian Service."

Perhaps the strongest statement favoring "amalgamation" and the ultimate destruction of the Bureau of Indian Affairs was made by O.K. Armstrong in a 1945 article for *Reader's Digest*. Armstrong claimed to have interviewed American Indians from the entire country and had found them with an "unmistakable determination" to "demand full rights of citizenship." Younger Indian people were going, he predicted, to lead a movement in the United States that would eventually set American Indians on their own or at least free them from the entanglements of government bureaucracy. Those Indians, he assured his readers, "who return from the service will seek a greater share in American freedom." Others, who had labored in factories and "tasted economic opportunity for the first time," would not be satisfied, as Armstrong put it, "to live in a shack and loaf around in a blanket."

Armstrong saved his heaviest ammunition for an attack on the Bureau of Indian Affairs. In the twelve years since John Collier had taken office as commissioner of Indian Affairs, Indian policy and the bureau had undergone great change. Since the passage of the Indian Reorganization Act in 1934 tribes could form governments, allotment of Indian lands had ceased, a revolving loan system had been set up to aid in the establishment of tribal businesses, and, in general, the policy of trying to destroy tribal cultures had been curbed. In Armstrong's eyes the Indian Reorganization Act marked a serious setback to the goal of Indian assimilation. According to him, the Indian New Deal had forced "a collectivist system upon the Indians, with bigger doses of paternalism and regimentation." Under it, also, bureaucracy had grown tremendously and with it "red tape" and a greater burden on the taxpayer. After attacking the Indian New Deal in conservative terms as befitting the period, Armstrong continued the assault in a more liberal tone. Since 1934, according to Armstrong, the Bureau of Indian Affairs had allowed the perpetuation of the reservation system and thus had maintained a policy of "racial segregation."

Villard's and Armstrong's statements and the sentiments expressed represented a striking paradox in American thought. Their ideas were well within the boundaries of both conservative and liberal American traditions. They were certainly conservative in that they advocated a policy of less government regulation and interference. At the same time they could wax very liberal. Liberalism in the United States had been, for the most part, nationalistic as well as elitist. It assumed that everyone was in the process of progressing toward the kind of democratic ideals, standard of living, and governmental system that had been developed in the United States. To welcome and promote acceptance of American philosophies and systems among outsiders became the ultimate in philanthropy. If American Indians accepted these ideals, they would "free" themselves and also free whites of long-held responsibilities.

Unlike Villard, however, Armstrong offered extensive solutions to the "Indian problem." He urged Congress to remove Bureau of Indian Affairs restrictions from Indian people. The move, according to Armstrong, would serve to "emancipate" American Indians as well as assist "all Indians to be self-supporting." He argued that the individual ownership of real and personal property would "furnish the same incentive for thrift and good management that are enjoyed by the Indians' white neighbors." Although Armstrong did not openly say that the reservations should be completely done away with, his statements about "segregation" and "emancipation" were to be extremely convincing arguments in favor of the termination policy of the 1950s.

Following the publication of Armstrong's article, the *American Indian* magazine, which was the editorial arm of the American Association on Indian Affairs, printed a series of rebuttals to his arguments. Haven Emerson, the president of the organization, led the attack. According to Emerson, Armstrong's article was "an ill-informed rehash of old fallacies and sentiments" and a "potential danger to the very freedoms which it demands." Emerson's remarks asserted that Armstrong sounded a great deal like the people who, in the previous century, had advocated the policy of allotment in severalty—a policy that proved itself to have been a disastrous mistake.

The remainder of the fall edition of the *American Indian* similarly attacked the Armstrong article. Both Emerson and historian Randolph C. Downes believed that Armstrong based his arguments on unsupported data. Downes insisted that the Indian New Deal under John Collier had actually promoted self-support and that Armstrong's remarks concerning this aspect of American Indian policy were completely unfounded. Emerson pointed out that a reservation was hardly an "outdoor prison," as Armstrong had suggested. Rather, reservations were land bases on which American Indians could work for economic freedom. Along the same lines another article, written by Walter C. Eells, simply stated that Indian veterans had virtually unlimited opportunities in education and thus were not trapped within the reservations.

Two years later Oliver La Farge recognized the ominous quality of Armstrong's solutions to Indian problems and attempted to refute some of them. La Farge, a Pulitzer prize-winning novelist, anthropologist, and proponent of the Indian New Deal, argued that reservations should be kept intact. He concentrated his arguments on the Navajo Reservation and firmly asserted that as an economic base the possession of land was absolutely necessary to American Indian survival. But in the article La Farge described deplorable conditions on reservations and told of a young Navajo war veteran who felt "boxed in" by the system. Even though he did not intend to do so, La Farge actually made a strong case for Armstrong's "reforms."

But views such as Armstrong's were far more compelling to white Americans fresh from a crusade against Nazi tyranny than the arguments presented in the *American Indian* or by La Farge. Indians had "fought for freedom" shoulder to shoulder with the white man yet returned to the grinding poverty of the reservations "segregated" from the society they helped to protect from Hitler. Not only that, but a government bureaucracy supported with public taxes was actively "restricting" the entrance of Indians into that society. Although most of these assumptions were somewhat fallacious, they provided the rhetoric of morality needed to dismantle New Deal institutions, especially the Bureau of Indian Affairs.

The process of "emancipating" American Indians and relieving the federal government of some very old responsibilities began almost immediately following the war. In 1946, Congress created the Indian Claims Commission in order to adjudicate various claims made by Indian tribes against the United States. In large part the establishment of the Commission was a genuine attempt to do justice to American Indians who had suffered at the hands of the government. On the other hand, the commission was designed also to take care of the suits in order to clear the way for an eventual withdrawal of the government from the "Indian business."

A year later lawmakers in Washington established the "Commission on the Organization of the Executive Branch of Government" and appointed as its head former President Herbert Hoover. Within the Commission's jurisdiction, Hoover set up an "Indian Task Force" in order to investigate and make recommendations on American Indian policies. In 1948, less than a year after its formation, the Hoover Commission issued a rather bland analysis of then-current programs directed by the Bureau of Indian Affairs. Although it condemned the policy of breaking up the reservations into individually held plots of land and urged caution in effecting rapid changes in policies, it nevertheless asserted that "assimilation must be the dominant goal of public policy" toward American Indians.

Nothing, it seemed, could alter the course that American Indian policy took in the ten years following World War II. Despite protests from the newly organized National Congress of American Indians and some objections from a few government officials, the government moved inexorably toward a policy of termination. Using the argument that the federal government was merely trying to grant the rights and freedoms of citizenship that American Indians had fought so hard for in the war, Congress reduced appropriations of the Bureau of Indian Affairs, urged the agency to promote "assimilation" programs such as relocating American Indians from the reservations to the cities, and pressed for the complete abolishment of federal responsibilities to American Indian tribes. By 1953, Congress, armed with the rhetoric of morality and democracy, was able to pass House Concurrent Resolution (H.C.R.) 108—a document that provided the power to terminate federal relations with individual tribes.

In 1954 the House and Senate Committees on Indian Affairs held hearings in consideration of the implementation of H.C.R. 108. During the deliberations, which eventually led to bills terminating several tribes in Utah, the Klamaths of Oregon, some Kansas tribes, and the Menominees of Wisconsin, Senator Arthur V. Watkins became the resolution's most active supporter. Watkins at once declared that termination was in keeping with democratic principles and would be "the Indian freedom program." Only incidentally would it be a means by which the government could disregard its treaties with American Indians and still maintain its outward moral integrity.

Termination was made fact because it came shrouded in liberalism and morality. American Indians marched off to war for various reasons; yet, whites took the tribes' participation as an unquestionable act of loyalty to the United States. Whites looked upon it as an American Indian effort to prove themselves worthy of "mainstream society." The fact that oppressed people could remain loyal to the United States served to illustrate the justice of America's cause. It tended, in the minds of Americans, to prove America's greatness every bit as much as winning the war had done. In this kind of intellectual climate, termination, no matter what its underlying motives, was easily passed as a liberal, democratic method of solving Indian problems. In the end, fighting the white man's war gained sympathy for American Indians, but it also fueled a fire that they did not want and eventually found difficult to extinguish.

For Further Reading

ON THE INDIAN NEW DEAL

Biolsi, Thomas. *Organizing the Lakota: The Political Economy of the New Deal on the Pine Ridge and Rosebud Reservations*. Tucson: University of Arizona Press, 1992.

Bromert, Roger. "The Sioux and the Civilian Conservation Corps." *South Dakota History* 8, 1978.

Busco, Elmer R. "John Collier: Architect of Sovereignty or Assimilation." *American Indian Quarterly* 15, Winter 1991.

Cash, Joseph H. and Herbert T. Hoover. "The Indian New Deal and the Years That Followed: Three Interviews." In Peter Iverson, ed., *The Plains in the Twentieth Century*. Norman: University of Oklahoma Press, 1985.

Hauptman, Laurence M. "The American Indian Federation and the Indian New Deal: A Reinterpretation." *Pacific Historical Review* 25, 1983.

——. *The Iroquois and the New Deal*. Syracuse, NY: Syracuse University Press, 1981.

Hurt, R. Douglas. "The Indian New Deal." In *Indian Agriculture in America: Prehistory to the Present*. Lawrence: University Press of Kansas, 1987.

Iverson, Peter. *"We Are Still Here": American Indians in the Twentieth Century*. Wheeling, IL: Harlan Davidson, 1998.

Kelly, Lawrence C. *The Assault on Assimilation: John Collier and the Origins of Indian Political Reform*. Albuquerque: University of New Mexico Press, 1983.

Kersey, Harry, Jr. "Florida Seminoles in the Depression and New Deal, 1933–1942: An Indian Perspective." *Florida Historical Quarterly* 65, 1986.

Koppes, Clayton R. "From the New Deal to Termination: Liberalism and Indian Policy, 1933–1953." *Pacific Historical Review* 46, 1977.

O'Neil, Floyd A. "The Indian New Deal: An Overview." In Kenneth R. Philp, ed., *Indian Self-Rule: First-Hand Accounts of Indian-White Relations from Roosevelt to Reagan.* Logan: Utah State University Press, 1995.

Parman, Donald L. "The Indian Civilian Conservation Corps." Ph.D. Diss., University of Oklahoma, 1967.

———. *The Navajos and the New Deal.* New Haven: Yale University Press, 1979.

Philp, Kenneth R. *John Collier's Crusade for Indian Reform, 1920–1954.* Tucson: University of Arizona Press, 1977.

———. "The New Deal and Alaska Natives, 1936–1945." *Pacific Historical Review* 50, 1981.

Rusco, Elmer R. *Legislation and Background of the Indian Reorganization Act,* Reno: University of Nevada Press, 2000.

Taylor, Graham D. *The New Deal and American Indian Tribalism: The Administration of the Indian Reorganization Act, 1934–1945.* Lincoln: University of Nebraska Press, 1980.

ON WORLD WAR II

Bernstein, Alison R. *American Indians and World War II: Toward a New Era in Indian Affairs.* Norman: University of Oklahoma Press, 1991.

Fixico, Donald L. "Warriors in World War II and New Attitudes." In *Termination and Relocation: Federal Indian Policy, 1945–1960. Albuquerque: University of New Mexico Press, 1986.*

Johnson, Broderick H. *Navajos and World War II.* Tsaile, NM: Navajo Community College Press, 1977.

Murray, Paul T. "Virginia Indians in the World War II Draft." *Virginia Magazine of History and Biography* 95, 1985.

Townsend, Kenneth William. *World War II and the American Indian.* Albuquerque: University of New Mexico Press, 2000.

United States Department of Interior, Bureau of Indian Affairs. *Indians in the War, 1945.* Chicago: Department of Interior, Bureau of Indian Affairs, 1945.

IV

1945–1960:
Termination, Relocation,
and Stereotypes

The postwar years of the late 1940s and 1950s represented a variety of changes for American Indians. They gained one benefit during the Truman years in 1946 when Congress created the Indian Claims Commission as a tribunal that provided Indians the means to obtain damages from the earlier loss of tribal lands. While the process resulted in substantial recoveries for some tribes, they were given only until 1951 to file their claims, which could not be granted with any accumulated interest. Worse, claims could only be made against the federal government, which restricted the claims that eastern tribes could make since much of their land was taken away by state, county, and private entities.

Affecting American Indians even more was the so-called "Termination Experiment" that began in 1953 and characterized the Eisenhower administration's policy toward Native Americans. Sponsored by Utah Senator Arthur V. Watkins, who claimed he wanted to set Indians "free," Congress passed House Concurrent Resolution (H.C.R.) 108, which sought to change the government's special relationship with Indian tribes by terminating recognition of them. The underlying philosophy was similar to that of the Dawes Act—to assimilate Indians into mainstream American society by reducing or eliminating federal services and protection. It applied specifically to smaller Indian tribes, such as forty Californian Indian rancherias, the Catawbas of South Carolina, the Poncas of Nebraska, the Ottawas of Oklahoma, the Menominees of Wisconsin, and several other groups. (Most, but not all of these, have since regained federal recognition, but had to do so by going through a bewildering bureaucratic process of appeals.) Termination meant, among other things, that exemptions from state taxing ended, federal programs to the tribes ceased, and state legislative and judicial authority were imposed on those Indians, which previous to this policy was perceived as unconstitutional. State jurisdiction was further extended in Indian Country in 1953 with the passage of Public Law 280. Termination also meant that thousands of Indians had to move off reservations to cities to find work and homes for their families. This was part of a planned "Relocation" effort in Indian policy that led to a new urbanization phenomenon for many American Indians.

But, as Peter Iverson explains in his revisionist chapter on the subject here, the discouraging 1950s became a time period "in which tribalism and Indian nationalism were reinforced." The policies "encouraged Indians throughout the nation to recognize their common bonds and needs," which led to the establishment of the National Congress of American Indians, the National Indian Youth Council, and to the growth of the Native American Church. These are examples of a very active agency that Indians retained in American society, as opposed to the hoped-for assimilation. It also led to policy changes toward self-determination in the 1960s and 1970s and helped inspire the Red Power movement.

Stereotypes about American Indians, however, persisted across the American cultural landscape. Popular culture, especially via Hollywood movies, continued to portray Native Americans in a less than realistic way. In her chapter "The Labor of Extras," Liza Black explores this dimension, and adds to our understanding of the roles that American Indians played in the films of this time period.

For additional reading on the topics of termination, relocation, urbanization, and the Indians as portrayed in popular culture, please consult the list of readings at the end of Part IV.

9

Building Toward
Self-Determination:
Plains and Southwestern Indians
in the 1940s and 1950s

Peter Iverson

Within the past decade more students of Indian history have turned their attention to the twentieth century. Until very recently the topical focus of this work has been primarily in the area of federal Indian policy, and the chronological focus, for the most part, has been on the years before World War II. This article represents a change in both topic and time. It attempts to analyze the period from World War II until the beginning of the 1960s, with specific consideration given to Indians of the Plains and the Southwest.

This era is often referred to in the literature as the era of termination. During this time many members of Congress and the Truman and Eisenhower administrations made sporadic but persistent efforts to reduce or eliminate federal services and protection for American Indians. The public rhetoric spoke of liberating the Indians by reducing governmental interference. Termination sought to immerse Indians in the mainstreams of their counties and states. This crusade resulted in significant hardship for many Indians. Tribes such as the Menominees in Wisconsin and the Klamaths in Oregon saw their reservation status ended. Indians who relocated to cities, with or without federal sponsorship, confronted many dilemmas. State and local agencies proved unwilling or unable to shoulder responsibilities previously bestowed upon the federal government. Economic development programs on reservations usu-

Reprinted from *Western Historical Quarterly*, Volume 16, Number 2 (April 1985) by permission of the Western History Association and the author.

ally did not markedly improve unemployment, housing, and other critical problems.

Yet to label these years as the termination era and to emphasize so exclusively the negative aspects of this generation is to present an incomplete picture. We cannot ignore federal policy in our consideration of any period, for it always has an important effect. But the 1940s and 1950s are more than a time of troubles. Just as new research is starting to reveal the late nineteenth and early twentieth centuries as a time when Indians in many areas made important and necessary adjustments to continue their lives as Indians, so, too, a closer examination of this more recent era shows it to be a period in which tribalism and Indian nationalism were reinforced. Indeed, to a significant degree the threat and the enactment of terminationist policy often strengthened rather than weakened Indian institutions and associations. In addition, the attitudes of state and local officials, as well as the perspectives of urban residents, encouraged Indians throughout the nation to recognize increasingly their common bonds and needs.

During the 1940s and 1950s, then, Indians in growing numbers tried to identify and take advantage of their own economic resources and tried to affirm their identities as members of tribes and as Indians. They rejected the conventional wisdom that they would be "less Indian" if they gained more education, acquired new jobs, or moved to a new residence. Actually, greater contact with the larger American society promoted greater awareness that the English language, new technological skills, and other elements of the American culture could be used to promote a continuing, if changing, Indian America.

A review of Indian actions in two important regions—the Plains and the Southwest—reveals a vital maturation in Indian leadership and a reaffirmation of Indian identity in the 1940s and 1950s. Far from vanishing, Indians emerged from this generation more determined than ever to be recognized on their own terms. The more publicized activism of the late 1960s and 1970s thus may trace its origins to these ostensibly more quiet years.

World War II marks a critical turning point in modern American Indian history. Indians took great pride in their involvement in the war effort. For example, Cecil Horse, a Kiowa, remembered his son John winning a bronze star and a purple heart and in turn receiving from his people a war bonnet and a giveaway ceremony in his honor. Navajos celebrated their code-talkers' role in the Pacific. In a publication of November 1945 the Office of Indian Affairs recorded the military honors earned by Indians and the investment by Indians in more than $17 million of restricted funds in war bonds. It quoted the instructions of Private Clarence Spotted Wolf, a Gros Ventre killed on December 21, 1944, in Luxembourg:

If I should be killed, I want you to bury me on one of the hills east of the place where my grandparents and brothers and sisters and other relatives are buried. If you have a memorial service, I want the soldiers to go ahead with the American flag. I want cowboys to follow, all on horseback. I want one of the cowboys to lead one of the wildest of the T over X horses with saddle and bridle on. I will be riding that horse.

The war generated more than memories and emotions. It meant that Indians had become more a part of the larger world in which they lived. As Ella Deloria, the Dakota linguist, wrote in 1944: "The war has indeed wrought an overnight change in the outlook, horizon, and even the habits of the Indian people—a change that might not have come for many years yet." Through the service, through off-reservation experiences, and through wage work, Indian perspectives and Indian economies began to change. Returning veterans and other participants in the war effort recognized the significance of better educational opportunities. Navajo Scott Preston put it simply: "We have to change and we have to be educated."

Change also demanded organization. Indian delegates from fifty tribes, hailing from twenty-seven states, met November 15–18, 1944, in Denver to organize the National Congress of American Indians (NCAI). In the words of one of the congress' first presidents, N.B. Johnson, the delegates set "an example for speed, diplomacy and harmony." Within four days they "adopted a constitution and formally launched the organization in an effort to bring all Indians together for the purpose of enlightening the public, preserving Indian cultural values, seeking an equitable adjustment of tribal affairs, securing and preserving their rights under treaties with the United States, and streamlining the administration of Indian affairs." In subsequent meetings in Browning, Montana, in 1945 and Oklahoma City in 1946, those in attendance proved to be, according to Johnson, "a cross-section of Indian population: old and young, full-bloods, mixed-bloods, educated and uneducated Indians from allotted areas and others from reservations," all of whom "were dissatisfied with many phases of the government's administration of Indian affairs." Improved health care and educational opportunities, protection of Indian land rights, and increased Indian veterans' benefits were advocated. The National Congress of American Indians urged the U.S. Congress and the current administration "not to enact legislation or promulgate rules and regulations thereunder affecting the Indians without first consulting the Tribes affected."

Such, of course, would not be the case. In both the Truman and Eisenhower administrations the federal government proceeded to pass legislation and carry out policies contrary to the will of the vast majority of American Indians. For many Americans the Indian war record had prompted concern that Indians be treated fairly. O.K. Armstrong's influential article in the August 1945 *Reader's Digest* urged America to "Set the American Indian Free!" House of

Representatives Majority Leader John W. McCormack read Armstrong's piece advocating the removal of "restrictions" from Indians and wrote to his colleague W.G. Stigler that he was "interested in seeing justice done for all—and this applies with great force to our fine American Indians." Cherokee/Creek historian Tom Holm has properly summarized what happened: "In the end, fighting the White man's war gained sympathy for American Indians but it also fueled a fire that they did not want and eventually found difficult to extinguish."

While they were not without effective allies, Indians had to lead the fight against Public Law 280, House Concurrent Resolution 108, and other features of termination. Protests against such measures soon resounded throughout the West. Through a variety of means, Indians attempted to ward off the implementation of a policy they realized could bring them great harm. In the early years voices from tribal councils and business committees rang out against a specific action in a particular locale. For example, Richard Boynton, Sr., and George Levi of the Cheyenne-Arapaho business committee telegrammed Oklahoma congressman Toby Morris to protest against the impending closing of the Cheyenne-Arapaho school in El Reno. Kiowa leader Robert Goombi argued that abolishing the Concho Indian School would be counterproductive. Yet as the wider pattern of the era emerged, multitribal associations were strengthened as a more effective means of presenting a more powerful Indian voice.

The National Congress of American Indians (NCAI) therefore continued to expand in its influence in the years that followed its establishment in 1944. Plains and Southwestern Indian peoples remained active in the executive ranks of the organization throughout the 1940s and 1950s. In the mid-1950s over half the elected members of the executive council would come from regional tribes, including the Osages, Gros Ventres, Gila River Pimas, Taos Pueblos, Blackfeet, Oglala Sioux, and Cheyenne-Arapahos. Colorado River tribes, Hualapais, Omahas, and the San Carlos Apaches appointed additional representatives. Oglala Sioux Helen Peterson served as executive director; Papago Thomas Segundo was regional representative.

The NCAI filled two critical functions. It helped Indians speak out against termination, but it also advocated programs that would contribute to Indian social, political, and economic revitalization. Through publicity releases from its Washington office, specially called tribal forums, and other means, the congress directly confronted the forces favoring termination. John Rainer from Taos Pueblo thus in 1950 attacked Commissioner of Indian Affairs Dillon Myer for imposing "drum head justice" upon Indians by denying tribes the power to choose their own attorneys.

The organization did more than criticize. It manifested a maturing capacity to articulate counterproposals when it offered suggestions to reduce Indian poverty, improvements for health care and educational facilities, and provisions to use reservation resources more effectively. A specific example—the Point Nine Program—was formulated and adopted by the congress in November 1954. It addressed critical questions relating to such matters as land and water resources, planning, credit, land purchase, and job training. Pointing to the assistance provided by the United States to underdeveloped countries around the world, Helen Peterson and other leaders demanded that this country apply the same principles within its borders.

Indians addressed the issues of the day through other forums as well. The Association on American Indian Affairs (AAIA), under the direction of Oliver La Farge, helped publicize both the dangers of federal policy and Indian moves to oppose it. Thus when the NCAI mobilized Indian representatives from twenty-one states and Alaska to come to Washington, D.C., on February 25–28, 1954, to protest impending legislation, *Indian Affairs*, the newsletter of AAIA, not only gave extensive coverage but also proper credit to NCAI for its actions. Other institutions and organizations put together symposia for the examination of contemporary Indian well-being. Tribal spokesmen from the Plains and the Southwest participated vigorously in such gatherings, be it the annual meeting of the American Anthropological Association in Tucson in 1954 or the annual conference on Indian Affairs at the University of South Dakota's Institute of Indian Studies.

By the end of the era new forums had been sought for the expression of Indian views. In 1961 representatives from sixty-four tribes, totaling approximately seven hundred delegates, met in Chicago to create the Declaration of Indian Purpose. They did not all agree with one another, but the so-called Chicago Conference was an important landmark in modern Indian affairs because of its size and its impact upon many of the participants.

Another example is the National Indian Youth Council (NIYC), which came into being soon thereafter. The NIYC had its roots in the annual conferences of the Southwest Association on Indian Affairs, beginning in 1956. This one-day session at the St. Francis Auditorium in Santa Fe brought Indian community people together with high school and college students, with the latter speaking to the former about their studies and the applicability of these studies to the communities. From this local beginning, the conference became regional in its focus in 1957 and was called the Southwest Regional Indian Youth Council. The council held annual conferences in the spring until April 1961, when the last meeting was held in Norman, Oklahoma. According to the Tewa anthropologist Alfonso Ortiz, "It was a core group from these youth councils, augmented later by alumni of D'Arcy McNickle's Indian Leadership Training Programs, who founded the NIYC in Gallup after the American Indian Chicago conference was held in June."

Other experiences and associations prompted heightened pan-Indian feelings. Relocation programs to American cities brought Indians into contact with non-Indians indifferent to tribal distinctions. Prejudice sometimes spurred pan-Indian identification. The formation of Indian communities and intertribal marriages in the cities also could foster such sentiments.

The Cherokee anthropologist Robert K. Thomas and other observers have noted that this movement frequently had a pan-Plains quality to it. Thomas also suggested that within the Southwest something of a pan-Puebloism could be perceived. Pan-Indianism, as it continued to evolve during this time, could be "very productive, as nationalist movements often are, in literature and the arts," but it also developed institutions dealing with non-Indians. One such development was the growth of powwows—a source of pleasure and pride for participants and enjoyment and education for spectators.

A final example of the pan-Indian movement in the 1940s and 1950s that should be cited is the Native American Church. It found significant support within the Plains and the Southwest, and leaders for the organization frequently hailed from these regions. At the tribal level, the Native American Church increased its membership during this period. Many Indians looked to participation within the peyote religion as a way of accommodating the various demands of modern life and reaffirming their identities as Indians. In Montana perhaps half the Crows and many Cheyennes embraced the church. Adherents included prominent tribal leaders such as Robert Yellowtail, Crow, and Johnnie Woodenlegs, Northern Cheyenne. Frank Takes Gun also emerged as an important, if controversial, church leader.

Attitudes toward the practice of the faith varied considerably, to be sure, from one Indian community to another and within communities. In the Navajo nation the peyote religion grew considerably in its membership during the 1950s, despite an antagonistic stance taken against it by the tribal chairman, Paul Jones. Raymond Nakai gained the chairmanship in 1963 in part because he pledged to stop harassing the Native American Church. On the Wind River Reservation in Wyoming, Northern Arapaho political and traditional leaders became more conciliatory toward the well-established practice. As was true of many tribes, the Arapahoes often added the Native American Church to prior participation in other religious ceremonies, be they Christian or traditional.

The reservation continued in the 1940s and 1950s as a centrally important place for religious observances, but for other reasons as well. The guiding philosophy of federal policy dictated that reservations were economic dead ends. After all, people were supposed to relocate because there were not enough jobs being generated at home. Since the land, families, familiarity, and indeed, everything that went into the definition of home continued to be valued so deeply, Indian communities within the Plains and the Southwest endeavored to keep more of their citizens at home. While organizations such as the NCAI could advocate local development of resources, such development had to be prompted and managed.

Navajo economic and political development has been described elsewhere in some detail. In the face of termination, Navajos who distrusted state governments and desired to maintain a working ethnic boundary between themselves and whites had little choice during the era but to pursue a more nationalistic approach. With large sums newly available to the tribal treasury from mineral revenues, the Navajo tribal government became far more ambitious. Federal assistance through the long-range rehabilitation program also assisted internal Navajo development. While the 1960s and 1970s would bring more fully to fruition some of these plans and programs, the 1940s and 1950s were crucial in the reinforcement of a working tribal identity and a commitment to a revitalized tribal economy.

Arts and crafts came to command a more important place in many tribal economies in the Southwest. For the Navajos, silversmithing and weaving continued to be vital sources of income. Pottery also gained widening acclaim, particularly at San Ildefonso, but also in other Pueblo communities along the Rio Grande and at some of the Hopi villages. Silverwork at the Hopi and Zuni pueblos, basket weaving especially among the Papagos and Hualapais, the paintings of such artists as Fred Kabotie, Hopi, and Harrison Begay, Navajo, and the sculpture of Alan Hauser, Apache, also found appreciative audiences. Though the boom in Indian art had yet to arrive, a foundation had been established.

Cattle ranching represented another important element in economic development. On the San Carlos Apache Reservation the cattle industry underwent significant alteration. The tribal council in October 1956 approved Ordinance 5–56 to reorganize and consolidate existing associations and implement various reforms in grazing regulations and practices. Improved range management could be combined with maintenance of cooperative efforts among the people of San Carlos. Cattle sales created some income for most families in the tribe. The quality of the Apaches' Herefords consistently attracted cattle buyers from throughout the West and generated a positive image of the Apaches to the non-Indian residents of Arizona.

Similarly, the Northern Arapahos gained greater control over their tribal ranch established during the Indian New Deal. With the assistance of an attorney, the tribe eventually was able to hire a ranch manager and to have the ranch's trustees be Arapahos appointed by the Arapaho business council. This sizeable operation returned a consistent profit to each Arapaho. As with the San Carlos Apaches, the ranching enterprise contributed to tribal self-esteem, the status of the tribal government, and an enhanced view of the Arapahos among outsiders, including the Shoshones who shared the Wind River Reservation.

In 1950 the tribal council of the Pine Ridge Reservation in South Dakota passed a tax of three cents per acre for grazing privileges on tribal lands. The tax met with strenuous objections by white cattle ranchers. In the face of such opposition the Department of the Interior quickly assigned the responsibility of collecting the tax to the Sioux. By 1956 white ranchers had challenged the tax in court, but in the following year the U.S. District Court judge ruled against them, contending that Indian tribes were "sovereign powers and as sovereign powers can levy taxes."

Greater assertion of Sioux power was not limited to Pine Ridge. Under the leadership of Chairman Frank Ducheneaux, the Cheyenne River tribal council approved a firm resolution against Public Law 280. Both on the Rosebud and on Pine Ridge, tribal voters in 1957 overwhelmingly defeated the assumption of state jurisdiction in South Dakota on Indian reservations. Opposition to repeated efforts to institute state jurisdiction led in 1963 to the formal organization of the United Sioux Tribes.

By 1959 the Rosebud Sioux tribal chairman, Robert Burnette, had filed complaints of discrimination under the Civil Rights Act of 1957 before the Civil Rights Commission. Burnette contended that Indians in South Dakota had been excluded from juries, had been beaten and chained in prisons, and generally had been greeted as people without equal rights in the state. While the commission was not very responsive to Burnette's allegations, the very act of publicly challenging local conditions indicated that a more activist stance would be assumed in the 1960s.

In the Dakotas, Wyoming, Arizona, and elsewhere, then, the growing importance of attorneys could be observed. For many tribes the establishment of the Indians Claims Commission in 1946 had prompted their first acquisition of some form of legal counsel. While the Bureau of Indian Affairs in the 1950s had often discouraged tribal use of attorneys or tried to dictate the choice of a specific firm, by decade's end it was clear that legal assistance would play a vital role in many realms of tribal life.

Williams v. Lee is a useful example of this evolution. Called by Chemehuevi attorney Fred Ragsdale "the first modern Indian law case," *Williams v. Lee* involved a non-Indian trader on the Navajo reservation who sued a Navajo in the state court to collect for goods sold on credit. While the Arizona Supreme Court ruled in favor of the trader, the U.S. Supreme Court reversed this decision. Justice Hugo Black, on behalf of the Court, stated: "There can be no doubt that to allow the exercise of state jurisdiction here would undermine the authority of the tribal courts over Reservation affairs and hence would infringe on the right of the Indians to govern themselves." This landmark decision served as a crucial statement in support of tribal sovereignty, presaging additional legal battles to be waged in the years to come.

Building Toward Self-Determination

In any reappraisal of the 1940s and 1950s, it is important to not overstate the case. The negative aspects of the period remain, even with the vital developments outlined above. And in a treatment of this length, some events of magnitude must be slighted. For example, the damming of the Missouri River created great hardship for the Indian peoples of that area. Scholars have correctly underlined the problems that seemed to exist everywhere, from the most isolated reservations to the largest city.

Nonetheless, a more careful examination yields a more balanced picture. In overdramatizing the difficulties of the time, we may not give sufficient credit to the enduring nature of Indians in this country. By the end of the 1950s tribal resources were more studied and better understood; tribal council leadership was often more effective. The Salish scholar and writer D'Arcy McNickle appreciated the transition that had taken place. He spoke in 1960 of the growing Indian movement toward self-determination. Indians in the future, he suggested, would "probably use the white man's technical skills for Indian purposes." McNickle affirmed that "Indians are going to remain Indian . . . a way of looking at things and a way of acting which will be original, which will be a compound of these different influences."

The 1940s and 1950s not only witnessed a change in Indian policy and a resurgence of pressures to assimilate Indians into the larger society, but also saw maturation and growth of Indian leadership at the local and national levels and efforts to develop tribal institutions, as well as a reaffirmation of identity and a willingness to adapt and change in the face of new conditions. In the immediate future seemingly new demands would resound for self-determination. Yet these demands were firmly based upon a foundation gradually constructed in the previous generation.

10

The Labor of Extras: American Indians in Hollywood, 1941–1960

Liza Black

Most Americans assume that Indians have rarely, if ever, played Indians in the movies, especially in the 1940s and 1950s. Studios hired men and women of many ethnicities to play Indian characters, including Irish Americans, Jewish Americans, multiheritage African Americans, Mexican Americans, Albanian Americans, Lithuanian Americans, Russian Americans, and American Indians. Studios hired Indians frequently and regularly, including Indian actors who lived in the southern California area and received union wages. These Indian actors made a lifelong career of playing Indian characters in the postwar era. The Indian men who played Indians remained at the level of supporting roles or bits. Only a few achieved a modicum of fame. On the other hand, non-Indians who played Indians often became famous as a result or at least augmented their fame.

Studios sought the employment of reservation Indians throughout the twentieth century. They flew their crews and equipment to places like Montana, Utah, Arizona, New Mexico, South Dakota and Alberta to capture the landscapes and the local Indians on film. The studios used reservation superintendents (both non-Indian and Indian) and non-Indian middlemen to recruit reservation Indians for employment. Indians also recruited themselves by simply making themselves a physical presence on the sets. Reservation Indian labor was critical in the production of movies in the postwar era that included

This chapter was originally a paper presented at the 39th Annual Conference of the Western History Association, Portland, OR, October 6–9, 1999.

Indian characters. In providing nonunion labor, the studios saved thousands of dollars. The studios used Indian extras for cheap, extremely temporary employment. Yet the Indians who worked in the film industry were neither powerless victims nor adept manipulators of the capitalist system. They worked for cash, and some felt they were gaining an exciting and very twentieth-century American experience of working on a movie set.

Directors, producers, and agents from reservations and Hollywood chased Indians for film work throughout the twentieth century. The irony was that the studios, as a modern medium, sought a premodern people, but they also sought to exploit them in ways that were very modern. They wanted Indians who would work cheaply, temporarily, with no benefits or physical protections.

Indians were workers living in the twentieth century, and studios sought these obviously modern Indians for movie work through modern mediums such as the Bureau of Indian Affairs. Yet they desired the employment of reservation Indians not just for authenticity but because of the very modern issue of avoiding union scales. The recruitments were sometimes spontaneous, but they were just as often handled in advance through reservation superintendents who oversaw the hires, ensured their legality, and dealt with correspondence. Twentieth Century-Fox dealt with James Stewart in hiring Navajos for *Buffalo Bill* (1944), and Paramount negotiated with Robert Yellowtail in hiring Crows for *Warpath* (1951). Whereas the hires of men who lived in southern California were largely casual and spontaneous, the hires of reservation Indians required planning, foresight, and a rudimentary knowledge of the workings of the Bureau of Indian Affairs.

Navajos were by far the most popular Indian extras in the 1940s and 1950s. Navajos and other reservation Indians who appeared in movies were not professional actors at all; they worked as extras anywhere from one day to two weeks. This was extremely temporary work that took place most often in June and July in western portions of the Navajo Reservation.

Hiring extras was overseen by the actors' and extras' guilds, but the guilds were only one part of the equation in hiring. In Hollywood, the guilds held power, but on reservations the superintendents maintained control of hiring. Hiring reservation Indians was not impossible, but it held obstacles different from those confronted when hiring actors, Indian and non-Indian. The studios recruited Navajos through a variety of means, but often they relied on reservation superintendents. Many studios wanted the efficiency of dealing with a union without paying union wages.

Although studios hoped to establish complete control over the Navajos, the federal government and Bureau of Indian Affairs asserted their own power in the negotiations over the Navajo hires.

When Fox producers attempted to secure the employment of Navajos in 1946 for *My Darling Clementine*, the superintendents and the Navajos actively participated in the employment negotiations. Fox's legal representative thought the hiring terms were clear for the Navajo extras, but the Navajos debated with the studio employees over issues that were not included in wage rates such as travel, cattle, and water. These issues went beyond wages, and the Navajos felt strongly about their necessary resolution. According to a Fox publicity document, the discussion went as follows:

Six weeks ago the first big salary pow-wow took place at Kayenta [Arizona]. Prices were set for cattle, for ponies, for the services of Indians, of squaws and even prices for papooses strapped to boards and unstrapped were discussed. The debates lasted weeks.
    How about bales of hay? How about water? Who will feed our cattle, our herds of sheep and goats when we bring them in? The Navajos talked to the 20th Century-Fox interpreters and business agents for days and days and nights and nights. Will those who bring their cattle from afar get more than those who bring in their cattle from nearby? Finally all plans were completed; the pow-wows were over. Far away in the mountains Navajo tribesmen had their local pow-wows, delegated their own appointees to take in the cattle to John Ford's location, 187 miles from a railroad in famous Monument Valley Pass.

The Navajos' hires were neither spontaneous nor "natural." Their labor was actively recruited by the studios, overseen by superintendents, and Navajos, in turn, actively participated in the negotiations.

The Navajo Reservation became a center of production, but studios filmed Westerns all over the country. Sometimes they filmed in the Southwest but used Apaches or Pueblos instead of Navajos. Other times, they filmed throughout the United States and even in Canada. On one fascinating occasion, they brought reservation Lakotas to Hollywood.

Warner Bros. actively recruited several Lakota men from the Standing Rock Reservation through the reservation superintendent at Fort Yates, North Dakota. Warner Bros. sought the Lakotas for their recreation of the Battle of the Little Bighorn in *They Died With Their Boots On* (1941). These men were perfectly glad to travel to Hollywood for the work, probably because it did not require a permanent or long-term stay.

Problems arose between the Lakota men and the crew almost immediately. On August 20, three of the men were sent home. On August 28, a studio bus was sent to fetch the men, but five of them were unable to be found as they had been out "on a spree." Mattison felt they should be sent back to North Dakota immediately. Either in spite of or because of these problems, Flying Cloud, Fast Horse, Village Center, Holy Bear, and Grey Eagle sent a telegram to Warner Bros. on September 2, inviting them to the "dinner and ceremonies at which Raoul Walsh will become Thunder Hawk, a blood brother in the Sioux

Nation" for the following evening. On September 3, however, Mattison admitted confidentially that "these Indians are beginning to give us a pain in the neck. It now appears they have a bunch of complaints which they have taken to the Guild and no doubt we will hear about them." On September 4, one of the men asked Frank Mattison if he could change his mind and stay with the rest of the men for the full term although he had previously decided to leave early. Mattison agreed and informed the studio he hoped they could "get through the rest of the picture without too much trouble."

The trouble, however, quickly escalated. On September 15, Mattison received a phone call from the Los Angeles Police Department at two o'clock in the morning informing him that Alvin Elknation and Joseph Fasthorse, Jr., had been in an accident. They were taken to the downtown Los Angeles emergency room, then Warner Bros. Dr. MacWilliams took them to Cedars of Lebanon Hospital. That same day, one of the Lakota men told Mattison that all of the men had agreed to return to Fort Yates the following day. The Lakotas reported a fight between some of the men, and Mattison requested permission to send them home.

Although they had assumed responsibility for the Lakotas while they were in Los Angeles, Warner Bros. balked at paying the Lakotas' hospital bill. Mattison received the bills and immediately suggested that the Legal Department attempt to force Louis G. Murray, the man who hit the Indian men, to pay the bills instead of Warner Bros. On September 23, Mr. Obringer wrote Arthur Freston of Freston & Files about the possibility of seeking payment of $71.60 from Murray for anesthesia, first aid, one x-ray, and room charges.

The story of these sixteen Standing Rock Lakota men, from "spree" to car accident, demonstrates the studios' intense desire to secure "real" Indians for their foreground and the complications that ensued. They used the men to give authenticity to their production. The men used them for wages and a free trip to California. Both groups sought to create public moments of interracial friendship amidst a private background of near constant wrangling and dispute.

The recruitment of Lakota men from the Standing Rock Reservation was an anomaly. On no other occasion in the 1940s and 1950s did a group of reservation Indians come to Hollywood for film work. Warner Bros. believed the results were disastrous. Studios had no idea of how to deal with the common, human dimensions of Indians' lives. They could not predict their behavior, and they could not control it. Although they assumed responsibility for these men, they attempted to shirk it the moment that it cost them money.

Studios repeatedly relied upon the acumen of reservation superintendents, both Indian and non-Indian, to secure the employment of Indian extras for film work. In 1941, the Crow Agency created a committee composed of Robert Yellowtail, William Bends, Mark Real Bird, and Harry Whiteman in production for *Buffalo Bill.* Together they drafted an agreement for renting teepees, filming ceremonies, and hiring Crows for film work.

Years later in the Southwest, Warner Bros. again turned to an Indian reservation superintendent for help in securing reservation Indians for labor. They contacted Lester Oliver, Apache Tribal Council Chairman, and he served as middleman. Oliver orchestrated the hiring of two hundred White River Apaches who played Modocs in *Drum Beat* (Warner Bros., 1954). The Apache extras traveled by bus to the set location in the Coconino National Forest in northern Arizona and replaced the Navajos who had left because of bad television reception.

Reservation superintendents were clearly an important part of the recruitment process, but local non-Indian technical advisors such as David Miller also played an important part. Miller, a non-Indian painter who lived in South Dakota during summers, became an important figure in several productions, including *Tomahawk* (Universal, 1951), *The Savage* (Paramount, 1952), and *The Last Hunt* (MGM, 1956). He was known for his ability to communicate with Lakotas and ably negotiated dozens of Indian hires for these films.

In 1951, David Miller organized all aspects of hiring for the Lakota extras. He reportedly had a method for obtaining their labor. He went to each of the ninety-four men who were ultimately hired for *Tomahawk* and gave them gifts. He spoke with them in Lakota about the movie until he secured their employment. He completed their time cards and kept detailed lists of their pay and taxes withheld. Some of the men included in this hiring were later hired in both *The Savage* and *The Last Hunt*: Ben American Horse, James Red Cloud, John Sitting Bull, Joseph High Eagle (nephew of Custer), Dewey Beard, and Andrew Knife. There were many others, including Benjamin Kills Enemy who appeared as an Indian years earlier in *The Overland Trail* (1925). Apparently Miller was not entirely thorough in his explanation of the movie. These six men left the set when they discovered the film was about Red Cloud and not Crazy Horse. It would be presumptuous to claim all Indians were concerned with film content, but these men certainly were.

When Universal shot *Pillars of the Sky* (Universal, 1956) in La Grande, Oregon, the studio hired Gilbert Connor, an Indian man from the Umatilla Reservation, to recruit Indian extras from the reservation about thirty miles southeast of La Grande. Connor recruited seventy-five men to appear in *Pillars*, but they never showed up for work after an intense night of stick game competition at the Pendleton round-up. Connor showed up nonetheless and received the bit part of Chief Elijah. Connor successfully recruited one other Indian man, Manuel Squakin (Okanagan), who worked as an extra. Similarly, Donald Deernose recruited other Crows for work in 1952 for *The Big Sky*

(RKO). He was paid $1400 for 42 days of work (about $33 a day). Recruiting Indians paid much better than playing Indians.

Because of the constant employment of southwestern Indians, several Indian men formed a casting company, which they ran out of Tucson. They hired a press agent, supposedly named Loose Tongue Harris, and the group was headed by two Navajo men, Charlie White Fish and Grey Eyes Judels. Universal became aware of the arrangement when they announced they would be filming in Tucson. Harris contacted Universal by phone. The casting office had approximately three hundred Indians signed up for movie work. Universal emphasized the modernity of the Tucson casting office: "The Indians are contacted on their reservation through a regulation telephone switchboard and not through smoke signals as someone suggested when the office was opened."

In still other cases, Indians simply recruited themselves and arrived at set locations. Paramount hired Navajos, Sioux, and Apaches for their Tucson location film, *The Last Outpost* (Paramount, 1951). The local Indians required no recruitment; the Indians simply showed up ready to work.

The location cameras for his big-scale Technicolor spectacle had barely been set up outside Tucson when a horde of job-seeking Indians swarmed on the scene lugging valises stuffed with tribal beads and feathers.

Thanks to the renewed popularity of Western films, any brave who can ride and draw a bow is fairly certain of finding work in the many outdoor pictures going before the camera. Thus, by car, by bus and by thumb, young Indians travel to the outdoor location centers—places like Phoenix, Flagstaff, and Tucson. More than 200 Navajos, Sioux and Apaches were hired for "The Last Outpost."

In 1951 and 1955, Indians not only arrived upon the location scene, they made clear their desire to be hired by the studio. During hires for *Tomahawk* (1951), sixty young Pine Ridge men showed up hoping to secure the role of Crazy Horse. Shoshone and Lakota men beat their drums outside the Alex Johnson Hotel in Rapid City, South Dakota, until director George Sherman hired them for *Chief Crazy Horse* (Universal, 1955).

There was no single way in which American Indians were hired for film work. Their labor was mediated through a variety of mediums. Both American Indians and the studios used a variety of approaches in negotiating labor in movies. No single person or agency, Indian or non-Indian, held total power in recruiting reservation Indians for film work.

Although these movie economies on reservations were temporary, they fit into the introduction of wage labor on reservations. Film studios had a significant impact on the communities they frequented. Kanab, Utah, for example, became a town that essentially existed on the financial support of film studios.

The studios' stays were brief but intense. They supported local businesses and often changed the people and the landscape.

For the most part, reservation Navajos and other reservation Indians who worked in movies were not interested in becoming actors or moving to Hollywood. They simply wanted to earn cash as quickly as possible in between their other household and community commitments. There are only a few examples of Navajos being star-struck, but they are there. One Navajo teenager was enamored with Virginia Mayo. Another young man apparently read magazines such as *Variety*, because he was well aware of the social world of Hollywood. Nonetheless, most Navajos did not want to move to Hollywood and become Indian actors. Most Navajos, in particular, were not especially interested in working off the reservation, let alone moving to another community. Only one Navajo, Grey Eyes (no first name given), came to Hollywood. His visit was temporary, and he brought his wife and son with him.

CONCLUSION

Actors, regardless of their ethnicity, received more than extras. Indian actors were paid much more than Indian extras playing Indians. The Indian extras who played Indians were paid very little, but they received cash in newly established wage economies and they did so without having to leave the reservation.

Indians were integral to film production in the 1940s and 1950s. The studios collected their names, social security numbers, and made deductions from their pay while making movies that, ironically, denied them their modernity. Indian extras consistently tried to receive more pay and better conditions; they sometimes demonstrated their knowledge of movies and the Hollywood scene.

The various categories comprising the Hollywood acting hierarchy (for example, leading role actors, bit part actors, and extras) do not allow for simplistic theories of dominance and victimization in which whites overpower and exploit Indians. Indian actors were sometimes paid more than non-Indian actors. Indian and non-Indian actors were always paid much more than Indian extras. Even the Indians who played Indians were not being duped by capitalism; they received work in newly established wage economies. Theories of dominance are applicable primarily by the fact that Indian actors were never allowed into the uppermost category of leads. This was strictly the domain of non-Indian actors. The best Indian actors could hope for was consistency in hires at the level of bit parts. The Indians who were involved in the film industry were in no way being hoodwinked. The studios used them, and they used the studios.

For Further Reading

ON TERMINATION AND RELOCATION

Ablon, Joan. "American Indian Relocation: Problems of Dependency and Management in the City." *Phylon* 66, 1965.

Burt, Larry W. "Roots of the Native American Urban Experience: Relocation Policy in the 1950s." *American Indian Quarterly* 10, 1986.

———. *Tribalism in Crisis: Federal Indian Policy, 1953–1961.* Albuquerque: University of New Mexico Press, 1982.

Deloria, Vine, Jr. "The Disastrous Policy of Termination." In *Custer Died for Your Sins: An Indian Manifesto.* New York: Macmillan, 1969.

Fixico, Donald L. *Termination and Relocation: Federal Indian Policy, 1945–1960.* Albuquerque: University of New Mexico Press, 1986.

———. *The Urban Indian Experience in America.* Albuquerque: University of New Mexico Press, 2000.

Iverson, Peter. *"We Are Still Here": American Indians in the Twentieth Century.* Wheeling, IL: Harlan Davidson, 1996.

LaFarge, Oliver. "Termination of Federal Supervision: Disintegration of the American Indians." *Annals of the American Academy of Political and Social Science,* 1957.

Neils, Elaine. *Reservation to City: Indian Migration and Federal Relocation.* Chicago: University of Chicago, Department of Geography, 1971.

Peroff, Nicholas. *Menominee Drums: Tribal Termination and Reservation and Restoration.* Norman: University of Oklahoma Press, 1982.

Philp, Kenneth R. "Stride Toward Freedom: The Relocation of Indians to Cities, 1952–1960. *Western Historical Quarterly* 16, 1985.

————. "Termination: A Legacy of the New Deal." *Western Historical Quarterly* 14, 1983.

————. *Termination Revisited: American Indians on the Trail to Self-Determination, 1933–1953.* Lincoln: University of Nebraska Press, 1999.

Rawls, James J. *Chief Red Fox Is Dead: A History of American Indians Since 1945.* Ft. Worth, TX: Harcourt Brace College Publishers, 1996.

Stefon, Frederick J. "The Irony of Termination: 1943–1958." *The Indian Historian* 11, 1978.

Wilkinson, Charles F. and Eric R. Briggs. "The Evolution of the Termination Policy." *American Indian Law Review* 6, 1978.

ON AMERICAN INDIAN STEREOTYPES AND POPULAR CULTURE

Berkhofer, Robert F. *The White Man's Indian: Images of the American Indian, from Columbus to the Present.* New York: Knopf, 1978.

Churchill, Ward. *Fantasies of the Master Race: Literature, Cinema, and the Colonization of American Indians.* San Francisco: City Light Books, 1998.

Deloria, Philip Joseph. *Playing Indian.* New Haven: Yale University Press, 1998.

Kilpatrick, Jacqueline. *Celluloid Indians: Native Americans and Film.* Lincoln: University of Nebraska Press, 1999.

Moses, L.G. *Wild West Shows and the Images of American Indians, 1883–1933.* Albuquerque: University of New Mexico Press, 1996.

Owens, Louis. *Mixedblood Messages: Literature, Film, Family, Place.* Norman: University of Oklahoma Press, 1998.

Rollins, Peter C. and John E. O'Connor, eds. *Hollywood's Indians: The Portrayal of the Native American in Film.* Lexington: University of Kentucky Press, 1998.

Trenton, Patricia and Patrick T. Houlihan. *Native Americans: Five Centuries of Changing Images.* New York: H.N. Abrams, 1989.

V

The 1960s and 1970s: Self-Determination, Activism, and Spiritual Rights

The era of termination faded into the era of self-determination for American Indians in the 1960s and 1970s. Self-determination refers to the logical notion that American Indians should have the right to determine the way their tribes and reservations are governed. It restores a degree of sovereignty that was taken away with the assimilationist policies of the 1950s. The Nixon administration is usually given credit for the change of policies due to the passage of the Indian Civil Rights Act of 1968, the Alaska Native Claims Settlement Act of 1971, and the Indian Self-Determination and Education Assistance Act of 1975. However, as Thomas Clarkin points out in his chapter here, the seeds of self-determination were planted and cultivated during the administrations of Presidents Kennedy and Johnson and were advocated by Secretary of the Interior Stewart Udall, who made it the cornerstone of his BIA policies.

Most of the reforms, of course, did not materialize by themselves. The 1960s witnessed the growth of American Indian activism that echoed other protest movements in the United States during that decade. But amidst all the activism for the civil rights of African Americans, the protests against the Vietnam War, and the beginnings of the women's liberation and environmental movements, few people stopped to consider the rights of American Indians. That changed very quickly in 1969 when a group of Native Americans led by Richard Oakes occupied Alcatraz Island in San Francisco. The story of Oakes and his group, the Indians of All Tribes, is retold here by Kent Blansett, and is important for understanding the beginning of the whole Red Power movement. Soon Indians from other parts of the country demonstrated against

U.S. policies. Most notable were the actions of the American Indian Movement (AIM), which occupied BIA headquarters in Washington, D.C., for six days in 1972, and occupied the town of Wounded Knee, South Dakota—the site of the 1890 massacre of the Sioux by federal troops—for two months in 1973. Led by such leaders as Russell Means, Dennis Banks, and Clyde Bellecourt, AIM demanded radical changes in reservation policies and insisted that treaty obligations be honored by the U.S. government.

One of the most important rights that began to be recognized during this time period was religious freedom for American Indians. The passage of the American Indian Religious Freedom Act of 1978 helped to change a long history of U.S. government misunderstandings regarding the spiritual rights of Native Americans. One of the points of contention was the use of peyote by many Indian tribes and as a much-practiced ritual by members of the Native American Church. The background history and geography of peyote, its use by American Indians, and its attempted regulation by U.S. authorities is detailed by Daniel Swan in the third chapter of this section.

For more information on any of these topics, please refer to the list of suggested readings at the end of Part V.

11

Federal Indian Policy and Self-Determination during the Kennedy and Johnson Years

Thomas Clarkin

In June 1961, some 800 Native Americans representing Indian communities from throughout the United States gathered in Chicago for the American Indian Chicago Conference (AICC). During a week of ceremonies and committee meetings, conferees crafted the *Declaration of Indian Purpose*, a forty-nine page document that included general statements and specific recommendations regarding the direction of federal Indian policy. The *Declaration* included a passage that may be regarded as a call for Indian self-determination:

The basic principle involves the desire on the part of the Indians to participate in developing their own programs with help and guidance as needed and requested. . . . The Indians as responsible individual citizens, as responsible tribal representatives, and as responsible Tribal Councils want to participate, want to contribute to their own personal and tribal improvements and want to cooperate with their Government [i.e., the U.S. government] on how best to solve the many problems in a business-like, efficient and economical manner as rapidly as possible.

By the end of the 1960s, this statement would seem rather conservative, but for its time the *Declaration of Indian Purpose* was a remarkable document, the product of the largest pan-Indian meeting ever held to discuss the problems that American Indians faced as a group. They had come together, as one conference member noted, because they "had a common sense of being under at-

This chapter was originally a paper presented at the 39th Annual Conference of the Western History Association, Portland, OR, October 6–9, 1999.

tack." The sense of crisis that American Indians experienced in 1961 stemmed from the crushing poverty that plagued them and from the federal policy of termination, which threatened the very existence of their communities. Termination sought to end the special relationship that existed between Indian tribes and the federal government, or, to use the language of a 1953 congressional resolution, "Indian tribes and individual members thereof, should be freed from Federal supervision and control and from all disabilities and limitations specially applicable to Indians." However, the "freedom" imposed on terminated tribes had been disastrous, marked by an increase in poverty and the loss of tribal assets. Thus, the AICC called upon the U.S. government to "abandon the so-called termination policy."

Among the non-Indians who attended the AICC were members of a special task force established by the new secretary of the interior, Stewart L. Udall, just days after he took office in January 1961. Udall held the primary responsibility for implementing federal Indian policy in the administrations of John Kennedy and Lyndon Johnson. In a speech given at the 1959 convention of the National Congress of American Indians, Udall blamed the administration of Dwight Eisenhower for failing "to lay emphasis on the step-by-step programs that make termination possible." Rather than pursuing immediate termination, Udall recommended "aggressive human and resource development which will make it possible for our Indian people to formulate their own plans for self-determination." At a congressional hearing eight years later, Udall declared, "I am a gradualist—gradual termination." Thus, Udall favored a gradual termination process without declared deadlines, one that emphasized development and Indian participation in the policy process.

In addition to regarding self-determination as a means to advance tribal termination, Udall held a narrow, limited concept of Indian self-determination, as his remarks at a 9 February 1961 task force meeting revealed. Udall told the task force members that it was important "that constantly throughout this process we test our thinking against the thinking of the wisest Indians and their friends." However, he added that "this does not mean that we are going to let . . . the Indian people themselves decide what the policy should be because some of them have special axes to grind, some of them view the problem from too narrow a point of vantage." Instead of advocating full Indian participation in the policy process, Udall declared, "I would hope when we finish there is a feeling among the Indians themselves, and I place great emphasis on this, that they have been fully consulted, that whether they agree 100 percent with our conclusions, that they had a full and fair hearing."

In keeping with Udall's charge to seek Indian counsel, task force members met with Indian delegations, visited several reservations, and attended the American Indian Chicago Conference, all of which led task force member and future commissioner of Indian Affairs Philleo Nash to claim that "98 percent of the [Indian] population was represented by the elected leaders that appeared before us and offered programs." In July 1961 the task force released its recommendations under the title "Report of the Secretary of the Interior by the Task Force on Indian Affairs." This report would serve as the blueprint for federal Indian policy for most of the following decade.

The task force report reflected Udall's support for gradual termination. Noting that "placing greater emphasis on termination than on development impairs Indian morale and produces a hostile or apathetic response," task force members sought to "create conditions under which the Indians will advance their social, economic and political adjustment to achieve a status comparable to that of their non-Indian neighbors," in part by "encourag[ing] Indians and Indian tribes to assume an increasing measure of self-sufficiency." Although the task force rejected "termination *per se* as a major objective of the Federal Indian program," it recognized as the final goal of that policy,"terminat[ing], at appropriate times, Federal supervision and services to Indians."

The task force neglected to define exactly what constituted "an increasing measure of self-sufficiency," or how that concept was related to self-determination. It also failed to establish bureaucratic mechanisms designed to bring Indians into the policy process, an omission that did not bode well for American Indians requesting a greater role in planning their futures. The task force report only called for the creation of an advisory board to the secretary of the interior consisting of unpaid Indian and non-Indian members, a vague recommendation that was never implemented and did not meet the Indian demand to participate in policy and program development.

The task force report was moderate, even timid, in its recommendations for a number of reasons. Udall's commitment to gradual termination, the lack of any bureaucratic tradition of including Indians in the policy process, and the persistence of the paternalism that for so long had marred the conduct of federal Indian policy all weakened the task force's recommendations. Uppermost in Stewart Udall's mind, however, was congressional opposition, especially from powerful western senators such as Clinton P. Anderson (D.-NM) who strongly supported termination. Philleo Nash later recalled that the task force "had to bear in mind that Congress provides the authority and the funds and you therefore could not fly in the face of congressional opinion." He added, "we therefore scaled it [the final report] very modestly."

Despite its weaknesses, the task force report's call for increased federal involvement and spending in order to develop Indian resources and improve the Indian standard of living represented a departure from the termination policy. For this very reason, Senator Anderson responded to the report with dismay. After reading the report, Anderson called for continued termination of Indian tribes without tribal consent. He and colleagues on the senate interior committee such as Gordon Allott (R.-CO) made it clear that they opposed any federal assistance that would slow or halt tribal terminations. As Richard Schifter, attorney for the Association on American Indian Affairs, noted in 1962, "the Anderson-Allott combination . . . is so strongly opposed to the Indian development concept that it will try to block Administration efforts" in that area.

Paradoxically, congressional opposition to legislation aimed at assisting Native Americans fostered conditions conducive to self-determination. With Anderson, Allott, and other interior committee members opposed to most legislation assisting Indians, government officials sought to include Indians in other federal aid programs, thereby allowing the Bureau of Indian Affairs to bypass the interior committee. Through the efforts of Commissioner Nash, other administration officials, and sympathetic congressmen, American Indians received assistance from federal programs intended to promote growth in economically underdeveloped regions of the country.

The Area Redevelopment Administration (ARA) was one such program. Originally intended to offer aid to economically depressed urban areas, the Area Redevelopment Act was amended to include rural regions in order to secure the support of congressmen who represented predominantly rural areas. The bill, which became law in 1961, created a "specific kit of tools to help communities rebuild their economic bases," including low-cost loans to attract industry, loans and grants to communities for infrastructure improvement, technical assistance for the creation of long-term development programs, and job training with subsistence pay for trainees. During hearings held in 1956, Senators Lee Metcalf and Michael "Mike" Mansfield (D.-MT) had argued that minor changes to the bill would "make certain that Indian reservations can qualify for its benefits." Section 6 of the amended bill listed Indian tribes among the public and private organizations permitted to propose loans or grants for public facilities. By 1964, the ARA had authorized eighty-four projects on Indian reservations at a total cost of $4.8 million.

In 1961, the chief counsel of the Public Housing Administration (PHA) determined that the United States Housing Act of 1937, which enabled "any state, county, municipality or other governmental entity" to qualify for public housing assistance, applied to tribal governments. Marie McGuire, who headed the PHA, met with BIA officials to coordinate such a project for the Oglala Sioux Housing Authority, which received over one million dollars to build eighty-eight units. Between 1964 and 1968, tribal housing authorities built 2,238 units.

The BIA worked with the Department of Labor so that the Manpower Development Training Act, which funded job training programs, applied to American Indians. Indian communities also qualified for federal assistance under the Public Works Acceleration Act. The original act, which President Kennedy signed into law in September 1962, did not specifically mention Indian reservations, an oversight corrected in October 1962 when Congress passed Lee Metcalf's amendment making Indian tribes eligible.

The decision to allow Indian reservations and their tribal governments to qualify for these and other federal programs constituted a significant and unintended recognition of tribal sovereignty that advanced Indian self-determination. Programs intended to assist Native Americans with economic development in order to ensure their eventual assimilation into the dominant American society empowered the very institutions that served to preserve and protect Indian identity.

The poverty programs of Lyndon Johnson's Great Society furthered the trend toward Indian self-determination begun during the Kennedy years. In his first State of the Union message, President Johnson announced that "this administration declares unconditional war on poverty in America," and called upon Americans to attack poverty "wherever it exists—in city slums and small towns, in sharecropper shacks or in migrant worker camps, on Indian reservations." American Indians largely had been ignored during early planning sessions for antipoverty legislation, but by the time congressional committees debated the Economic Opportunity Act of 1964, Secretary Udall had prepared a statement detailing the benefits that Native Americans would receive. Udall maintained that the Community Action Program (CAP), which allowed community residents to organize Community Action Agencies (CAAs), craft proposals, apply for grants, and administer local programs without interference from local, state, or federal officials, "offers an unprecedented opportunity for Indians to carry out local community improvement."

Udall was correct. Although chronically underfunded, poverty programs administered by the Office of Economic Opportunity (OEO) brought numerous benefits to Native American communities, prompting Russell Means, Yankton Sioux, to note in his 1995 autobiography, "OEO was the best thing ever to hit Indian reservations." In addition to bringing much-needed social programs and additional federal dollars to the reservations, OEO allowed American Indians control over program planning and operations. Means claimed that "those OEO programs and others that helped communities form and manage their own organizations, to find solutions to their own problems[,] inspired hope."

Because American Indians ran the war on poverty programs, they received training in administrative and bureaucratic procedures necessary to run tribal governments and business enterprises. From grant writing to record keeping to personnel training, OEO programs gave Indians the opportunity to acquire the skills needed for the successful management of their interests. OEO also offered young and ambitious American Indians new leadership opportunities—a generation of tribal chairmen and activists got their starts as OEO directors and employees. As LaDonna Harris, Comanche, declared in 1986, "Indian leadership developed out of that program." Peter McDonald and Peterson Zah of the Navajo Nation serve as two examples of tribal leaders with OEO backgrounds.

Stewart Udall recognized the possibilities that war on poverty programs offered to American Indians, and hoped to emulate them with Department of the Interior initiatives. At a BIA conference held in Santa Fe, New Mexico, in April 1966, Udall praised a memorandum written by William King, a reservation superintendent at Salt River. King gave credit to OEO because "it has allowed Indians to redefine their relationship with the Federal Government." He contended that "much of the actual power of the Superintendency, and virtually all of that additional power which many reservation Indians feel it possesses, must be shifted to an Indian power locus, logically the Tribal Council." King suggested that "the Government . . . contract with tribes to carry out many of the activities presently performed by the Bureau." Udall distributed copies of the King memo at a press conference and declared, "the suggestion in the letter . . . in regard to strengthening tribal government by transferring functions to tribal government is a suggestion that we are seriously considering."

Despite his enthusiasm for the recommendations found in the King memorandum, Udall proved unable to extend the ideal of Indian self-determination to the larger arena of policy formulation. In 1967 he proposed what he called "foundation legislation," a comprehensive bill that would rival the 1934 Indian Reorganization Act in terms of its influence on American Indian life. Known as the Indian Resources Development Act of 1967, Udall's grand legislative scheme came to naught because he failed to work with American Indian leadership in crafting his proposals. Once again, the tradition of paternalism prevented well-intentioned government officials such as Udall from recognizing the limits that they placed on Indian participation in the policy process.

Yet the concept of Indian self-determination gained support within the Johnson administration, as the president's March 1968 Special Message to the Congress on the Problems of the American Indian revealed. Johnson proposed "a policy of maximum choice for the American Indian: a policy expressed in programs of self-help, self-development, self-determination." Declaring that "the greatest hope for Indian progress lies in the emergence of Indian leadership and initiative in solving Indian problems," Johnson looked forward to a day "when the relationship between Indians and the Government will be one of full partnership—not dependency." The tone of the message evidenced the changes that had taken place since 1953, when, under the banner of liberation, the federal government had tried to terminate that historic partnership.

In a 1998 interview, Stewart Udall claimed that "the idea of self-determination . . . this really bubbled up in my time there [in the Department of the Interior] . . . self-determination, the idea was kicking around pretty strong." Why, then, did this idea take so long to bear fruit, and offer so little in the way of tangible achievements by the end of the decade? Robert Bennett, commissioner of Indian Affairs from 1966 to 1969, offered an explanation in a 1968 memo to Udall. Bennett asserted:

Cutting across the broad field of Indian legislation as well as the administration of Indian affairs in general is the Indians' fear of termination of federal trusteeship and services. Positive attempts to bring about the development of the Indian people—to equip them with the tools necessary to that development—to imbue in them a sense and desire for independence and self determination, meet with outright suspicision [*sic*] by the Indians which must then be laboriously overcome.

While the move toward Indian self-determination constituted a success for the Kennedy and Johnson administrations, their failure to repudiate termination presented the greatest obstacle to the stated goal of promoting Indian self-sufficiency. Although the programs operated under the authority of the Public Housing Administration, the Area Redevelopment Administration, and the Office of Economic Opportunity contributed to improvements in the Indian standard of living, created new employment opportunities for some individuals, and bolstered tribal sovereignty, American Indian participation in those programs was predicated upon poverty levels, not upon the historic federal obligations to Indians. Sharing the benefits of federal development and antipoverty programs with American Indians raised the specter of termination in two ways. First, program sharing hinted at the eventual abolition of the BIA, long a goal of terminationists. Second, it redefined American Indians as poor people, ignoring the cultural and social values that many Indians wished to protect. Concerned with acquiring funds for reservation development, federal officials never imagined the long-term benefits or questioned the long-term consequences that program sharing might have for Indian communities.

12

A Journey to Freedom: Richard Oakes, American Indian Activism, and the Occupation of Alcatraz

Kent Blansett

It was a crisp cool fall day in 1969 when Richard Oakes and others stepped onto dock number 40 in the San Francisco Bay. A crowd of reporters had gathered to witness the Indian "takeover" of Alcatraz Island. The reporters snapped photos of Oakes holding up strips of red cloth and beads, mocking, with a smile, an attempt to purchase the island from the government. Finally a boat was found to take the "occupiers" to the island. One by one, people climbed on board the *Monte Cristo* and other boats and started out. The rough currents were sliced by the motion of the boat, and the faces of the passengers reflected the excitement. As the winds picked up, many glanced back at the pier and the enormous crimson superstructure of the Golden Gate Bridge. Eventually, the focus returned to the weathered concrete of the "Rock." Dressed in blue jeans, a sweater, and his cherished pair of cowboy boots, Richard Oakes made his way to the side of the boat. Looking over at the waves and the island, he turned to the crowd and motioned, "Come on, let's go. Let's get it on!" Within a few seconds, his shirt was off and his large frame disappeared into the chilled November waters, his boots still on as he swam for land.

Oakes never looked back. He continued to swim through wave after wave. He seemed to lack fear. The danger of being swept out to sea, or, worse yet, drowning never entered his consciousness. After two hundred and fifty yards, he was pushed in by the waves. He reached for the shore, pulling himself up on

This chapter was originally a paper presented at the conference "American Indian Leaders: Red Power and Tribal Politics," University of Kansas, Lawrence, KS, September 15–17, 2000.

the sea-stained rocks. A lone dog approached and began to lick the fatigue and salt from his body. Richard Oakes had made a long journey, a journey to freedom.

The life of Richard Oakes, a St. Regis Mohawk, is crucial to any discourse on contemporary American Indian leadership. Oakes helped organize the highly publicized Alcatraz, Fort Lawton, and Pit River "takeovers." His assassination in 1972 galvanized the Trail of Broken Treaties march on Washington, D.C., and unified a movement that eventually ushered in the era of self-determination in the mid-1970s. But Oake's life served yet another purpose: it inspired and enlightened future generations of Native leaders. This chapter will explore the life of Richard Oakes Ranoies [A Big Man] and illustrate how his actions reflected the unique voice of indigenous leadership within the Red Power movement of the 1960s–1970s.

Just before Richard Oakes was admitted to San Francisco State University, the campus became caught up in one of the most violent riots in all of American college history. In 1968 the Third World Liberation Front, La Raza Unida, the Black Student Union, and the American Federation of Teachers had joined in a campus-wide strike. By the end of the strike, "more than 700 arrests, countless beatings, and daily occupation of the campus" finally produced negotiations. The negotiators for La Raza, a Chicano student organization that also represented Native students, convinced the university to create a Native American Studies department. As a result, in February of 1969 Richard Oakes and eight other students were admitted to the first Native American Studies (NAS) department at San Francisco State.

Oakes, now coordinator for Native American Studies, and other students helped build the program by participating in the search committees for faculty positions and by attending various conferences throughout California. The first positions open for the NAS community advisory board were filled by Belva Cottier (Lakota), Jeanette Henry (Cherokee), and Rupert Costo (Cahuilla). Belva Cottier had mentioned to Oakes that she and other Lakota had tried to "take over" Alcatraz Island in 1964, drawing on the Fort Laramie Treaty of 1868. She informed Oakes that under the treaty any surplus land the government had abandoned could be reclaimed by the Lakota people. Oakes listened as Cottier explained that the media had ignored their actions and by the next day, the occupation was over.

For many years Alcatraz Island, a former federal prison in the San Francisco Bay, remained unused. Both the state of California and the federal government sought proposals for what to do with the island. In 1969, Lamar Hunt, the son of a Texas oil millionaire, hoped to develop Alcatraz into a theme park; others wanted housing developments. But the proposals never went past the drafting board. Oakes, now a student at San Francisco State, would offer the ultimate proposal: Native occupation of the island.

Professor Louis Kemnitzer at San Francisco State described Oakes as being, "the major thinker and actor in this process" of creating the foundation for NAS. Oakes enrolled in the Native American Heritage course taught by Kemnitzer in the fall of 1969. Throughout the course, Oakes was influenced by the writings of Vine Deloria, Jr. (Standing Rock Sioux), N. Scott Momaday (Kiowa), Stan Steiner, and other authors. Kemnitzer's course revolved around the establishment of a clear mission for the Native American Studies program. In September, Kemnitzer invited spokesmen from the "White Roots of Peace Caravan" to lecture in his course. Inspired by the speakers, Oakes and the other students became more vocal on campus for NAS.

Jerry Gambill (Mohawk) was one of the speakers who worked with White Roots of Peace and was also the editor of *Akwesasne Notes*, a national Native newspaper. Gambill later described Oakes as "a strong, good humored man, always kidding and laughing and cajoling people into committing themselves deeper in their causes. He was the sort of natural born leader kind, although he himself searched for guidance and direction—he had just become aware of his Indian heritage in a political way as a young adult." Oakes not only became aware of his political heritage, he took his message to college campuses across California.

At a local conference, Native students and community members from across California gathered to discuss the current status of their respective NAS programs. Oakes stood before the students and proposed that they help join the occupation of the abandoned Alcatraz Island. Oakes' announcement was met with a few snickers, uncertainty, and then hope. After a brief silence, an elder from the community stood and said to the students, "[A]ll you young people listen: we have been looking forward to this day when there would be something for you to do. You are our leaders." Oakes' next step turned the many questions into strategy meetings. The occupation was still in the planning stages when a small group of students began to debate the idea at the American Indian Center in San Francisco.

This meeting produced an approximate date for the proposed occupation: the summer of 1970. It was at these meetings that Richard Oakes met Adam Nordwall (Red Lake Chippewa) and the plans took a different turn. Oakes recalled, " One fellow had jumped the gun and was already making plans with local reporters to develop the first news release in November 1969." Nordwall invited Richard and Anne Oakes to a press party at the house of Tim Finley, a local reporter with the *San Francisco Chronicle*. Apparently, Nordwall proposed the idea to the media and announced the date of the occupation as November 9, 1969. Nordwall's date conflicted with the students' plans. They had hoped to occupy the island during the summer when classes were out.

Another event in the early hours of October 28 convinced the students of the new date when a fire ravaged the San Francisco Indian Center. The three-story center had served thirty thousand Native people in the Bay area since 1958. Arson was suspected as the cause of the fire, but no one was ever brought up on charges. The community was devastated—it had lost a place that provided health care, employment, legal aid, social programs, important documents, and more. For many, the destruction of the center became yet another driving force that accelerated the Native community's claim to Alcatraz.

On the morning of November 9, 1969, reporters showed up by the dozens to witness the historic moment when the new organization, Indians of All Tribes (IAT), planned to take over the island. The crowds grew, but no boat was in sight. Oakes asked Adam Nordwall about the boat that was supposed to take them to the island. Nordwall made some quick phone calls and finally secured a boat. Meanwhile, Oakes and others read the proclamation for the IAT. As the boat pulled out of the harbor and headed for the island, Richard Oakes, Jim Vaughn (Cherokee), Ross Harden (Hochunk), Walter Heads, and Joe Bill (Hooper Bay Inuit) jumped from it and swam toward the island. Each followed Oakes' lead and dove into the cold waters of the bay. Once on the island, the group of six men made plans to come back that night and "take it over." After fifteen minutes, the group was taken back to the mainland. Reports seized upon the moment to dramatize the events of the day. Back at the pier, dripping wet and freezing, Oakes found new hope. He realized that the eventual occupation was just a matter of time.

On the evening of November 9, 1969, a group of about fourteen individuals, including Oakes, converged at the docks. As Edward Castillo (Cahuilla) recalls, "Oakes located the designated boat, but the skipper suddenly erupted into an agitated harangue. After a short while, Oakes walked back to the caravan of cars to tell us that the 'chicken-shit coward' now refused to transport us to the island."

Meanwhile, LaNada Means (Shoshone-Bannock) had secured the back-up boat, the *New Vera II*, after long discussions with the captain. Just as the boat was pulling out to Alcatraz, Oakes and the caravan were seen running to the docks. Reluctantly, the captain turned the boat around and picked up Oakes and the others. The *New Vera II*, with twenty-five occupiers, made a dangerous docking; only fourteen made their way onto the island. Some, like Earl Livermore (Blackfoot), stayed behind to notify the press of the takeover. As the activists made their way onto the island they were cautious of the lone security guard as they split up, hunting their way through a maze of pitch-black concrete. All night long the group hid from the security guards and the Coast Guard, both of whom were searching the island for the activists. Oakes described the night:

They soon gave up the search, and we split up into three groups, just to be safe. . . . The next morning we did a lot of exploring, looking for food, wood supplies, places to sleep, and generally getting the lay of the land for the next landing. The place was desolate. It was so run down that it was already beginning to feel like a reservation.

Oakes and the others hid until morning when T.E. Hannon, regional director for the Government Service Administration, the Coast Guard, and various reporters arrived. Ultimately, the reporters discovered Ross Harden and his group hiding out in the cellblock. They told the group of occupiers that the Coast Guard would not press charges if they surrendered. They made the wise decision to accept a bargain with the authorities and vacated the island. The rest of the occupiers met the authorities at the dock and read the proclamation, stating that they claimed the island by right of discovery. They vowed to return.

Oakes and others had decided that getting arrested would only have pushed back the date of when the "real" takeover could happen. Obviously, with more people it would be more difficult for the Coast Guard to evict them from the island. After eleven days, a total of eighty-nine students and community members gathered on November 20, 1969, for the final attempt to claim Alcatraz as "Indian Land." In the beginning, organizers decided that they would not have one leader but that all would play a role in leading the occupation. Therefore, they created the name "Indians of All Tribes." Still, a spokesperson and ultimately a leader emerged in Richard Oakes. By the third landing, it was clear that Richard had been the main catalyst for this movement. Once again IAT chose to occupy the island at night. The previous missions had all been viewed as experiments. Oakes described the events to follow: "The Coast Guard put up a blockade. They tried to take our boat that night, but some of us jumped on the Coast Guard boat and told them that if they tried to take our boat, we'd take theirs. . . . Also, that night, there were helicopters, circling overhead. With the Coast Guard's searchlights and all, it was quite a spectacle."

Overnight, Indians of All Tribes staged a total of six supply drops on Alcatraz Island. One of the drops was undertaken by Joe Bill, who secured the island's only rowboat and crossed the choppy bay waters to retrieve more supplies. Opposite the Golden Gate side of the building, a group built a large bonfire, distracting the Coast Guard's attention, while others used rickety ladders tied together with ropes to descend steep cliff walls to reach the shore and gather in key supplies. This routine of cat and mouse with the Coast Guard went on until daybreak. By the next day, the occupiers were on edge, expecting U.S. Marshals, the Coast Guard, or someone to evict them from the island. As afternoon approached, the waters of the bay filled with boats, largely pleasure cruisers, which distracted the blockade on the island. Under maritime law, motored boats must yield to sail or wind-powered boats and the Coast Guard was outnumbered in maintaining their perimeter. Several boats easily slipped past the blockade and brought the occupiers their much needed supplies.

Around 4 P.M., IAT organizers and attorneys Aubrey Grossman and R. Corbin Houchins met with GSA official Thomas Hannon and a representative from the Department of the Interior. At first all negotiations to remain on the island stalled, but a compromise was soon accepted. The compromise called for only one supply boat to land in the evening and demanded that the occupiers vacate the island by noon the next day. At that time federal officials were unaware that this takeover would last another nineteen months, despite repeated negotiations. Government officials counted on a lack of organization and media attention to drown out IAT's hopes for a prolonged occupation.

Despite the government's wishes, IAT was highly organized. It included a mainland branch office, donated by Dr. Dorothy Lonewolf Miller (Blackfeet) who administered all accounts, bookkeeping, and the IAT bank account. On the island, a council was elected that included Richard Oakes, Al Miller (Seminole), Ross Harden, Ed Castillo, Bob Nelford (Inuit), Dennis Turner (Luiseño), and Jim Vaughn (Cherokee). The council established the housing and security committee and began a new school. Everyone on the island was employed to work on sanitation, day-care, cooking, laundry, supply lines, or repairs. Rules were established that advocated total sobriety and a drug-free environment for all residents. During the first few days of the occupation, the council met five to six times a day to establish an independent government absent of federal authority. The Big Rock school eventually received full funding from a grant written by Dr. Dorothy Miller, who assisted in establishing a twenty-four hour radio service between the mainland and Alcatraz, a healthcare system complete with one doctor and a registered nurse, and an IAT newsletter. Not only was IAT becoming a permanent feature on the island, it also was active on the mainland.

Reporters targeted Richard Oakes as the "spokesperson" for the occupation; his experience in the takeover was what lured the press to the twenty-seven-year-old Mohawk. The newspapers dubbed Richard Oakes the "Mayor of Alcatraz." On the nightly news, Bay area residents watched TV reports of boats running the Coast Guard blockade. San Francisco became enthralled by the takeover as individuals and organizations flooded Alcatraz with donations. The Richard Nixon White House viewed reports of the takeover on the national news and quickly postponed any attempts at removal. At the time, President Nixon was drafting his new Indian policy that would eventually usher in the era of self-determination. Eventually, Richard Nixon signed a remarkable twenty-six pieces of legislation that altered the government's relationship with Indian Country forever.

But the media attention had its drawbacks as well. Richard Oakes had to attend frequent meetings with reporters and government officials both on and off Alcatraz. Whenever he had a free moment, Oakes returned to Alcatraz, offered support, ran supply lines, or used his blue-collar skills for needed repairs across the island. By Thanksgiving, hundreds of native people had gathered on the island for an all-out celebration. A powwow began in the cellblock and the proclamation was presented to the press. Afterwards, donations poured in from across the Bay. Hundreds of people, later known as "fire-keepers," withdrew money from their paychecks to support the occupation. Plumbers and other skilled laborers made their way to the island and opened up the old water lines for Alcatraz. By late afternoon an enormous movement was underway. The federal deadline to vacate or relocate passed without notice.

By late November Oakes had moved his family from the dorms of San Francisco State to Alcatraz Island. His family lived in an apartment within the old officer quarters on the island. The apartment door, tagged in red paint, read simply "Oakes Place." Graffiti soon blanketed Alcatraz as slogans of Red Power, tribal affiliations, and "Indians Welcome, United Indian Property" replaced the earlier signs, barren walls, and brittle concrete. As publicity peaked, Alcatraz became a haven for celebrities like Jane Fonda and Anthony Quinn. The support gelled when the *Merv Griffin Show* taped one episode dedicated to the occupation. The rock group Creedence Clearwater Revival donated a boat named *Clearwater* for IAT to use in retrieving supplies and ferrying residents. Benefit concerts by musician and songwriter Buffy Sainte-Marie (Cree) raised money for food supplies on the island. Al Silbowitz, manager of KPFA, a radio station out of Berkeley, created "Radio Free Alcatraz," a radio show led by John Trudell (Santee Sioux), who conducted interviews and presented educational programming and Indian news for the San Francisco Bay area.

As November turned into December the cold and rain took its toll on the residents. Storms drenched the night fires and the portable heaters supplied little warmth to battle the winter nights. Richard Oakes later reminisced about the nightlife on the island: "We did a lot of singing. We sang into the early hours of the morning. . . . A few of us would go off alone and start talking about our experiences on the different reservations, about the more advanced problems and finding solutions to them." It was this type of unity that drove hundreds and thousands to Alcatraz, which soon became the Mecca of Indian Country. Oakes stated later that such unity was undreamed of. It was something that had not taken place since the Ghost Dance of the late-nineteenth century. Unity was the key to creating one of the most powerful symbols of the 1960's Red Power movement: "Alcatraz."

Life on the island was never a utopia; tragedy struck Oakes' family on January 3, 1970, when thirteen-year-old daughter Yvonne Sherd Oakes fell three stories down a stairwell in the officers' quarters on Alcatraz and died. The island was stunned by the news. Oakes briefly mentioned the event: "About a week before the accident, my wife Anne told me of dreams and feelings of premonition she was having. She was afraid, that someone in our family would be hurt if we stayed on the island. She felt that it was time to leave."

For several weeks prior to this tragedy, the island had slowly divided into pro-Oakes and anti-Oakes factions. A major source for the split lay with the use of the money donated to Alcatraz. IAT received donations from many sources through the mail. Letters in the mailroom were sorted between individuals and those addressed to IAT. Many began to suspect that Oakes was stealing money from the movement. Yet, no proof existed to give credence to this charge. One witness who asserted that these factions plotted to remove Oakes claimed that he saw Yvonne being pushed from the stairs. This speculation led Oakes to pressure FBI to investigate Yvonne's death. Instead, the government used Yvonne's death as an opportunity to push for removal of the Alcatraz residents. After three months of living on Alcatraz, the Oakes family finally moved to Anne's home at Kashia Pomo in Northern California.

In March 1970, the next "occupation" inspired by Alcatraz occurred at Fort Lawton, in Seattle, where celebrities such as Jane Fonda came to support the popular struggle over fishing rights in the Northwest. Bernie Whitebear (Colville) was inspired by IAT and Alcatraz when he founded the United Indians of All Tribes. The first occupation ended in the arrest of dozens of activists for trespassing. The second led to the arrest of the popular actress. A third would end in eighty arrests. Newspapers across the country flashed the headlines about Fort Lawton and pulled the fishing rights protests to the front page. Oakes was in Seattle with others from Indians of All Tribes working on the strategy of the takeover. One account stated that, "as they stood and sat in the crowded brig of the abandoned post, Oakes used his gift for oratory to encourage and inspire the activists." Soon the occupiers were rushed by a detachment of military police. After the Fort Lawton success, Oakes returned to California to work on regaining land for the Pit River Nation in Northern California. This cause was to command most of his energy for the remainder of his life.

Perhaps the most dramatic legacy of Richard Oakes lay with the Trail of Broken Treaties. But even more importantly he served as a role model of Red Power from his early childhood until his assassination. Oakes achieved prominence in the move to occupy Alcatraz, in pressuring for land claims for Pit River, in advocating fishing rights in the Northwest, and in training new leaders in White Roots of Peace. He helped to establish the first wave of organizational leadership for the Red Power movement of the 1960s and 1970s. Oakes' life cannot be defined solely by the occupation of Alcatraz. Rather, the summation of his life experiences reveals those of a leader, A Big Man. From a young age and throughout his life, Richard Oakes struggled to ignite a generation that would fight to maintain the independent and sovereign status of Native nations.

13

The Peyote Religion and the Native American Church

Daniel C. Swan

I have been using Peyote for forty-five years. I have had my own experiences with Peyote. It has given me what I want in this life. It has given me a clear mind and good health. I pray to Peyote for these blessings. The Great Spirit has given us Peyote to help us. I have come to feel pity for everyone. Peyote has taught me. I feel sorry for everyone who does harm. I know what is right and wrong. Peyote has taught me. I have prayed and Peyote has given me help. It has given me the right vision to feel sorry for people and to pray for them. I pray for people whether they are rich or poor. We are all the same. We are all taken care of by God, and we all go to the same place when we die. I myself have made up my mind about Peyote. Peyote has given me vision. He gave me visions telling me how to study our existence, how to think right. Peyote was put here for the people to use so that they can study life, have good thoughts and live right. God taught Peyote to teach his children the good ways, to have good thoughts and clear minds before they leave here. God chose Peyote to do this for him. (Elk Hair, Delaware Peyotist)

Lophophora williamsii is a small, spineless cactus that grows on the caliche- rich bluffs of the Rio Grande valley in Texas and the northern plains of Mexico. Called peyote, from the Aztec word *péyotl*, it has been used as a physical and spiritual medicine by the Indians of the Americas for thousands of years. When

Reprinted from Daniel C. Swan, *Peyote Religious Art: Symbols of Faith and Belief*, Jackson: University of Mississippi Press, 1999, pp. 3–22, by permission of the University of Mississippi Press.

first contacted by the Spanish in the sixteenth and seventeenth centuries, the Aztec, Cora, Huichol, Tarahumari, Tarascan, Zacateco, and numerous other Indian groups all had ceremonies that centered on the use of peyote. In what is now the United States, the Lipan Apache, Carrizo, Tonkawa, Karankawa, Mescalero Apache, and various Caddoan groups all knew of peyote and had included it in their native pharmacopoeias.

Native American use of peyote has always focused on its value as a source of spiritual and physical well-being. Peyote was employed by Native Americans to cure illnesses, to foresee future events, to combat fatigue, and as a route to spiritual instruction and knowledge. In Mexico, peyote also played an important role in the collective social and ceremonial lives of Native American communities. Today the Huichol, Tarahumari, Cora, and other Mexican tribes continue this tradition of community festivals and religious ceremonies, which often include a complicated pilgrimage to obtain peyote plants, ritual performances, feasts, and social dancing. A number of elements found in the nineteenth-century Peyote religion of the southern Plains were present in their Mexican precursors. These include the use of drums and rattles, ritual corn-husk cigarettes, fire and incense as cleansing agents, meat and corn as ceremonial foods, and, most importantly, peyote as a holy sacrament.

The origin of the modern form of Peyotism has received considerable attention from anthropologists, and several generalizations regarding its early history and development can be made. In the late seventeenth century, peyote use was well documented among the Carrizo, a group that was clearly central in the development of the ritualized use of peyote and its spread north of the Rio Grande. Their ceremonies incorporated features of the religion that emerged on the southern Plains in the late nineteenth century, including an all-night ceremony, rounds of individual singing and drumming, and a ritually maintained fire.

The Carrizo taught their form of the Peyote religion to the Lipan and Mescalero Apache in the late eighteenth and early nineteenth centuries. These groups brought new elements to the ceremony, including the use of a tepee as the place of worship, the focus on meditation and quiet prayer, and the incorporation of Christian elements and symbols. The Lipan Apache are widely regarded as the source of the modern Peyote religion on the reservations of Oklahoma Territory. Two brothers, Pinero and Chebahtah (also referred to as Chiwat or Chivato), married and lived among the Comanche in the late 1870s and are credited with teaching the religion to the Comanche, Kiowa, and Plains Apache.

The Comanche, Kiowa, and Apache reservation of southwestern Oklahoma quickly became what Omer Stewart has described as the "cradle of Peyotism," where a ready number of converts adapted the religion to local traditions and circumstances. By 1880, the ceremonial structure, ritual instruments, and core theology of Peyotism became more uniform, and the religion spread to other tribes within Oklahoma. The growth of Peyotism was influenced by the development of a trade system that ensured a dependable and affordable supply of peyote, the increased use of English as a common language among tribes, new forms of intertribal contact through prisoner-of-war camps and boarding schools, increased exposure to Christianity, and the growing inability of traditional religions to explain and rationalize the changing conditions in which Native Americans were living.

Although Peyotism spread through a number of contacts and sources to particular tribes, some groups and individuals had distinguished roles in the rapid growth of the religion. The Comanche and the Kiowa were primary in proselytizing the religion, introducing it to the Oto, Southern Cheyenne, Caddo, Southern Arapaho, Pawnee, Wichita, Ponca, and Shawnee by 1890. The Caddo were important for their introduction of Peyotism to the Delaware, Osage, Quapaw, Oklahoma Seneca-Cayuga, and Oklahoma Band of the Modoc in northeastern Oklahoma in the late 1890s.

By 1900 the Peyote religion had spread to the majority of Oklahoma tribes, which was greatly facilitated by patterns of intertribal visiting and intermarriage. The greatest factor in the early diffusion of Peyotism, and the rationale often given for its acceptance at the individual level, was the role of peyote in curing illness. The following testimonial from a Menominee Peyotist is representative of the events that have been instrumental in conversion to the Peyote religion:

Some years ago I had an old aunt, 65 years old. She got sick, and she was sick a long time, so we took her to the hospital. After awhile the doctor said, "It's no use, she's going to die, no medicine will help her." So we took her home, so she could be comforted in her last hours. The doctor said that he would be out with the hearse in two days. We were sitting around talking when suddenly somebody said, "Those Peyote people, they have a Medicine. Go! Talk to them. Tell them about her. Maybe they can help." It happened that they were having a meeting just then. . . . So we took her over, and all that night we sat in the teepee with her. It was rough for us. We didn't understand the songs, we didn't understand anything. We took some medicine, to help her and the others fed it to her all night. The next morning she was still, so we thought she was dead. But we felt of her and her heart was still beating, and she was warm. Then later that day we took her home. After a little while she got up! She said she felt good. The next morning the doctor came out, with the hearse just behind. He asked where she was. We told him, "Inside, go see for yourself." He went in. There she was preparing breakfast. He stopped: He was surprised so much he could not talk. Then he said, "My God! What happened? What medicine did you give her?" We said, "Never mind what medicine. That is the work of the Almighty." He went to his car talking to himself. That was all I needed. . . . So I go to some more meetings. I learn more. I listen to them songs. I watch the people pray. Finally, I see; "This is where we Indians belong. This is our church."

The Peyote Religion and the Native American Church

By 1915 Peyotism had spread to Indian reservations in Kansas, Nebraska, Iowa, South Dakota, Wisconsin, Montana, Wyoming, Colorado, Utah, and New Mexico. Among the tribes impacted were the Potawatomi, Omaha, Winnebago, Sac and Fox, Dakota, Lakota, Iowa, Kickapoo, Menominee, Chippewa, Northern Cheyenne, Crow, Northern Arapaho, Shoshone, Ute, and Taos Pueblo.

Not all the members in each reservation and community adopted Peyotism, and some were violently opposed to it. Many individuals maintained strong ties to tribal religions and continued their participation in traditional ceremonies. Others became strong supporters and members of Christian denominations. Still others participated in several religions simultaneously, including Peyotism. In each community local traditions, practices, and variations were incorporated into the religion, while its basic structure and ideology remained consistent. This proved that Peyotism was flexible and adaptable and thus readily adopted in new settings and situations.

In the 1920s and 1930s the Peyote religion continued to gain converts among the Indians of the northern Plains, Great Basin, and Southwest regions. Important events in this period were the diffusion of the religion into Canada and the adoption of Peyotism by the Navajo. In these years the Peyote religion was introduced to members of the Sioux, Blackfoot, and Cree tribes in both the United States and Canada and into communities of the Bannock and Shoshone in Idaho; the Goshute and Western Shoshone in Utah; the Washo and Northern Paiute in Nevada and California; and the Mandan, Hidatsa, and Arikara inhabitants of the Fort Berthold Reservation in North Dakota.

A number of individuals played important roles in the spread of Peyotism. Among them are two early leaders who were distinguished missionaries of the religion. Quanah Parker may well have been the most influential and effective leader among early Peyotists. The son of a Comanche father and a white mother, Quanah was among the earliest Peyotists in Oklahoma and a leader of considerable reputation. He is credited with introducing the religion to groups including the Cheyenne, Arapaho, Oto, Pawnee, Ponca, Delaware, and Caddo.

Another notable teacher of Peyotism in its first decades was John Wilson, a Caddo-Delaware with some French ancestry. Wilson developed a variant form of the religion that became known as Big Moon Peyotism, which found converts among the Caddo, Delaware, Osage, Quapaw, Wichita, Shawnee, Seminole, Oklahoma Seneca-Cayuga, and Oklahoma Band of the Modoc. Other Peyotists that were instrumental in spreading Peyotism included Jim Aton (Kiowa), Jim Blue Bird (Lakota), Truman Dailey (Oto), Bill Denny (Rocky Boy's Cree), Albert Hensley (Winnebago), Jonathan Koshiway (Oto), Ben Lancaster (Washo), and John Rave (Winnebago). Numerous others, most who received no formal recognition, played important roles in the introduction and adoption of the Peyote religion throughout North America.

THE PEYOTE PLANT

Peyote is generally referred to as "medicine" by members of the Native American Church. It is also referred to as "the sacrament" or "this holy herb." Native words for peyote are quite variable, including generic terms for cacti, words for medicine, phrases that describe the physical characteristics of the peyote pant, and localized pronunciations of "peyote" as a loan word. The use of the term "medicine" with respect to Native American religious beliefs and practices is somewhat problematic, considering difficulties inherent in cross-cultural interpretations and the ethnocentric manner in which Indian societies have been represented. Much of this misunderstanding stems from the fact that there is no distinction between religion and medicine in most Native American societies; the mind and body function as one entity, with no differentiation between mental and physical afflictions.

Considerable confusion regarding the identification of peyote has existed in both scholarly and popular discussions of the plant and its uses. Often referred to as "mescal," peyote has been confused with both the alcoholic drink distilled from the century plant, *Agave angustifolia*, and the hard shell beans of the evergreen bush *Sophora secudiflora*. Early anthropologists, government officials, and missionaries often used "mescal buttons" to refer to the dried cactus tops. The history of the botanical classification of peyote has also been imprecise and variable. It was not until 1894 that a separate genus for peyote, *Lophophora*, was devised. A second species, *Lophophora diffusa*, found in the state of Querétaro, Mexico, was named by Edward Anderson in 1969.

In the United States, peyote ranges in a thin habitat strip that extends from the Big Bend region of western Texas along the Rio Grande valley to Brownsville. The range of peyote is more vast in northern Mexico, extending from the international border south to San Luis Potosi between Monterrey and Torreón.

The primary source of peyote for members of the Native American Church is a region that extends from near Oilton, Texas, south to Rio Grande City on the Mexican border. The overwhelming majority of peyote used by members of the Native American Church grows in four counties in southern Texas: Starr, Jim Hogg, Webb, and Zapata. This semiarid environment has seasonal rainfall in early summer and larger amounts in the early fall. The environment is characterized by a wide range of vegetation, primarily dense growths of thorny trees, bushes, and cacti including scrub mesquite, black acacia, prickly pear, pencil cholla, and yucca.

Native Americans refer to this region as the "peyote gardens" or simply "the gardens." My travels in this region quickly taught me that the dense vegetation and topographic homogeneity make navigation and orientation extremely difficult. On numerous occasions I spent considerable time relocating the road after focusing on the ground looking for peyote led me to become lost in the dense undergrowth. This disorientation was compounded by the inhospitable vegetation and the large numbers of rattlesnakes. I never left the area without wounds from thorns, barbs, and cactus spines. It was only after I witnessed the successful "hunt" for peyote by an Osage elder and his devotional experience as he prayed and ate a green peyote that I began to understand the nature of this name for the area. As the source of peyote, the region is the garden from which many blessings and cures originate. Parallels to the biblical "Garden of Eden" are easily drawn.

The peyote cactus is small, generally ranging from one to three inches in diameter. It grows close to the ground, showing a light, grayish-green top that is sustained by a long, carrotlike tap root. The exposed tops of the plants display ribs that form a spiral design, with four or five ribs generally seen in younger plants and as many as fourteen ribs possible in mature plants. Peyote can grow in a variety of patterns and distributions, ranging from young, singular plants of a half inch in diameter to large clusters of numerous plants, some several inches in diameter. Peyote reproduction is primarily sexual, beginning with the production of flowers that range from pink to white and ending the following season with the ripening of fruit and the release of small, dark seeds. However, peyote can also reproduce through the growth of roots from cut tops and the emergence of new plants from the root stock.

The peyote cactus contains a complex set of alkaloids and related compounds, some of which produce physical and mental exhilaration. These alkaloids cause peyote to have an extremely bitter taste and can produce serious nausea and vomiting. In terms of physical and mental effects, the most important chemical ingredient in peyote is mescaline. The concentration of mescaline in a dried peyote plant is approximately one percent. Mescaline causes a wide range of effects in humans, including a slight increase in blood pressure and heart rate, dilation of the pupils, increased motor action, a rise in blood sugar, flushed skin tone, increased salivation, and sweating. Mescaline also is psychoactive in the brain and central nervous system, affecting synaptic function and the action of neurotransmitters, specifically serotonin.

A great deal of the antipeyote literature of the early twentieth century reported the deleterious effects of peyote on the Indians who used it, based on claims of numerous deaths and mental damage. There has never been a confirmed death resulting from the ingestion of peyote, and members of the Native American Church have not suspected that peyote could cause death. The issues of addiction, tolerance, and genetic damage have also been raised and examined with regard to peyote. Extensive research among the Huichol Indians of west-central Mexico, who may consume peyote ceremonially dozens of times per year beginning in childhood, showed no chromosomal damage when compared to control groups of Huichol who were not peyote users. There is no evidence whatsoever that peyote and its active ingredient mescaline are habit-forming or even mildly addictive. The scientific debate regarding increased tolerance of peyote through repeated usage is mixed, with no clear findings.

In the dozens of peyote meetings that I have witnessed, I have never seen behavior that I would even remotely equate with intoxication. Omer Stewart, a long-time student of Peyotism, provides an excellent summation of the physical effects of peyote: "[The ritual consumption of peyote] produce[s] a warm sense of euphoria, an agreeable point of view, relaxation, colorful visual distortions and a sense of timelessness that are conducive to the all night ceremony of the Native American Church." In my conversations with members of the church regarding the concept of visions (what western science would call hallucinations), I have never encountered reports like those supplied by users of LSD, psilocybin, and other synthesized drugs. The following statement, made by a Menominee Peyotist in 1949 responding to a question about peyote-induced visions, is characteristic of my experience: "I suppose that's what a whiteman would say. But these are not visions. They are what you see. Your eyes are open, you're not asleep. It is in your mind's eye you might say, but these things happen because the Holy Spirit from the Peyote fills you. The Peyote is injected by the word of God with the Holy Spirit. It stands to reason that if you partake of it you are filled with the Spirit."

OBTAINING PEYOTE: PILGRIMAGE AND TRADE

This herb here . . . this Peyote . . . this little green thing grows in the desert. There ain't no water where it grows, but it's got plenty water in it. When you eat it you ain't thirsty. It fills you up. You ain't hungry. . . . It grows where the Creator put it. It grows in them Gardens in Texas, in Arizona and all over Mexico. There is millions of them. Each one of them little herbs is singing his own songs the Creator give him. Any Indian member in good standing can hear them all singing if he go on a run down there to get the Medicine. It is the music that the Creator put on this earth to make the mind of humans good and clear. It is for happiness and good health. (Washo Peyotist)

As the religious use of peyote spread to new communities farther from the natural source, the process of securing an adequate supply of the sacrament evolved into an elaborate process rich in social, economic, and legal detail. In the late nineteenth century, Native Americans began to augment their harvests of green plants by purchasing dried cactus tops from Mexican American traders. Called *peyoteros*, these individuals developed a system that involved harvesting, processing, and distributing peyote to members of the Native American Church.

The trade in peyote most likely began in the early 1870s. Once harvested and dried, the peyote was packed in wooden barrels for wagon transport to Laredo, Texas, where it was shipped to Oklahoma and other regions. Traders in Laredo became the principal distributors of peyote to Native Americans in the late 1880s. Laredo traders acted as middlemen, buying peyote from the *peyoteros* and shipping it north to Native Americans via rail.

In the first half of the twentieth century the peyote trade between *peyoteros* and Native Americans continued much as it had from its beginning. Although numerous states passed laws prohibiting the shipment of peyote to Native Americans within their boundaries (including Texas in 1937), the activities of the *peyoteros* and their Native American clients largely went unhindered. It was not until 1953, when a well-known *peyotero* was arrested, that the Texas law was enforced. The Native American Church retained a lawyer for his defense; on the recommendation of the prosecuting attorney, the grand jury failed to act on the warrant. In 1954, peyote was officially exempted from the Texas Narcotic Drug Act. Regulation of the peyote trade was initiated in 1969, when the Texas Dangerous Drug Act was amended to permit peyote use by Native Americans for religious purposes under state supervision. Dealers were required to obtain licenses, to keep sales records, and to sell only to individuals with membership credentials from the Native American Church. In the early 1970s, regulation of the peyote trade was transferred to the Texas Department of Public Safety.

The price of peyote has increased considerably over time, a result of a shrinking plant supply and increased costs on the part of *peyoteros*. Competition for a smaller amount of dried peyote must also be viewed as a factor. In 1955, the price for one thousand dried plants ranged between $9.50 and $15.00, and in 1981, the price was about $80.00 per thousand dried plants. In 1995, the price ranged between $145.00 and $190.00 per thousand for dried plants and averaged $120.00 for one hundred green plants. The increased cost of peyote and its limited availability has led many church chapters to decrease the amount used in the ceremonies.

Visits to the peyote gardens have long been an important part of the religious activity of Peyotists. Among the members of the Native American Church such trips are really religious pilgrimages, as it is easier to purchase peyote through the mail from a licensed dealer. These trips usually take place between February and April, often close to Easter weekend. Trips to the gardens are important social activities for church members. They may arrive several days before a planned peyote ceremony to visit "old Mexico" and to socialize with *peyoteros*. Church members often travel by caravan on the old state highways that were used by their parents and grandparents.

Many organizations, including the Native American Church of North America, the Native American Church of Oklahoma, and individual tribal chapters, hold annual peyote meetings in the gardens. At this time individual Roadmen bring their Chief Peyotes, large, perfectly formed cactus tops used as a central symbol in the church services, back to the gardens so that they might see their "home."

In addition to securing a supply of peyote from a licensed dealer, members of the Native American Church seek mementos from this region, which they consider to be a holy land. The most important is a new Chief Peyote, ideally cut fresh in the gardens accompanied by a prayer and ritual cigarette offered to convey the sacred intent of its use. Soil from the area is taken home to build the ceremonial altar, or "moon." Round, multicolored rocks about the size of large marbles are used as bosses to tie the small water drum during the ceremonies. Wood from local trees is gathered to be carved into ceremonial drumsticks. Also, quartz pebbles are collected and placed in gourd rattles.

Social interaction between members of the church and the licensed peyote dealers is an important aspect of these journeys. Relationships between these two groups extend over several generations and produce great loyalty and affection. The Osage Peyotists whom I have worked with extensively have a long-standing relationship with Mrs. Isabel Lopez, a *peyotero* from Oilton, Texas. She has been harvesting peyote for sixty years and is a highly respected dealer with a large corps of loyal customers. She began in 1937, when her family rented a house from Frank Cordina, an early *peyotero*, and went to work harvesting peyote for him. Mrs. Lopez has said that she can smell peyote and uses this skill to aid her hunt for large patches. Today she works as an independent dealer, harvesting peyote with her husband and son and relying on the peyote trade as her principal source of income. Mrs. Lopez relates that on a good day she and her husband locate and cut upwards of 5000 peyote plants.

Mrs. Lopez's home sits on approximately an acre of land that borders a state highway and backs up to the chaparral brush country that dominates the region. The front room of her home serves as her office, with business conducted at a dining-room table. A separate house has been converted into a dormitory with two or three beds in each room to provide lodging for visiting church members. An area has been cleared to provide space for erection of a tepee for holding church services, and a number of sets of tepee poles are stored on the site for this purpose. At the church services that I witnessed at Mrs.

Lopez's, she opened her home to the visiting guests, allowing women to sleep in her house and use her kitchen to prepare meals for the worshippers.

A chain-link fence surrounds the area used to process and store the harvested peyote plants, which are placed on wire racks to slowly dry in the warm climate. These racks are covered with corrugated sheet metal to protect the green plants from the harsh sun and thus regulate the drying process. As the plants mature in the curing process, they are transferred to shallow, cardboard boxes, where they are regularly turned to promote even drying.

THE FUTURE OF PEYOTE: ACCESS, CONSUMPTION, AND CONSERVATION

The peyote plant, its trade, and its use by Native Americans as a holy sacrament are inherently tied to the future of the Native American Church. Issues surrounding the legal status of peyote will quickly become secondary to its conservation and its availability in sufficient quantity to meet the needs of the Native American Church. The natural population of peyote has diminished in the last half century due to a number of factors and events. Recent efforts to examine this situation and reverse the trend have focused on three areas: access, consumption, and conservation.

The issue of access to the peyote gardens involves legal, social, and economic factors. Increased regulation of the trade in peyote has kept the majority of church members from harvesting peyote themselves. While it is possible to acquire the necessary permits and authorizations, few Peyotists obtain peyote in this way. The primary limitation is access to lands on which peyote grows. In the area of southern Texas in which an abundant supply of peyote can be found, the overwhelming majority of land is privately owned. Strict trespassing laws and frequent patrols by federal, state, and local law-enforcement agencies combine to make unauthorized access something to be avoided. Over the past thirty years, *peyoteros* and Native Americans have increasingly found their access to private land restricted.

In the late 1960s, non-Indians identifying with the popular drug culture thronged to southern Texas in large numbers, hoping for a Carlos Castaneda-like experience with peyote. Often illegally entering lands, cutting fences, and breaking down gates, the "hippies" became a general nuisance. Many land owners lobbied for stricter trespassing laws and more effectively secured their lands with stronger, locked gates. Interest in commerce in sport-hunting leases has also caused land owners to protect access to their properties and to erect tall chain-link fences to inhibit game movement. This competition for access to peyote has led land owners to lease harvesting rights to *peyoteros* at considerable cost.

While the demand for peyote has steadily increased over the past forty years, the northern extent of its range in the United States has receded dramatically. In pioneering work documenting the extent of the peyote trade, George Morgan estimated that 1.1 million plants were sold between September 1972 and August 1973. In 1993 the State of Texas, which requires *peyoteros* to account for the amount of peyote sold, reported that 1.9 million plants were harvested and sold through the legal peyote trade. This rising trend continued in 1994, when a record number of 2.1 million plants were reported sold. The spread of Peyotism to the Navajo Reservation and its rapid adoption has made the Navajo people the largest consumers in the peyote trade. It is estimated that eighty percent of the peyote sold is going to Navajo Peyotists.

An additional, and perhaps more immediate, threat to peyote is the destruction of its habitat through the conversion of land to commercial pasturage. The use of this region for grazing began in the 1750s with Spanish settlement and quickly led to overgrazing and an increase in brush vegetation. In the 1930s increased use of brush eradication through chopping and dragging temporarily disrupted the natural growth pattern of peyote. This practice has been replaced by root plowing and sowing of native and nonnative grasses, a much more destructive practice. Peyote growth continues only in those areas that evade such plowing. Government incentives to promote root plowing were halted in the late 1980s when peyote was placed on the endangered species list in Texas.

The future of peyote depends on increased habitat conservation, the promotion of harvesting techniques that stimulate plant growth, and most importantly, increased cooperation among members of the church, *peyoteros*, and land owners. Leaders of the Native American Church have been exploring alternate methods of obtaining an adequate supply of peyote, including importing plants from Mexico, and cultivation. However, neither avenue is finding support from federal and state officials in the United States. George Anderson, the leading peyote botanist, remains optimistic that peyote will survive as a species but considers it questionable that peyote will be available in sufficient quantities to support the current demand.

THE LEGAL STRUGGLE FOR RELIGIOUS FREEDOM

Peyotists have been the target of numerous organized efforts to deprive them of their use of peyote as a holy sacrament. Much of this campaign stems from the classification of peyote as a "drug" by the dominant society, its association with recreational or pleasure drugs, and the toll that the drug trade takes on American society. Despite tremendous medical, scientific, and cultural information that exists to support the use of peyote by members of the Native

American Church, Peyotists continue to come under legal attack. This legacy of religious persecution reflects the marginal political, economic, and social position of Native Americans. Because many drugs with proven deleterious effects, such as caffeine, nicotine, and alcohol, are legal in our society, the distinction between legal and illegal drugs is evidently not based on scientific knowledge.

The first recorded efforts to prohibit peyote use by Native Americans came quickly on the heels of European knowledge of its existence. In sixteenth-century Mexico officials of the state and church used cruel and extreme methods to identify and prohibit native religious and medicinal practices. The Spanish Inquisition in Mexico deemed the use of peyote as evil and contrary to their efforts to missionize the Indians, placing peyote use on the same level as human sacrifice and cannibalism. Learning that peyote use had spread to non-Indians in the colonies, in 1620 Spanish authorities issued a general decree that banned the use of peyote by any person. Despite these efforts, the use of peyote as a spiritual sacrament and medicine continued in Mexico, in some instances leading to a syncretic mix of native and Catholic beliefs and practices.

In the United States the situation was similar, with efforts to suppress peyote coming quickly on the heels of its discovered use among Native Americans. The first concerted campaign began in the late nineteenth century in Oklahoma Territory, when Indian agents and missionaries tried to extend the federal laws prohibiting liquor on Indian reservations to include peyote and other "intoxicating" substances. In 1888, the agent of the Kiowa and Comanche reservation in southwestern Oklahoma Territory posted a general order prohibiting the use of peyote. These early efforts were futile. The courts upheld the claim that the federal laws related solely to liquor and individual agents had no authority to enforce their decrees without the backing of appropriate legislation.

An effort to ban peyote use was attempted at the Oklahoma Constitutional Convention, where Peyotists testified in what was one of the earliest legislative hearings on the subject. Quanah Parker continued his efforts to protect the religious use of peyote by testifying before the first Oklahoma Legislature:

The mescal bean cannot be eaten; a drink is made from it, but it's the peoti bean we eat or use as a medicine. My boy was at Carlisle School when he was taken sick with consumption, he was sent home when I took him to Mexico and he died. My girls took sick with the same disease. Then we gave them peoti which cured them and they are now well. . . . I do think peoti beans have helped Indians to quit drinking. I do not think this legislature should interfere with a man's religion, also these people should be allowed to retain this health restorer. These healthy gentlemen before you use peoti and those that do not use it are not so healthy.

Quanah's testimony contains many of the arguments that Peyotists and their supporters would offer in future efforts to protect the religion: First Amendment rights, the success of peyote in promoting sobriety, and its value in curing illness and promoting health.

The failure to gain federal antipeyote legislation did not cease the efforts of the commissioner of Indian Affairs and his agents to stop the religious use of peyote. The 1908 Indian Bureau Appropriation Act called for the appointment of a chief special officer to deal specifically with the peyote issue. W.E. "Pussyfoot" Johnson was selected as the first special prosecuting officer, based on his previous efforts to halt the illegal liquor traffic to reservations. Unable to stop peyote use through the threat of withholding annuities and rations, Johnson set out to suppress it at its origin. In the spring of 1909, he traveled to Laredo, Texas, purchased and burned 166,400 dried peyotes, and attempted to persuade local dealers to not sell peyote to the Indians.

In 1912, efforts to pass a federal law were renewed by the Board of Indian Commissioners. The board had support from a powerful lobby that included scholars, missionaries, and the Society of American Indians, a highly organized group of Native Americans that was opposed to the use of peyote. Antipeyote legislation was introduced in Congress each year between 1912 and 1916 without success.

Sir: We the undersigned members of the Osage Tribe of Indians, respectfully ask that the use of "peyote" be allowed in religious worship and church services among the members of our tribe. We understand that the Constitution of the United States provides that "Congress shall make no law respecting an establishment of religion, or prohibiting the free exercise thereof." We have never known or heard of a single instance in which the use of peyote in our religious worship has resulted in injury to either the mind or body. There is a strong fear among the members of our tribe that if the use of peyote is prohibited that our people will return to strong drinks and other evil habits. . . . God is truth! Religion is one's belief as to what this truth is, and we all hold certain opinions, and all working for the same goal, notwithstanding that there are many views on this subject. In using the peyote we are living more peacable, honorable and Christ like. . . . While using peyote our people have advanced along many lines, to wit, stock raising and improving our farms. We are educating our children as best we can to make useful men and women and that our prosperity will equal that of any race of people. . . . We beg you to give this matter your most serious and careful consideration, as it is a very grave and important matter to us; and we will greatly appreciate anything you will do for us so we may continue the use of peyote in our church work.

In 1918, a lengthy set of peyote hearings were held before a subcommittee of the U.S. House of Representatives. Testimony was taken from Native Americans on both sides of the issue, chemists, physicians, Indian agents, and anthropologists. While the defenders of Peyotism won this battle by a narrow margin, they realized that a new strategy was needed if they hoped to halt the seemingly endless debates and efforts for antipeyote federal legislation.

As early as 1906, Peyotists began to view formal organization as a religious defense, when a number of loosely defined organizations emerged on the local level. Fashioned after fraternal and denominational organizations, they included the Mescal Bean Eaters, the Union Church, the Peyote Society, the American Indian Church Brotherhood Association, and the Kiowa United American Church. The next step in the evolution of organized Peyotists took place in 1914 among the Oto of Red Rock, Oklahoma. Following the example of the Indian Shaker Church of the Pacific Northwest, Jonathan Koshiway filed an application for the incorporation of the First Born Church of Christ in Oklahoma City.

The intense efforts to gain a federal antipeyote bill in 1918 prompted greater communication and cooperation among Peyotists and brought them into contact with sympathetic non-Indians, including a number of anthropologists from the Smithsonian Institution. After a series of intertribal conferences, a group of Peyotist leaders from the Comanche, Kiowa, Cheyenne, Ponca, Kiowa Apache, and Oto tribes, with the assistance of the Smithsonian ethnologist James Mooney, filed an application with the Oklahoma secretary of state for incorporation. The Native American Church of Oklahoma was granted a charter on October 10, 1918. The principal purpose of the church was put forth in its articles of incorporation:

The purpose of this organization is to foster and promote the religious belief of the several tribes of Indians in the State of Oklahoma, in the Christian religion with the practice of the Peyote Sacrament as commonly understood and used among the adherents of this religion in the several tribes of Indians in the State of Oklahoma, and to teach the Christian religion with morality, sobriety, industry, kindly charity and right living and to cultivate a spirit of self-respect and brotherly union among the members of the Native Races of Indians, including therein the various Indian tribes of the State of Oklahoma.

As the religion spread to more communities outside of Oklahoma, some church leaders wanted to expand the charter to better reflect the national scope of its membership. In 1934 the charter of the Native American Church of Oklahoma was amended to permit affiliation with chapters in other states. In 1944 the formal name of the organization changed to the Native American Church of the United States.

In 1946 a split developed in the organization over the issue of a further expansion to include the growing number of Peyotists in Canada. In 1950 Oklahoma-based Peyotists renamed the organization the Native American Church, with affiliated tribal and local chapters within the state. The Native American Church of the United States filed a new charter in Oklahoma that same year;

they amended the charter to incorporate Peyotists in Canada in 1955. This new organization was called the Native American Church of North America. Today a number of formal organizations, including the Native American Church of North America, the Native American Church of Navajoland, and numerous state and local chapters account for over 250,000 registered members.

Although incorporation brought significant improvements in the organization of Peyotists, it did little to halt attempts by government officials and white Christian denominations to prohibit the religious use of peyote. Efforts to pass antipeyote legislation at the federal level continued between 1919 and 1934. The BIA published an antipeyote pamphlet in 1919 and distributed it to agencies throughout the country. Several legislatures enacted antipeyote laws at the state level, which led to the arrest and prosecution of many individuals. Some relief came in 1934 through the appointment of John Collier as commissioner of Indian Affairs. Among the many reforms instituted during his administration was the replacement of the BIA antipeyote pamphlet with a circular entitled, "Indian Religious Freedom and Indian Culture." This action was immediately countered via privately published and circulated antipeyote pamphlets by a number of missionary organizations and groups.

Two additional bills calling for federal antipeyote legislation were introduced to Congress in 1939 and 1963, although neither gained passage. The period of 1963–1990 was relatively successful for Peyotists. On religious grounds, they gained exemptions from the expanded and modified federal drug policies of the era. The arrests and convictions of Native Americans for violation of state laws for peyote possession were all overturned on appeal to higher courts on the grounds of First Amendment protection. Peyotists also gained protection in certain states through court rulings or legislative actions that exempted church members from state drug laws.

The American Indian Religious Freedom Act of 1978 federally protected the rights of American Indians to practice traditional religions and to access and use sacred sites and objects. Although it was assumed this federal law would extend to members of the Native American Church and thus support previous federal rulings on the religious use of peyote, one final chapter in the struggle for religious protection remained.

The most serious threat to Peyotism came in 1990 with the ruling of the U.S. Supreme Court in the case of *Employment Division of Oregon v. Smith.* The case involved two members of the Native American Church who were fired from their jobs as drug and alcohol counselors based on their religious use of peyote. When denied unemployment benefits because their membership in the Native American Church was a direct violation of the Oregon law prohibiting peyote use, one individual sued the State of Oregon. In appeal the Supreme Court ruled in favor of Oregon, declaring that a state could enforce its laws even if in doing so it infringed upon the religious freedom of a minority interest in that state. This effectively established a constitutional precedent for states to prohibit the religious use of peyote. Despite wide-ranging protests from constitutional law experts and religious organizations, the Supreme Court refused to reconsider their decision.

In 1994, Congress reacted to the Supreme Court ruling with an amendment to the American Indian Religious Freedom Act that included explicitly worded legislation that protects the members of the Native American Church in the religious use of peyote.

Despite the optimism engendered through this action, it remains to be seen if the legal struggles of the Native American Church have finally been put to rest. Intolerance for minority rights, particularly those related to religion, appears to have no limits. The Native American Church has survived one hundred years of criticism, persecution, and legal attack, largely due to the deep religious conviction and tenacity of its members.

For Further Reading

ON SELF-DETERMINATION

Castile, George Pierre. *To Show Heart: Native American Self-Determination and Federal Indian Policy, 1960–1975*. Tucson: University of Arizona Press, 1998.

Clarkin, Thomas. *Federal Indian Policy in the Kennedy and Johnson Administrations, 1961–1969*. Albuquerque: University of New Mexico Press, 2001.

Forbes, Jack D. *Native Americans and Nixon: Presidential Politics and Minority Self-Determination, 1969–1972*. Los Angeles: American Indian Studies Center, UCLA, 1981.

Iverson, Peter. *"We Are Still Here": American Indians in the Twentieth Century*. Wheeling, IL: Harlan Davidson, 1996.

Kennelly, Janet. "President Richard M. Nixon and the Reform of Federal Indian Policy." Paper presented at the Western History Association conference, San Antonio, TX, 14 Oct. 2000.

Letgers, Lyman H. and Fremont J. Lyden, eds. *American Indian Policy: Self-Governance and Economic Development*. Westport, CT: Greenwood Press, 1994.

Nelson, Robert A. and Joseph F. Sheley. "Bureau of Indian Affairs Influence on Indian Self-Determination." In Vine Deloria, Jr., ed., *American Indian Policy in the Twentieth Century*. Norman: University of Oklahoma Press, 1985.

Philp, Kenneth R., ed. *Indian Self-Rule: First-Hand Accounts of Indian-White Relations*. Logan: Utah State University Press, 1995.

Reagan, Ronald. "Statement on Indian Policy." In Alvin M. Josephy, Joane Nagel, and Troy Johnson, eds., *Red Power: The American Indians' Fight for Freedom*. Lincoln: University of Nebraska Press, 1999.

Smith, Dean Howard. *Modern Tribal Development: Paths to Self-Sufficiency and Cultural Integrity in Indian Country*. Walnut Creek, CA: Alta Mira Press, 2000.

Tyler, Dan, ed. *Red Men and Hat Wearers: Viewpoints in Indian History*. Boulder, CO: Pruett, 1976.

White, Robert H. *Tribal Assets: The Rebirth of Native America*. New York: H. Holt, 1990.

Winslow, Kate. "Reagan on Indian Affairs." *American Indian Journal* 6, 1980.

ON AMERICAN INDIAN ACTIVISM

Blue Cloud, Peter. *Alcatraz Is Not an Island*. Berkeley: Wingbow Press, 1972.

Bonney, Rachel H. "The Role of AIM Leaders in Indian Nationalism." *American Indian Quarterly* 3, 1977.

Brave Bird, Mary with Richard Erdoes. *Ohitika Woman*. New York: Grove Press, 1993.

Churchill, Ward and Jim Vander Wall. *Agents of Repression: The FBI's Secret War Against the Black Panther Party and the American Indian Movement*, Boston: South End Press, 1988.

Costo, Rupert. "Alcatraz." *The Indian Historian* 3, 1970.

Dewing, Rolland. *Wounded Knee: The Meaning and Significance of the Second Incident*. New York: Irvington Publishers, 1985.

Fortunate-Eagle, Adam. *Alcatraz! Alcatraz!: The Indian Occupation of 1969–1971*. Berkeley: Heyday Books, 1992.

Johnson, Troy R. *The Occupation of Alcatraz Island: Self-Determination and the Rise of Indian Activism*. Urbana: University of Illinois Press, 1996.

———, ed. *Alcatraz, Indian Land Forever*. Los Angeles: American Indian Studies Center, UCLA, 1994.

———, ed. *You Are on Indian Land!: Alcatraz Island, 1969–1971*. Los Angeles: American Indian Studies Center, UCLA, 1995.

———, Joane Nagel, and Duane Champagne, eds. *American Indian Activism: Alcatraz to the Longest Walk*. Urbana: University of Illinois Press, 1997.

Josephy, Alvin M., Jr., Joane Nagel, and Troy R. Johnson, eds. *Red Power: The American Indians' Fight for Freedom*. Lincoln: University of Nebraska Press, 1999.

Lyman, Stanley David. *Wounded Knee, 1973: A Personal Account*. Lincoln: University of Nebraska Press, 1991.

Matthiessen, Peter. *In the Spirit of Crazy Horse*. New York: Viking Books, 1991.

Means, Russell with Marvin J. Wolf. *Where White Men Feared to Tread: The Autobiography of Russell Means*. New York: St. Martin's Press, 1995.

Nagel, Joane. *American Indian Ethnic Renewal: Red Power and the Resurgence of Identity and Culture*. New York: Oxford University Press, 1996.

Peltier, Leonard. *Prison Writings: My Life is My Sun Dance*. New York: St. Martin's Press, 1999.

Sayer, John William. *Ghost Dancing the Law: The Wounded Knee Trials*. Cambridge, MA: Harvard University Press, 1997.

Smith, Paul Chaat and Robert Allen Warrior. *Like a Hurricane: The Indian Movement from Alcatraz to Wounded Knee*. New York: New Press, 1996.

Stern, Kenneth S. *Loud Hawk: The United States Versus the American Indian Movement*. Norman: University of Oklahoma Press, 1994.

"Voices from Wounded Knee, 1973, in the Words of the Participants." *Akwesasne Notes*, 1974.

West, W. Richard, Jr., and Kevin Gover. "The Struggle for Indian Civil Rights." In Frederick E. Hoxie and Peter Iverson, eds., *Indians in American History: An Introduction*. Wheeling, IL: Harlan Davidson, 1998.

ON PEYOTE AND THE NATIVE AMERICAN CHURCH

Aberle, David. *Peyote Use Among the Navajo*. Chicago: Aldine Publishing Co., 1966.

Anderson, Edward F. *Peyote: The Divine Cactus*. Tucson: University of Arizona Press, 1996.

Dekorne, Jim. *Psychedelic Shamanism: The Cultivation, Preparation, and Shamanic Use of Psychotropic Plants*. Yakima, WA: Breakout Productions, 1998.

Deloria, Vine, Jr. *God Is Red: A Native View of Religion*. Golden, CO: Fulcrum Publishing, 1994.

Fikes, Jay C. *Reuben Snake, Your Humble Servant: Indian Visionary and Activist*. Santa Fe: Clear Light Publishers, 1996.

LaBarre, Weston. *The Peyote Culture*. Hamden, CT: Archon Books, 1975.

Marriott, Alice and Carol K. Rachlin. *Peyote*. New York: Thomas Crowell Co., 1971.

Meyerhoff, Barbara. *Peyote Hunt: The Sacred Journey of the Huichol Indians*. Ithaca: Cornell University Press, 1976.

Mount, Guy. *The Peyote Book: A Study of Native Medicine*. Arcata, CA: Sweetlight Books, 1988.

O'Brien, Sharon. "A Legal Analysis of the American Indian Religious Freedom Act." In Christopher Vecsey, ed., *Handbook of American Indian Religious Freedom*. New York: Crossroad, 1991.

———. "Freedom of Religion in Indian Country." *Montana Law Review* 56, 1995.

Roseman, Bernard. *The Peyote Story*. Hollywood, CA: Wilshire Books Co., 1966.

Slotkin, J.S. *The Peyote Religion: A Study in Indian-White Relations*. Glencoe, IL: The Free Press, 1956, 1975.

Smith, Huston and Reuben Snake, eds. *One Nation Under God: The Triumph of the Native American Church*. Santa Fe, NM: Clear Light Publishers, 1998.

Steinmetz, Paul. *Pipe, Bible, and Peyote Among the Oglala Lakota: A Study in Religious Identity*. Syracuse: Syracuse University Press, 1998.

Stewart, Omer. "Peyote and the Law." In Christopher Vecsey, ed., *Handbook of American Indian Religious Freedom*. New York: Crossroad, 1991.

———. *Peyote Religion: A History*. Norman: University of Oklahoma Press, 1987.

Swan, Daniel C. *Peyote Religious Art: Symbols of Faith and Belief*. Jackson: University of Mississippi Press, 1999.

Wachtel, David. "Peyotism," *American Indian Journal* 7, 1981.

VI

The 1980s–2000: Contemporary American Indian Issues

The final part of this book deals with four contemporary American Indian issues: the evolving role of Native women in American history, repatriation of artifacts and Indian remains, gaming and casinos on Indian reservations, and the conflicts over natural resources in Indian Country.

Certainly American Indian women's issues are not unique to the time period of 1980 to 2000. But, as Devon Mihesuah shows in the first chapter here, the way that they have been studied and interpreted has changed the most in the last twenty years. Her chapter challenges readers to consider matters of gender, class, race, culture, economics, tribal social systems, and inter- and intra- tribal relations in any analysis of the history of Native American women. She also urges us to recognize the contributions made by *all* Indian women, not just the leading figures or wives of leaders who have received the most attention in the past.

The second chapter, by Walter Echo-Hawk and Roger Echo-Hawk, examines the critical issues of repatriation, reburial, and religious rights. The question of human skeletal remains, and why American Indians have a right to protect them, is the central topic here. The authors discuss museum artifacts, the legalities involved in returning them to American Indian tribes, and the implications involved for religious freedom. In doing so, they place the entire issue in a historical and constitutional (First Amendment) context, and provide a case study of the Pawnee Tribe's efforts to repatriate and rebury their tribal ancestors.

Christopher Miller's chapter does the same for the question of American Indian gaming and casinos. Here, the history and legalities of reservation gambling is cast in light of the significant court cases and legislation that were involved in its evolution in the last twenty years. Overall, as Miller points out, the gaming question is part of the larger picture of recognizing the American Indian presence in contemporary society and understanding the nature of Native American sovereignty.

Finally, we conclude with a chapter that harkens back to the first essay of the book: American Indians and the environment. This chapter, written by Donald Fixico, explores the dilemma of natural resource development in Indian Country. As the energy crisis and demand for natural resources has increased in the past twenty years, developers have sought to extract oil, coal, natural gas, minerals, and water from Indian reservations. The temptation to "develop" Indian lands in this way has intensified relations between reservation leaders and white Americans and has created problems among Indians by exacerbating the tension between traditionalists and progressives. Fixico addresses the political and legal questions involved in this dilemma and the Indians' roles in negotiating with government agencies.

14

Commonality of Difference: American Indian Women and History

Devon A. Mihesuah

Literature about American Indian women has increased dramatically during the past twenty years. Recent works reflect the efforts ethnohistorians have made in re-creating Indian women's histories and their publications illustrate sensitivity to their positions as interpreters of the lives, cultures, and histories of others. While women scholars who study American Indian women have made significant inroads into their histories, many interpretations remain incorrect and undeveloped, providing only partial answers to complicated questions about Native women. Their studies also do not connect the past to the present, which is why we should be writing history in the first place.

Numerous feminist scholars express concern over the propensity of writers to ignore the heterogeneity among women, particularly among women of color. American Indian women are especially multifaceted, and with few exceptions this aspect is overlooked. Further, most writings are devoid of Indian voices and are thereby only partial histories. To analyze American Indian women, scholars must look beyond gender and class. This essay briefly discusses some of those ambiguous elements: race (or races), tribal social systems, factionalism, culture change, physiological appearance, and personal motivations.

Reprinted from the *American Indian Quarterly*, volume 20, number 1 (winter 1996) by permission of the University of Nebraska Press. Copyright © 1996 by the University of Nebraska Press.

COMMONALITY OF DIFFERENCE

There was and is no such thing as a monolithic, essential Indian woman. Nor has there ever been a unitary "worldview" among tribes and, especially after contact and interaction with non-Indians, not even among members of the same group. Cultural ambiguity was and is common among Indians. Traditional Native women were as different from their progressive tribeswomen as they were from white women and often they still are. Even within a single tribe (and sometimes within the same family), females possess a range of degrees of Indian blood, skin and hair colors, and opinions about what it means to be Indian.

Indian women share the common context of gender and the "common core" of struggle against colonialism (genocide, loss of lands, encroachments onto their lands by European Americans and other Indians, intermarriage with tribal outsiders, population loss from disease, warfare, and removal), and the consequent tribal cultural changes and identity confusion. Even what may appear to be similarities may actually be differences, however, because cultural disparities between tribes, such as religion, social systems, and economies caused Indian women to react to common experiences of externally induced adversity and change in dissimilar ways.

Authors can challenge notions of fixed identity among Indian women by investigating their allegiances to tribal traditions, their definitions of ethnicity and self, their emotions and physical appearance. Reconstructions of the intricacies of Indian women's lives must be specific to time and place, for tribal values, gender roles, appearances, and definitions of Indian identity have not been static.

"CLASS"

Do economics account for Indian women's inferior status (as Marxist feminists might argue)? Or are socialist feminists correct in their assertion that a low economic position combined with gender are better explanations? While Indian women may be oppressed because of their lesser economic status, capitalism and gender should not be construed as the only forces of oppression brought against them. Native women were gender oppressed (most notably after contact with European Americans) and, like other women, still are. What many feminist theorists ignore is that women of color also are subjugated because of their race. In regard to Indian women, because of their varied economic situations, social values, appearances, and gender roles, they are oppressed by men and women—both non-Indians *and*, interestingly enough, other Indians.

We know of the oppression of Indian women at the hands of non-Indians, but what about inter- and intra-tribal racism and sexism among Indians? Tribes have long experienced factionalism between those who cling to tradition and those who see change as the route to survival, either tribal, familial, or personal. Intratribal factionalism might also be termed "culturalism," a form of oppression that dovetails with racism. Indians in tribal power positions, either political or economic or social, often use expressions of culturalism against those who do not subscribe to their views.

After Indians adopted new value systems, members of a single tribe often viewed each other from different economic and social "classes." Indians with a high "level of acculturation" might view themselves as "more enlightened" than others whom they deem as "less enlightened," "uncivilized," or "heathens." Usually, but not always, mixed-bloods had more money and material goods than fullbloods, and they maneuvered themselves into tribal leadership positions. These wealthy families often were educated, progressive, Christian, and did not value tribal traditions. Many saw themselves as morally superior to the uneducated, non-Christian, and less wealthy traditionalists (usually, but not always, fullbloods). Their "white blood" also contributed to their feelings of importance. From their point of view, they were in the superior "class."

Women situated in the upper level of one "class" did not necessarily belong to the higher echelon of the other. Lack of wealth placed some Indian women in a low economic category, but as far as they were concerned, their cultural knowledge put them in a higher social grouping. Those who valued tribal tradition and resisted acculturation believed themselves to be "more Indian" than the "sell outs." Many biracial Indians may have been more wealthy and educated than fullbloods, but among traditionalists, these were not enviable social traits. LaVera Rose, a Lakota, makes the observation in her master's thesis on biracial Lakota women that the fullblood Lakotas looked down on the biracial women because of their cultural naiveté, and many still do.

To complicate the issue, fullbloods often adopted attitudes similar to progressives. Ten years ago I conducted an interview with a 98-year-old Cherokee woman. When I asked if she spoke Cherokee and attended stomp dances—a logical question considering that she was a fullblood and descended from a prominent Cherokee leader—she answered, "Hell, no, I'm no heathen." There are other examples too numerous to recount, but the point is that the issue of who held tribal political and social powers and why is one of the threads that should wind through almost every aspect of our studies of Indian women.

INDIAN WOMEN AS ACTIVISTS

Chandra Talpade Mohanty writes in her anthology, *Third World Women and the Politics of Feminism*, that women of color, or "third world women," all have the "common context of struggle." Indeed, women of color may still struggle against colonialism, racism, and stereotypes, but as multiheritage progressive Indian women illustrate, these struggles have not always been the same nor are their strategies of resistance.

White feminists tend to focus on gender oppression and overlook racial issues, thus alienating many Indian females. Traditional Indian women have been more concerned about tribal or community survival than either gender oppression or individual advancement in economics, academia, or in other facets of society. In *The State of Native America*, Annette Jaimes argues that some Indian women hold white feminists in disdain because they view them as constituents of the white supremacy and colonialism that oppress Indians. In fact, some Indian women see some biracial Indian women feminists in almost the same light.

Indian women who participated in the takeover at Wounded Knee in 1973 washed clothes, prepared food, and stayed in the background while the flamboyant males spoke to the media. Deb Lamb's research on the takeover reveals that some Indian women could not have cared less about the opinion white feminists had about what appeared to be their subservient roles. Many Indian women concede that male American Indian Movement leaders were and are sexist, having learned misogynist ways of thinking in white society; nevertheless, the women agree that combating racism against their tribes is more important than personal gain. One woman present during the takeover sums the differences between white and Indian ways of thinking about feminism: "In your culture you have lots of problems with men. Maybe we do too, but we don't have time to worry about sexism. We worry about survival." To some feminists, domestic duties may seem less important than some men's roles, but these women felt empowered in their domestic sphere. Numerous Indian women assert that they are not "unfulfilled." They refuse to be victims of gender oppression by taking charge of their lives, reveling in their roles and status as women who hold their tribes together.

Two alternative terms to describe Indian women may be *tribalist* and *womanist*, but most of them are either comfortable in their "subservient" positions and/or are too busy working to preserve their cultures to worry about the labels non-Indians assign to them.

MULTIHERITAGE WOMEN

Shortly after tribes' contact with European Americans, a generation of mixed-race Indians emerged. Some of these individuals still appeared phenotypically Indian and retained their cultural values. Others may have adopted the ways of their non-Indian parent (it was almost always their father, initially), but appeared to be Indian. Continued intermarriage with European Americans and other mixed-bloods resulted in multiheritage women with a spectrum of physical characteristics and cultural values. The appearances and cultural affiliations of some women were indistinct, not only to themselves but also to researchers.

Defining the racial backgrounds and cultural adherences of Indian women is crucial to forming an accurate portrait of their lives. To date, studies of multiheritage Indians that portray them as "cultural brokers" or "cultural mediators" make broad generalizations without a sociological understanding of the mixed-heritage person. Elements of a person's racial identity include their physical appearance, acceptance by the racial reference group, commonalities of culture and psychological identification with the group, and percentage of biological heritage. How do these elements contribute to the psychological and sociological make-up of Indian women with bifurcated racial and cultural backgrounds? Did multiheritage Indian women mirror Stonequist's model of "marginal" people—those of mixed heritage who live lives of frustration, unable to fit comfortably into any group, or did these women absorb cultural traits of all their heritages, making them more like McFee's proposed "150% Man"? What are the categories between?

For the most part, scholars have slighted the role that appearance played and still plays in Indian women's lives. Appearance is the most visible aspect of one's race and has determined how Indian women defined themselves and how others defined and treated them. Their appearance, whether Caucasian, Indian, African, or mixed, either limited or broadened Indian women's choices of ethnic identity and ability to interact with non-Indians and other Indians.

Appearance has played a crucial role in status and ease of travel (that is, both physical and sociocultural "traveling") to different cultural groups or societies or "worlds" as defined by Maria Lugones. Consequently, many mixed-heritage white-and-Indian women had numerous "worlds" open to them while most fullblood Indian women and those of mixed black-and-Indian heritage did not.

Progressive, biracial Indian women, especially those who appeared to be largely Caucasian (some looked white after one generation of intermarriage), often defined their identity by the terms of white society, not of traditional tribal societies. For example, by the early nineteenth century, many Cherokee and Choctaw women possessed as little as 1/128 Indian blood, looked to be white, and had adopted the value systems of their white or mixed-blood fathers, including Christianity, acquisitiveness, and the use of African slaves. Many of these women and those of subsequent generations had little or no knowledge of their tribes' cultures, yet they retained an Indian identity.

While enrolled in early twentieth-century boarding schools, some Indian women were influenced by publications such as *Godey's Ladies Book* and strived for the Victorian ideal of the "True Woman." Because many of these Indian women were educated, wealthy, and appeared Caucasian, they felt at ease in the white world. Women who looked phenotypically Indian or African American (many Oklahoma freedwomen enslaved by Indians possessed significant amounts of Indian blood) were not as welcome in white society. They also were barred from Indian society.

Many biracial Indian women who looked Caucasian were not concerned with issues of race, just of gender and economic and social class. Some Indians—especially educated, Christianized ones—aspired to be like whites. At the same time, many traditional, dark-skinned women had no desire to fit into white society. Phenotypical-looking Indians often felt inferior when they began judging themselves by white standards. After all, they could alter their cultural adherence but not their appearance. How did this desire to be white affect their behavior toward other women and men in the tribe, and how did other Indians react to them?

How have like experiences compared for mixed-race women and men? Have mixed-heritage women had an easier time blending into white society than have mixed-blood men? Census records of the five civilized tribes reveal that many white men married full and mixed-blood women, but few white women married Indian men—even those of mixed blood. Why did whites see these women as desirable but not the men? (And why are so many white women today attracted to Indian men?) Perhaps one reason is that opportunistic white men targeted wealthy Indian women to marry to better themselves. Another reason Indian women were desirable was that women of some tribes were viewed as more "civilized" than others because many of them were Christian and educated (but, so were many Indian men). What compelled women of some tribes to marry whites and to adopt the lifeways of non-Indians? Some may have believed that by marrying someone from the "superior" race, they were improving their lot. Perhaps they married out of affection for one another, but this angle has only been explored in works of fiction.

WOMEN AND POWER

Some anthropologists argue that Indian and white men did not take power away from women at some point because women never had it to begin with. Many disagree with literature that portrays men as leaders and women as followers, with no say or control in tribal affairs. In many cases Indian women did indeed have religious, political, and economic power—not more than the men, but at least equal to men. Women's and men's roles may have been different, but neither was less important than the other. If we look at tribal societies at contact and trace the changes in their social, economic, and political systems over time through interaction with European Americans and intertribal relations, we will find that women did have power taken from them and so did Indian males.

Gender roles changed over time, and Europeans were among the catalysts for this change. Intermarriage with white men meant for some Indian women that children no longer belonged to their clans, property was no longer theirs, and men made the rules. Among some southeastern tribes, women were farmers, but after contact and intermarriage, they were forced indoors to use the looms while Indian men were obliged to work the fields. After the loss of bison and confinement to reservations, men of the Plains tribes could no longer hunt.

The spiritual traditions of many tribes include a female divine spirit. European Americans pressured tribes to convert to Christianity, which included the acceptance of the male God only, thus reinforcing the superiority of males. European Americans preferred to deal only with men, perhaps moving women into less pivotal positions. Intratribal conflicts developed between those who preferred the old ways and those who adopted European American values. Is it frustration and confusion over the loss of traditional gender roles and the adoption of white society's values that has contributed to spousal abuse among Indians today? Writers have explored how colonialism changed tribal life, but few have written about how Indian women have made the best of what colonialism has wrought.

CONTRIBUTIONS

Because many authors write from a patriarchal or white feminist perspective, the value of Indian women is vastly underrated. Despite overwhelming oppression at the hands of whites, Indians have persevered, but it has not been only the men who were the catalysts for survival, adaptation, and development. Women have been just as crucial to the economic, social, religious, and political survival of tribes.

Indian women are usually evaluated by standards set by white society—and that usually means male bias. Writings on the history of Indian women have focused on the most notable Indian women—Pocahontas, Sacajawea, Susan LaFleche, and a few others because of their interaction with whites or their success in the white world. But while Sacajawea was helping Lewis and Clark, surely other Shoshone women were doing something important within their tribes.

Scholars need to chronicle the accomplishments of Indian women but should use different means of evaluation besides white society's standards. If women's work is evaluated according to male or feminist bias, then Indian females' duties appear inferior to men's roles. Indians from tribes in Indian Territory earned terminal degrees in the mid-1800s, and while some non-Indians may have respected an Indian woman with a doctorate, not all Indians saw it as an admirable accomplishment (many still do not). How do we evaluate the behavior of progressive Indians? If we use white standards, then obviously it is impressive that these women were so much like whites; if we use traditional standards, their aspirations to imitate whites were tragic because they abjured their own culture. What were the standards of the tribe? When tribes are fractured along social and cultural lines, writers need to look at several sets of standards.

INDIAN WOMEN AS REAL PEOPLE

Aspects that have gone mostly unaddressed in historical works are the feelings and emotions of Indian women, the relationships between them, and their observations about non-Indians. We have intrinsic knowledge of how women interacted with each other during events such as childbirth and healing and puberty ceremonies. We also know what was required of women in certain tribal roles. There are photographs showing us clothes women wore and how they styled their hair during various time periods. The intriguing mystery is: what was behind their solemn gazes?

Women worked and socialized together throughout their lives, but we have not read much about their relationships with their families and friends. What did northern Plains women discuss as they sat together during the long, cold months making clothes and doing bead and quill work? Were their conversations much different from what their modern descendants talk about during winter days while performing the same work? What about southwestern women, who spent hours together grinding corn and preparing food? Did they gossip, joke, and seek advice from each other as they do today?

Colonialism was a powerful force that affected women in countless ways. How did women feel about Eurpean Americans who intruded upon their lands, the devastation of their ways of life, the cultural changes they underwent to survive? Did Indian women discuss resistance strategies against the onslaught of colonization, or did they conspire with men? Surely they pondered the intruders as intently as European Americans speculated about them. Thoughts and personal dramas hold our attention and are what endear the women to us, especially if we encounter a semblance of ourselves in them. Historians might argue that depictions of personal conflicts, confusions, and expressions of happiness and anger are best left to novelists, but I believe that without the inclusion of feelings and an understanding of motivations, histories of Indian women—of all Indians—are boring, impersonal, and, more importantly, merely speculative and not really Indian history.

SOURCE MATERIAL

If writers want to find out what Indian women think, they should ask Indian women. If they want to know about past events and cultures they should do the same thing. More authors—non-Indian *and* Indian—need to follow the examples of Marla N. Powers and Ruth McDonald Boyer, women who spent a good portion of their lives getting to know the people they write about and making certain that the women's voices are heard. Unfortunately many scholars, historians in particular, have been loath to use Indian oral accounts as source material. Almost every "resource guide" or "annotated bibliography" lists the requisite secondary source material, government documents, and tribal records, but none informs researchers about oral history collections, recorded interviews, or locations where personal narratives might be stored.

Even fewer writers use literature and poetry, but greater numbers of Indian historians are beginning to explore these works. Because many Indian women writers possess empirical data that cannot find acceptance in historical or anthropological works, literature is one effective outlet for their stories.

Scott Momaday has commented that "Language is the repository of . . . knowledge and experience." Why then, would not the textualization of oral stories or of literature composed from influences of oral stories have messages of import for readers? Works written by culturally aware Indian women are derived from their consciousness, filled with experience and knowledge of tribal ritual. Chicana feminist Alvina Quintana says that when women writers free their writings of patriarchal discourse, language becomes "a vehicle for the demystification through self-representation of that unity we call woman." Indeed, it is through their writings that we learn Indian women were and are powerful; they were and are as complex as their cultures are diverse. Their works are worth a look.

If modern Indians have no knowledge of their tribes' stories, or even if they have plenty of it, writers also must read written accounts for information. The problem is that most of the observations of Indian women were written by European American men, who judged them by the same standards they used to judge women of their own societies. Many non-Indians misunderstood tribal kinship systems, female and male roles, and tribal spiritual and social values. Their observations also reflected their biases and, perhaps, their desire to manipulate reality to accommodate their expectations.

For example, almost all the historical and cultural studies of the Choctaws examine only the male tribal members. Choctaw women are rarely mentioned, not even the wives of prominent tribal leaders. When discussed, their roles as Choctaws are described by non-Indian men who evaluate women's roles by their own European, male-oriented standards. Some early commentaries portray Choctaw women as useful tribal members (because they prepare food or bear children), but they are also characterized as subservient drudges with no economic, political, or social influence on the tribe.

These viewpoints are incorrect. In the precontact period Choctaws were successful agriculturists; the women tilled soil, sowed seed, and harvested crops. Men hunted deer and turkeys and fished the numerous Mississippi and Alabama waterways, while women dressed and prepared the game. In addition, women made clothes, reared children, and held positions of religious importance. Descent was matrilineal, and women retained control of tribal property.

We know that some Europeans' views of Indian women were distorted, but to assess properly women's lives, information on the Europeans' value systems and women's spheres must coordinate with the tribes' accounts of their past.

There is much to do to give voice to Indian women. Many books and articles about Indian women desperately need new interpretations. Their social, religious, political, and economic roles have been the focus of numerous articles, but few authors use demographic data or Indian women themselves as sources of information. Those who eschew an analytic treatment of women but who utilize one or two informants believe that is sufficient to write the "New Indian History." It is not.

Granted, the myriad lifestyles of Indian women render them difficult to write about. Taking the less arduous route of writing descriptive, nonanalytical history—which has been the traditional method for the majority of scholars who study Indians—will continue to have serious repercussions on American Indian history, for without understanding the complexity of Indian women, we cannot hope to comprehend the whole of tribal existence.

15

Repatriation, Reburial, and Religious Rights

Walter R. Echo-Hawk and Roger C. Echo-Hawk

Collisions have occurred with increasing regularity in recent years between federal agencies, U.S. museums, and other non-Indian institutions, on the one hand, and American Indian communities, on the other, over issues related to Native religious freedom. One such issue concerns the treatment of human skeletal remains. This chapter considers how museums and other public and private institutions have dealt with Indian remains and explores some of the circumstance under which Indian bodies have entered the basements and display cases of museums throughout the United States. In addition, as a case study in contemporary problems for Indian religious freedom, this chapter describes the efforts of the Pawnee Tribe to repatriate and rebury their tribal ancestors exhumed from graves in Nebraska and Kansas.

The free exercise of Indian religious belief and practice in the United States has historically been undermined, regulated, obstructed, and suppressed in a broad array of contexts—from the slaughter of Ghost Dancers at Wounded Knee to the denial of unemployment benefits to members of the Native American Church in the state of Oregon. The passage in 1978 of the American Indian Religious Freedom Act represents an acknowledgment of this history and a symbolic affirmation that constitutional protections under the First Amendment extend to Indian people. Nevertheless, a fundamental reality of Indian

This chapter originally appeared in Christopher Vecsey, ed., *Handbook of American Indian Religious Freedom*, New York: Crossroad Publishing Co., 1991, pp. 63–80, and is reprinted here by permission.

religious life is that Indians must at times deal with a variety of agencies, institutions, legislatures, and courts if they wish to conduct their religious affairs in accordance with what the First Amendment promises.

In recent years this reality has dominated relations between Indian communities and federal agencies, museums, and many other institutions—particularly with regard to the treatment of Indian dead. When non-Indian institutions possess Indian sacred objects and living gods and when they control the disposition of the dead, they become little more than quasi-church facilities imposed upon Indian communities, regulating the "free" exercise of religion for dispossessed Indian worshipers. First Amendment religious freedoms are clearly controlled from the pulpit of science when museums elevate scientific curiosity over Indian religious belief in the treatment of the dead. Should Indians protest, some scientists are a quick to raise the specter of research censorship, comparing such protesters to "book-burners" and referring to Indian plans for the disposition of their deceased ancestors as the "destruction of data." The inner sanctums of many museums and institutions throughout the United States have been troubled places in recent years, as administrators have struggled with the fact that—all predictions to the contrary—Indians have not died out, and now there is the problem of explaining to living Indians how so many tribal ancestors ended up as scientific and commercial "property."

While many of the present controversies involve a wide array of federal agencies, tourist attractions, and other institutions, much of this chapter focuses on the issue as it relates to museums. Since their inception, American museums have maintained an interest in American Indians that has been both beneficial and antagonistic. On the beneficial side, museums serve as a bridge between cultures by addressing the heritage and history of Indian societies for the benefit and enjoyment of both the tribes and the public at large. Indeed, museums can effectively convey to American society a broader understanding and respect for Native peoples and their tribal religions. This would offer a meaningful benefit to tribes beleaguered by very substantial contemporary threats to their religious freedom. This potential role for contemporary museums resembles earlier assistance rendered to Indian tribes during crisis periods in American Indian history, when the federal government practiced actual genocide and sought to assimilate Indians by force into mainstream American society. To some extent, perhaps, museums could be viewed as historical places of refuge for important tribal religious symbols threatened by oppressive pressures exerted by U.S. missionaries and government officials. For their part, museums are also beneficiaries of positive Native relationships: they stand to gain a deeper understanding of their collections from close working ties with the cultures they portray and preserve. There is optimism that the beneficial aspect of the "love-hate" relationship can be fulfilled to its utmost potential. Indeed, it should be entirely possible for museums to educate the public about Indians without violating the cultural or religious integrity of the people concerned.

Unfortunately, present-day museums are heirs to massive collections of dead Indian people and to staggering amounts of Indian cultural patrimony, and they have inherited a number of serious social problems that must be solved before the Indian/museum relationship can reach its fullest potential. These problems draw upon a larger historical context not entirely of the museum community's making, and their resolution must be found by recognizing the basic character of this inheritance as a problem of religious rights and ethical responsibilities.

THE PLUNDERING OF NATIVE NORTH AMERICA

An understanding of the historical context for the present crisis in American Indian religious freedom helps to clarify the origins and nature of the problem. A defining factor of Indian/white race relations in the United States has been the systematic transfer of the material possessions of Native Americans to non-Indian control. Under any definition of this relationship, Indian tribes have been virtually "picked clean" by the dominant society: land, natural resources, personal possessions, and even the dead left Native hands in surprisingly massive amounts within a relatively short time span.

By the 1870s, vast amounts of Indian lands had been swallowed up by the federal government, and the tribes had been successfully relocated onto ever-diminishing reservations. Hunger for Indian possessions did not stop at real estate. Between 1875 and 1925, trainloads of Native artifacts left Indian hands for American and European museums and mansions. One wealthy collector, George Heye, managed to acquire over one million artifacts. Statistically, he collected more than one object from every American Indian who was alive during that time! This remarkable, massive one-way transfer of material possessions has been summarized by Douglas Cole:

During the half-century or so after 1875, a staggering quantity of material, both secular and sacred—from spindle whorls to soul-catchers—left the hands of their Native creators and users for the private and public collections of the European world. The scramble for skulls and skeletons, for poles and paddles, for baskets and bowls, for masks and mummies, was pursued sometimes with respect, occasionally with rapacity, often with avarice. By the time it ended there was more Kwakiutl material in Milwaukee than in Mamalillikulla, more Salish pieces in Cambridge than in Comox. The city of Washington contained more Northwest Coast material than the state of Washington and New York City probably housed more British Columbia material than British Columbia itself. . . . In retrospect it is clear that the goods flowed irrevocably from Native hands to Euro-American ones until little was left in possession of the descendants of the people who had invented, made and used them. This situation, often regretted and sometimes deplored, in which Natives are divorced from the products of their heritage, has created some demands for repatriation, demands like those of the Greeks for the return of the Elgin Marbles.

The "need" for such massive transfers of Native property and even dead bodies was predicated at the time upon the "Vanishing Red Man" social theory and spurred by the demand for collections made by newly founded American museums.

As to the collecting process itself, much was done under normal trade and intercourse with the tribes. However, some museum collecting crews conducted their work in fierce competition with each other, and many operations have been better described as "rip and run" raids, rather than as scientific expeditions. In other instances, Native sacred objects were stolen, taken as spoils of war, improperly sold by Indians who did not have title, or illegally expropriated from federal lands by pothunters. The manner in which sacred objects left Indian hands and found their way into federal museums was reviewed in 1978 by a federal task force convened to carry out Section 2 of the American Indian Religious Freedom Act:

Museum records show that some sacred objects were sold by their original Native owner or owners. In many instances, however, the chain of title does not lead to the original owners. Some religious property left original ownership during military confrontations, was included in the spoils of war and eventually fell to the control of museums. Also in times past, sacred objects were lost by Native owners as a result of less violent pressures exerted by federally sponsored missionaries and Indian agents.

Most sacred objects were stolen from their original owners. In other cases, religious property was converted and sold by Native people who did not have ownership or title to the sacred object.

Today in many parts of the country, it is common for "pothunters" to enter Indian and public lands for the purpose of illegally expropriating sacred objects. Interstate trafficking in and exporting of such property flourishes, with some of these sacred objects eventually entering into the possession of museums.

The deleterious impacts of the expropriation of Native religious property upon the practice of traditional Indian religion in the United States has been much discussed in the literature. In addition, competing property rights to this sacred material have also been analyzed. This chapter will focus on the problem for American Indian religious freedom caused by the digging up and carrying away of dead bodies.

INVASION OF THE BODY SNATCHERS

It has been estimated that museums, federal agencies, other institutions, and private collectors retain between 300,000 and 2.5 million dead bodies taken from Indian graves, battlefields, and POW camps by soldiers, museum collectors, scientists, and pothunters. Examples of contemporary insensitivity to the treatment of Native dead in the United States abound. The Smithsonian Institution alone, for example, presently displays about 150 dead Indians in its showcases and warehouses over 18,500 Indian remains, and this does not even rank as the nation's largest "collection" of dead people. Many of the Smithsonian's dead bodies were taken from fresh graves and battlefields by army personnel under an 1867 order of the U.S. surgeon general to procure Indian crania for government-sponsored studies. In such a context, the racial slur "the only good Indian is a dead Indian" takes on a stark reality in the lives of Indian people today. In Montana for example, when the government failed to provide much needed rations during the early 1890s and Blackfeet Indians were dying from starvation, an army surgeon surreptitiously dug up more than a dozen graves and decapitated the remains in order to provide the Army Medical Museum with examples of Blackfeet crania. Last year, on the Island of Maui, Hawaii, a private developer dug up one thousand dead bodies from a Native Hawaiian burial ground in order to build a hotel. In 1987, two men paid a landowner $10,000 for the "right" to loot Indian graves located on his Kentucky farm and literally mined the dead in order to dig up 650 graves. In 1986, the Louisiana Court of Appeals decided a bizarre case in which an amateur archeologist dug up 150 Indian graves and then tried to sell 2.5 tons of "goods" looted from these burials to the Peabody Museum. Even federal agencies, such as the U.S. Park Service, claim dead Indian bodies as their "property" under existing federal law and have issued permits to dig up and carry away untold thousands of deceased Indian people. Motives for Indian body snatching range from interests in race biology, to museum competition for anthropological "collections," to commercial exploitation, to just "carrying out orders."

Non-Indians have methodically exhumed untold thousands of dead bodies and literally hundreds of thousands of associated burial offerings from Native graves. All tribes throughout Indian Country, including Alaska and Hawaiian Natives, have been victimized by what has become the most grisly and frightening problem confronting Native Americans today. The impact of this activity upon Native people, regardless of the motive, is always the same: emotional trauma and spiritual distress.

The reburial issue, as illustrated by the following case study, raises two basic human rights issues. First, Natives are confronted with a discriminatory denial of equal protection under the laws. Systematic disturbances of non-Indian graves, on one hand, are abhorred and avoided at all costs, while Indian people are actively searched out, dug up, and placed in museum storage. Criminal statutes in all fifty states very strictly prohibit grave desecration, grave robbing, and mutilation of the dead—yet they are not applied to protect Indian dead. Instead, the laws and social policy, to the extent that they affect Native dead, do not treat this class of decedents as human, but rather define them as "non-renewable archaeological resources" to be treated like dinosaurs or snails, "federal property" to be used as chattels in the academic marketplace, "pathological specimens" to be studied by those interested in racial biology, or simple "trophies or booty" to enrich private collectors. The huge collections of dead Indians are compelling testimony that Indians have been singled out for markedly disparate treatment.

Second, the refusal of agencies or institutions to allow tribes to bury their desecrated dead undermines basic religious freedom rights of living Native Americans. Native religious beliefs regarding the sanctity of the dead are not idiosyncratic beliefs peculiar only to American tribal peoples. On the contrary, humans have *always* treated their dead with reverence, religion, and respect. These are universal values that have been held by all societies in all ages, including the United States, where the sanctity of the dead is firmly ingrained in the common law and statutes of all fifty states. Aside from these basic human right issues, the problem also affects political rights of Indian tribes that are based upon treaties and inherent sovereign powers of tribal governments to repatriate tribal or ancestral dead.

CASE STUDY: THE DISINTERMENT AND REBURIAL OF PAWNEE REMAINS

As with other American Indians, the Pawnee Tribe of Oklahoma has suffered harm from massive grave looting and desecration by non-Indians of every description: through the mutilation of their dead by soldiers, from the commercial exploitation of tribal ancestors, and from museum expropriation of deceased tribal citizens who have been exhumed from cemeteries located throughout the Pawnee central Plains homeland. This case study will briefly describe the mortuary traditions and history of the Pawnee Indians, recount the history of non-Indian desecration and expropriation of tribal dead who came to the attention of the tribe in recent years, and then summarize the repatriation and reburial efforts of the tribal government to correct this problem.

Pawnee History and Mortuary Traditions

The Pawnee Tribe of Oklahoma is a federally recognized Indian tribe with a citizenship of about 2,500 persons. The tribe includes four confederated bands of Northern Caddoan Indians (Skidi, Chaui, Kitkahahki, and Pitahawirata), located on a small reservation in northern Oklahoma. The cultural traditions of the Pawnee Tribe draw upon an ancient and complex human heritage, and the Pawnees today continue to value those traditions in spite of a more recent history of religious suppression and other destructive pressures directed at Pawnee culture by the United States.

Human history in the central Great Plains extends back in time for at least several thousand years, and this history is dominated by the Pawnee people and their northern Caddoan relatives and ancestors, who resided in earthlodge towns and settlements along the streams of Nebraska and Kansas. Recognized as accomplished warriors and agriculturalists by neighboring tribes, the Pawnee also enjoyed a complex ceremonial and religious life. The people relied upon the great herds of buffalo and crops of corn, squash, and beans for their subsistence. They also took advantage of diverse plant and animal life, together with other natural resources, and they traded extensively with other tribes and peoples.

Treaties made by the Pawnees with the United States between 1833 and 1857 dramatically reduced the Pawnee land base until all the bands were consolidated upon one small reservation on the Loup River near present-day Genoa, Nebraska. The lack of protection from white encroachment and the threat of war with local settlers ultimately made reservation life for the Pawnees in Nebraska intolerable, and during the mid-1870s the tribe was forced to leave its central Plains homeland. The federal government moved the entire tribe four hundred miles south to its present reservation in Oklahoma. One consequence of this "Trail of Tears," of course, was that the Pawnees were forced to leave behind tribal cemeteries filled with their deceased relatives and ancestors.

The Pawnees have historically buried their dead in cemeteries and graves located near their tribal communities. According to one description in 1851: "On the highest mounds in the prairie, we often observed little hillocks of earth, which we were informed were the places of sepulture [sic] of their chiefs and others of their tribe." The Pawnees have always responded to the occurrence of death by following well-established religious beliefs and practices regarding the appropriate treatment of the dead. These traditions guide the preparation of remains, interment procedures, graveside observances, and other customary activities associated with the disposition of human remains. The general purpose of these practices is to influence the spiritual condition of both the dead and the living. Nevertheless, death evokes deep sorrow in all human communities, and the Pawnee people are no exception. One traveler witnessed the funeral of a young Pawnee man at Fort Kearney in 1858 and reported: "They placed him in a grave amid the acclamations and lamentations of the whole tribe."

Pawnee funerals are traditionally conducted by priests who exercise the authority to hold such services by hereditary right and training. Superficial differences have apparently distinguished the "way of burial" of each priest according to the mandates of the various traditions handed down within their families. Other factors can influence funeral arrangements as well, including the reputation and position of the deceased and circumstances of death, age, and gender. No substantive differences exist among the four Pawnee bands in mortuary practices.

The dead are prepared for burial through a variety of ritual activities, during which the body of the deceased is consecrated and then considered holy. Following a period of public visitation, the remains are conducted by procession to a burial site within a nearby tribal cemetery and interred with further ceremony, together with a variety of offerings designed to provide for the spiritual benefit of the dead. During the days, months, and years following interment, additional activities at the graveside and within the community include the funeral feast, ceremonial sacrifices, the offering of more gifts, and mourning visits. An example of one form of offering was described by a Pawnee agency school teacher who attended the funeral of a Chaui elder during the 1860s or early 1870s:

At his death the agent and many of the employees followed him to his burial overlooking the beautiful valley of the Loup. A most remarkable phenomenon occurred as we awaited the burning of the dried buffalo meat which his wife had drawn aside to offer for his support as he traveled to the distant land of the dead. As the smoke of the offering ascended, from out of the clear azure above us came a long roll of distant thunder.

The improper disposition or handling of grave offerings can have serious repercussions for the living. A Pawnee historical tradition mentions the occurrence of drought and the absence of buffalo when grave offerings were not properly positioned on one occasion, but with the correction of this problem "there came a great rain storm accompanied by thunder." The spirits of the dead become restless when their possessions are disturbed. Spiritual danger is also associated with the theft of grave offerings. One Echo-Hawk family elder recalls a childhood friend who took some articles out of a partially exposed grave and fell sick. When attempts to spiritually purify the boy failed, he soon died. This tragic incident serves as a stern warning concerning the sanctity of Pawnee graves and associated funerary objects.

This overview briefly summarizes the array of religious observances that surround the traditional Pawnee treatment of the dead. Human bodies are regarded as holy remains to be interred with dignity in a permanent resting place. Associated grave offerings are sanctified as the spiritual possessions of the dead. The total assemblage of elements associated with Pawnee burials is closely related to the spiritual condition of the deceased; the strong proscriptions serve to protect the grave from future disturbance. In short, burials among the Pawnee represent the outcome of highly religious (and emotional) events in the life of the community.

The Spoils of Conquest

Following the removal of the Pawnees to a new reservation in the South, non-Indian settlers began an unrestrained plundering of tribal cemeteries in Nebraska, opening graves to search for grave offerings of any apparent value or interest. One Pawnee caught a troubling glimpse of this cavalier treatment of Pawnee graves in 1898, when he visited the site of the last Pawnee town in Nebraska: "Where my sisters graves were is now cornfield. What few graves I did find were open and robbed of what little—if any—trinkets were found on the dead [sic]." According to research commissioned by the Pawnee Tribe, the looting of Pawnee graves by private citizens also extended to human remains, as archeologists later found in 1940 at the site of a Kitkahahki Pawnee cemetery:

At the site 25HM2, archeologists noted that extensive looting had occurred. Of the seven burial pits excavated at the site, only two retained burials. Archeologist Robert B. Cumming observed that Field Burial #7 lacked a skull and stated that "the region had been potted before and the owner of the land remembers digging up skulls here 55 years ago."

But these disturbances of Pawnee graves were not the first instances of American interest in the dead of the Pawnee Nation. In 1820, the United States organized the Long Expedition, a military and scientific reconnaissance party, and sent it through Pawnee country into the central Great Plains. This party of American scientists acquired the skull of a man whom their guides described as a Pawnee killed two years earlier. Several years later, Samuel Morton apparently included this skull in his comparative study of human crania, which demonstrated a "scientific" basis for perceiving the intellectual inferiority of Indians and Blacks to White Americans.

Other Pawnee bodies fell into the hands of U.S. scientists before the tribe left Nebraska; these wound up in Washington, D.C., in the Army Medical Museum and the Smithsonian. Among these individuals are at least six skulls of Pawnees who were killed by the army in January 1869 and beheaded in compliance with the 1867 order of the surgeon general, which requested the submission of Indian heads from army surgeons in the field for a new collection of crania at the Army Medical Museum.

These Pawnees were themselves veterans of the Pawnee Scouts, a military unit that operated in alliance with the U.S. Army against other Indian tribes. The post surgeon at Fort Harker, Kansas—an avid collector of Indian heads—directed the decapitation of these former Pawnee Scouts for the Army Medical

Museum. Surgeon B.E. Fryer described his initial difficulties in "collecting" the Pawnee heads: "I had already obtained for the Museum the skull of one of the Pawnees, killed in the fight you speak of, & would have had all had it not been that immediately after the engagement, the Indians lurked about their dead & watched them so closely, that the guide I sent out was unable to secure but the one."

Reminiscing about the killing of these Pawnees years later, a former Pawnee agency teacher wrote that the federal government "had taken no notice of the foul deed," but the army had indeed taken notice. Unknown to the Pawnee Tribe, the skulls were carefully measured by government scientists as a contribution to the "progress of anthropological science." From the measuring of seven or eight hundred Indian crania, the curator of the Army Medical Museum was able to determine in 1870 that "American Indians must be assigned a lower position in the human scale than has been believed heretofore." These Pawnee skulls later underwent the scrutiny of Ales Hrdlicka, a Smithsonian anthropologist who believed that his research could be used to justify white supremacism in the United States. Ignorant of the circumstances under which these Pawnee skulls entered the keeping of the Army Medical Museum, Hrdlicka concluded that several of the crania might be white, and in 1989, Smithsonian anthropologists cited Hrdlicka's work to Pawnee tribal leaders in an effort to cast doubt upon the Pawnee identity of these remains.

Archeologists entered the hunt for Pawnee bodies and grave offerings during the 1920s. By this time, recognizable Pawnee cemeteries had been thoroughly rifled and the graves plundered. Still, the search for graves continued. Asa T. Hill was a used car salesman and amateur archeologist who became known as the "father" of Nebraska archeology and served as the director of the Nebraska State Historical Society Museum. He referred to himself—at least in correspondence with his white friends—as Nebraska's "champion pothunter." During the 1920s Hill managed to locate a Pawnee town that scholars now agree is the earthlodge town that Zebulon Pike visited in 1806. Hill immediately began to hunt for graves. Referring to the exhumation of Pawnee bodies, Hill described his activities to the press as a form of recreation and compared the Pawnee cemetery to a golf course for the pleasure it brought him. Between 1920 and 1950 hundreds of Pawnee bodies were disinterred by archeologists for scientific study—all without the knowledge or approval of the Pawnee Tribe.

Near Salina, Kansas, during the 1930s, the remains of Pawnee tribal ancestors were exposed in their graves and placed on public display for commercial profit by a farmer and a police sergeant, who later acknowledged the "scientific help" of A.T. Hill of the Nebraska State Historical Society and Waldo Wedel of the Smithsonian Institution. This business enterprise took advantage of tourist traffic on the nearby interstate and served for over fifty years as Salina's primary "tourist attraction"—one that featured the public viewing of open graves for a "modest fee." Few cities can lay claim to such a distinction. Had another enterprising Depression-era family opened the Topeka city cemetery in a similar fashion, public outcry would have demanded swift punishment. Instead, elementary school teachers brought their classes to view the Indian remains near Salina, and the cemetery was designated by the National Park Service as a National Historic Landmark in 1964.

The Pawnee Struggle for Reburial

During the mid-1980s, Pawnee tribal leaders became involved in Indian repatriation and reburial issues when they learned that the human bodies on display at the "Salina Indian Burial Pit" were ancestral to the Pawnee people. Tribal leaders called for the closure of this "tourist attraction" and joined in efforts to devise legislation that would shut down the "burial pit" as a commercial enterprise and offer protection for unmarked graves in Kansas. The Kansas State Historical Society cooperated with Indian representatives in forming a writing committee that would produce a bill for the state legislature. The resulting legislation was introduced in 1988, and the Pawnee business council endorsed it by resolution in January. This legislation, however, foundered on the issue of compensation for the operator-owners of the Indian cemetery near Salina. The Kansas attorney general subsequently issued an opinion holding that landowners were not entitled to compensation when the state exercised its police power to regulate the disposition and protection of dead bodies.

In that same year the Pawnee Tribe also learned that the Nebraska State Historical Society (NSHS) had a "collection" of Pawnee dead bodies. In March, the tribe was formally notified by the NSHS that it had from five hundred to one thousand human remains, together with associated funerary objects, and that some of these could be identified as Pawnee. The tribal government immediately requested the return of these people for proper reburial according to Pawnee religious traditions, but this request was soon denied. Tribal attorneys at the Native American Rights Fund (NARF) were directed to continue negotiations with the NSHS. As in Kansas, a writing committee was formed by the Nebraska Indian Commission to develop state-level legislation, and this committee was composed of Indian and NSHS representatives. The attorneys for the Pawnee Tribe also requested more information from the society about the Pawnee remains, but access to documents concerning the acquisition and identity of these human remains was denied by the NSHS until society researchers could respond to NARF's request for information.

The Pawnees also initiated negotiations with the Smithsonian Institution for the return of tribal ancestors held at the National Museum of Natural History after receiving information from the Smithsonian regarding its collection of dead Pawnee Indians. In August 1988 the tribe submitted a formal repatriation demand to the Smithsonian for "all Pawnee Indian remains and associated burial goods" and in late September followed with a request for a response to this demand. In Late January 1989, the Smithsonian finally responded with a letter that asserted that only two remains out of a total of nine possible candidates could be reasonably identified as Pawnee. However, based upon the analysis of a 1988 Smithsonian "Master List of Specimens," Pawnee tribal historians suspected that many more individuals might prove to be ancestral to the Pawnees. Those suspicions were subsequently confirmed by tribal researchers.

Through the spring and summer of 1988, the Pawnee Tribe could only wonder how Pawnee bodies had entered the keeping of the NSHS. In late August, the society finally responded to NARF attorneys. They reported that approximately 204 remains could be reasonably identified as Pawnee, and that these bodies had been acquired during the 1930s and 1940s in the course of federally funded archeological excavations in Pawnee cemeteries dated "between A.D. 1750 to 1870 or later." The NSHS defined remains from earlier sites as "prehistoric, that is they originate from archeological sites created before written records were made in the Nebraska region," and asserted that due to periodic population "disruptions," these "prehistoric" remains could not be assigned an ethnic identity. The NSHS archeologists advised the Pawnee Tribe that all such remains "must remain objectively anonymous and the subject of skeptical enquiry." But the tribe felt that the NSHS might have Pawnee bodies from sites dating before 1750, since tribal traditions suggest a lengthy residence in the central Plains. However, until full access to NSHS archives could be obtained, the Pawnees were forced to rely on NSHS census information.

When tribal researchers were again denied access to NSHS archives in September, the attorneys for the tribe filed a motion to Nebraska's attorney general, Robert Spire, under the state public records law for an order opening the society's files, and on October 6, he ordered the NSHS to cooperate with the Pawnees. A second order on October 21 was required before the tribe's researchers could gain access to archival records.

Tribal attorneys prepared lengthy memoranda for the NSHS, clarifying the society's legal and ethical obligations to return identifiable Pawnee human remains and associated grave offerings. The tribe's legal research was supplemented by the Nebraska attorney general, who issued an opinion holding that in litigation the First Amendment rights of the Pawnees would take precedence over the state interest in withholding tribal remains from burial. The NSHS director responded to this authority by citing a federal regulation that allegedly prohibited compliance with the Pawnee request, but NARF subsequently found that this law *did not exist.*

In September, members of the writing committee for Nebraska legislation learned that the NSHS—in spite of the fact that it had a representative on the committee—had secretly produced its own bill, without any Indian input. Efforts to meet with the NSHS and merge the two versions of human remains legislation proved futile, and the Nebraska Indian Commission and Indian tribal representatives went ahead with their version. Both bills were eventually introduced in January of 1989, but the NSHS version failed to generate any support and died in committee.

In November, the tribe rejected a proposal circulated by a member of the NSHS board of directors that would have arbitrarily limited repatriation of Pawnee ancestral remains to bodies dated after 1750 C.E.—but only if the Pawnee Tribe would agree to place the skeletal remains in a protective vault designed to prevent decomposition, preserving the skeletal remains for future scientific interest. This plan also postponed any decision on the return of burial offerings—the NSHS would keep them for yet further rounds of negotiation. With this wholly inadequate proposal, the board of directors hoped that the Pawnee Tribe would endorse a plan already known by the board to be completely repugnant to tribal religious traditions and spiritual beliefs—a plan that called for the Pawnees to compromise away a substantial portion of their heritage and history. In December, good faith negotiations broke down completely when the board of directors rejected a reburial policy proposed by the Pawnee Tribe and adopted its own proposal. The NSHS director also contended that an ownership interest by the federal government prevented return of any skeletal remains, but the Department of the Interior immediately disclaimed any alleged federal ownership. Even so, the NSHS board of directors still refused to reconsider its decision. The Pawnee Tribe and its representatives had conducted lengthy and expensive negotiations with the NSHS to no avail. Pawnee government officials, religious leaders, elders, historians, and tribal attorneys all failed to sway the NSHS—the board remained unmoved even by letters from numerous Pawnee schoolchildren. The tribe then turned its efforts to the Nebraska legislature, where Senator Ernie Chambers introduced LB 340, the Nebraska Unmarked Burial Sites and Skeletal Remains Protection Act, on behalf of Nebraska's Indian people and the Pawnee Tribe.

The tribal researchers, headed by Dr. Orlan Svingen, released a preliminary report on their initial research in January 1989. This report described the manner in which the NSHS acquired its "collection" of Pawnee bodies and burial offerings. Dr. Svingen estimated that the NSHS had exhumed about 304 Pawnee men, women and children from tribal cemeteries dated between 1500 and 1875. A more complete census of NSHS human remains ancestral to the Pawnee Tribe was later begun under yet a third order from the state attorney general, overruling the continuing objections of NSHS director James Hanson.

The Pawnee Tribe moved to support new Kansas legislation in 1989, developed under the auspices of the Kansas State Historical Society: House Bill 2144, the Kansas Unmarked Burial Sites Protection Act. That effort was supported by tribal attorneys, who negotiated an agreement between the owners of the "Salina Indian Burial Pit," state officials, and the Pawnee, Arikara, and Wichita tribal governments. The "Treaty of Smoky Hill" of January 1989 called for the reburial of the 146 exposed human remains at the "burial pit" and promised support for state compensation to the owners. The state legislature subsequently passed the burial protection bill, together with appropriations to fund the purchase of the Salina Indian cemetery and to carry out the "Treaty of Smoky Hill." As a result of these successful efforts, the Pawnee, Arikara, and Wichita tribes began planning the reinterment of these 146 deceased tribal ancestors.

The passage of LB 340 in Nebraska, mandating the return of all reasonably identifiable human remains and associated grave offerings to tribes of origin upon request, was bitterly opposed in Nebraska by the NSHS and a small group of anthropologists associated with the University of Nebraska and the National Park Service. Nevertheless, the Nebraska Unicameral eventually passed LB 340 and it was signed into law. By the end of spring 1989, the Pawnee Tribe stood before the one-way mirror of Nebraska anthropology to view documents filled with accounts of desecration and anguish, but the reburial of their restless ancestors in the central Plains was at last in sight.

Dissatisfied with Smithsonian inaction, the Pawnees and other tribes with similar requests decided to seek federal legislation directing the National Museum to repatriate Indian remains to tribes of origin on request. At a July 1989 congressional hearing on the National Museum of the American Indian Act (H.R. 2668), the NARF Pawnee tribal attorney was joined by other tribes and national Indian organizations in insisting that appropriate repatriation language be included in the bill. Subsequently, negotiations with the secretary of the Smithsonian were held in an effort to find a solution for the national moral crisis surrounding the treatment of Native dead. These negotiations produced the historic "Smithsonian Agreement," which directs the return of human remains and funerary objects to tribes where a cultural affiliation is shown to exist by the preponderance of available evidence. That agreement was incorporated into the bill before Congress, and despite the active opposition of the Society for American Archaeology (which consistently resists tribal reburial efforts at the national level), Congress passed the bill, and it was signed into law. Under this new repatriation law—which hopefully marks a turning point in federal policy—all culturally affiliated human remains and associated funerary objects will be identified and repatriated.

This case study describes prolonged and vigorous repatriation efforts by one small Indian tribe to rebury its desecrated dead—ultimately requiring extensive lobby efforts, several attorney general orders and opinions, negotiated agreements, four pieces of state legislation, and one act of Congress. Throughout the time in question, while Pawnee bodies were being dug up, state law spelled out very stringent conditions for exhuming the dead, but those statutory requirements for court orders, permits, and so forth, which are intended to safeguard the sanctity of the dead and the rights of the living, were simply not followed when it came to Indians. Thus, hundreds of dead bodies were dug up without any regard for the feelings or rights of the Pawnee people, providing a clear denial of equal protection under the laws. In Kansas, open commercial exploitation of an entire Indian burial ground existed for years because of a "loophole" in Kansas statutes, despite systematic efforts by the legislature to comprehensively protect burial grounds and cemeteries of every conceivable description. And, of course, the 1867 order of the U.S. Army surgeon general, under which the heads of slain Pawnees were taken, was racially motivated conduct patently discriminatory against American Indians under any interpretation of the Equal Protection Clause.

However, the Pawnee struggle for repatriation was motivated by the adverse impact of this disparate racial treatment upon long-standing tribal religious traditions, which require that Pawnee dead be respected and properly laid to rest. The unfolding facts of this history were met with shock and outrage among the Pawnee people. The spiritual implications of such vast disturbances of the dead required that the government of the Pawnee Tribe take immediate action. As such, the case study reveals the deep impact that grave desecration and body snatching can have upon living communities of American Indians and their religious beliefs and mortuary conditions. Under these circumstances, the withholding of the dead from proper burial by the government, acting through its museums and federal agencies, directly infringes upon very clear religious beliefs and practices that require Indians to lay their dead to rest properly.

CONCLUSION: IMPLICATIONS FOR INDIAN RELIGIOUS FREEDOM

As we have seen, tribal repatriation to rebury the dead is religiously impelled action taken by tribal governments to protect basic religious freedoms and the sensibilities of their citizenry. Indian religious obligations, such as those embraced by Pawnee mortuary traditions, often exist between living Indians and the spirits of deceased ancestors. This relationship imposes a duty upon the living to bury the dead properly and to ensure that the spirits and sanctity of the dead are not disturbed. Such religiously motivated conduct is readily understandable, because death and burial have always been deeply held religious matters for all peoples. As one commentator notes, "[No] system of jurisprudence permits exhumation for less than what are considered weighty, and sometimes compelling reasons."

Thus, denial of sepulcher to deceased Indians, when done by the state acting through its museums, agencies, or other public institutions, directly burdens the free exercise of Indian religion by preventing Native people from burying their dead. Government interference with Native religion through the withholding of the dead infringes upon fundamental beliefs and practices of the universal type mentioned above.

The federal government recognized in 1979 that Native American sepulcher involves the basic religious liberty of Native people. As found by the federal task force in the *American Indian Religious Freedom Act Report*:

Native American religions, along with most other religions, provide standards for the care and treatment of cemeteries and human remains. Tribal customary laws generally include standards of conduct for the care and treatment of all cemeteries encountered and human remains uncovered, as well as for the burial sites and bodies of their own ancestors. Grounded in Native American religious beliefs, these laws may, for example, require the performance of certain types of rituals at the burial site, specify who may be at the site or prescribe the proper disposition of burial offerings.

The prevalent view in the society of applicable disciplines is that Native American human remains are public property and artifacts for study, display, and cultural investment. It is understandable that this view is in conflict with and repugnant to those Native people whose ancestors and near relatives are considered the property at issue.

Most Native American religious beliefs dictate that burial sites once completed are not to be disturbed or displaced except by natural circumstances.

The courts have not been called upon to decide whether the withholding of the dead by the state violates the First Amendment rights of kin to bury the deceased in accordance with their religious beliefs. This is presumably the case because it would be an extremely rare situation indeed, given the strong public policy that all persons are entitled to a decent burial, for the state to withhold the dead permanently from burial over the objection of the closest relatives. However, in *Fuller v. Marx* the court suggested the obvious when it intimated that a failure by the state to return human remains to next-of-kin for burial can indeed violate a First Amendment right to bury a decedent as required by the religious beliefs of the next-of-kin. There, a civil rights action was brought by a widow against a doctor who performed an autopsy on her deceased husband and failed to return certain organs. The widow asserted that the failure to return all organs with the body violated her "First Amendment right to bury her husband in a manner consistent with her religious beliefs." The court did not doubt that such a First Amendment right exists, but ruled that the widow failed to show that her right had been infringed upon under the facts of that case, because she could have retrieved all of the organs had she followed procedures that were available to her.

Under *Fuller*, should Indian tribes prove in particular cases that denial of sepulcher by the state impairs religious practices, then the burden of proof under the traditional First Amendment test shifts to the state to prove that its withholding of the dead is necessary to serve materially some compelling state interest—one that cannot be served in a manner less restrictive of religious liberty than a permanent withholding of the dead from burial. In regard to the state's burden of proof under the test, the Nebraska attorney general issued an opinion in 1988 upholding the Pawnee religious rights involved in that case and stated in part: "I am not convinced that scientific curiosity or the possibility that future scientific advances will permit further study of the remains, are sufficient reasons to overcome the strong impulses in the law to allow human remains to rest in peace in a grave or other proper sepulcher."

Although other constitutional, common law, and federal Indian law rights are at stake, it is the protection of Indian religious liberty that cries out the loudest. Felix S. Cohen, a noted scholar and father of the field of federal Indian law, once noted that society's treatment of America's Native people is a social barometer for the basic freedoms and well-being of all Americans: "The Indian plays much the same role in our American society that the Jews played in Germany. Like the miner's canary, the Indian marks the shift from fresh air to poison gas in our political atmosphere; and our treatment of Indians, even more than our treatment of other minorities, reflects the rise and fall in our democratic faith."

Similarly, the way in which society treats the dead, especially the dead of minority cultures, is also a social barometer for the respect and well-being it accords to the living. Museums and other institutions that have inherited a legacy of insensitivity and oppression toward Native communities must address this heritage as a major priority if they wish to open their halls to living people with as much enthusiasm as they have for the dead. The formation of productive and positive relationships between culturally diverse people should be based upon bonds of mutual respect—not chains of religious oppression. Indians have long been yoked to museums, historical societies, universities, and federal agencies by such chains. But through repatriation, reburial, and the recognition of fundamental religious rights, Indian people hope to be free to visit such places as equal partners in the sharing of human traditions, rather than as dispossessed victims and humiliated plaintiffs in court proceedings.

16

Coyote's Game: Indian Casinos and the Indian Presence in Contemporary America

Christopher L. Miller

When you walk into the Spirit Mountain Casino, operated by the Grand Ronde Reservation community in western Oregon, you are immediately struck by the seemingly comic figure of Coyote dancing and frolicking about the gambling hall. His picture dominates the casino's official logo and he is omnipresent. Change and continuity are embodied in Coyote, and so is survival. In many ways Coyote may be the perfect symbol not only for Spirit Mountain, but also for an entire movement, and perhaps a new moment of rebirth for those to whom Coyote is sacred.

Perhaps no other idea has remained as constant in the United States' national culture than that of the "vanishing Indian." From the first days of fifteenth-century European colonization to the present time, Indians have been perceived as a doomed people. For some, like the Puritans in seventeenth-century Massachusetts, this was to be the natural outcome of Indian depravity—the consequence of original sin, in which Indians participated, and the lack of intervening grace, in which they did not; both apparent in the native refusal to embrace the modern world. For others, this was to be the natural outcome of Indian innocence—the absence of original sin, itself seen as a consequence of the Indians dwelling outside of time and away from the seductions of modern existence. The causes might be debated, but neither side doubted, for one moment, the inevitability of the consequences.

This chapter was originally a paper presented at a W.K. Kellogg Foundation-sponsored colloquium on American Indian Gaming, Humboldt State University, Arcata, CA, March 27, 1998.

No other issue in modern Indian affairs has done more to tear away the anchor of certainty about Indian extinction than that of reservation-based casino gambling. Not that gambling was anything new; gambling in one form or another is as ancient in North America as the Indians themselves. Gambling paraphernalia is a regular part of the archaeological record, stories about gambling punctuate native oral histories and folklore, and various games of chance have been recorded by both casual and professional observers, forming a major component in the ethnographic record. Such ceremonial, social, and charitable gambling, however, bears little resemblance to what is occurring in the glittering modern gaming houses that have sprung up on reservations across North America since 1983. In these gambling establishments, the objective is money—lots and lots of money.

Two federal court cases provided the mechanisms for the transition. In the first of these, *Seminole Tribe of Florida v. Butterworth* (1983), the U.S. Fifth Circuit Court of Appeals ruled that because the State of Florida did not prohibit bingo off Indian reservations, it could not do so on them. More importantly, because the power to regulate commerce with the Indians was specifically reserved for the federal government by the Constitution, the state could not impose its regulations relating to bingo onto the Seminole tribe. The second, *California v. Cabazon Band of Mission Indians* (1987), went even further. In this case the Supreme Court specified that if any given state permitted gambling in any form, it could not prevent similar gambling activities on Indian reservations within the state, nor could it impose its authority over that of a sovereign tribal government by placing controls over such activities. These legal cases were the first big challenge to prevailing notions about Indians, announcing in headlines around the country that they had not vanished at all. Indians were suddenly a presence in contemporary America. Even Donald Trump, never known for having a sensitized social consciousness, had to come to grips with the fact.

The fact of an Indian presence in contemporary America was disturbing enough to a population primed for their extinction, but what made matters worse was the question of sovereignty. In both *Seminole* and *Cabazon*, the courts drew the line right where the Constitution said they should, but it still caught most Americans off guard.

Internal sovereignty is one of the identifying features that sets Indian organizations apart from any other domestic group in the United States, and it is rooted deep in the very fiber of the Constitution itself. The full body of both constitutional provisions and case law forms a complicated tapestry of many interwoven threads, but legal scholar Felix Cohen summarized the situation in a landmark statement nearly sixty years ago:

1. An Indian tribe possesses, in the first instance, all the powers of any sovereign state.
2. Conquest renders the tribe subject to the legislative power of the United States, and in substance, terminated the external powers of sovereignty of the tribe . . . but does not by itself affect the internal sovereignty of the tribe.
3. These powers are subject to qualification by treaties and by express legislation of Congress, but, save as thus expressly qualified, full powers of internal sovereignty are vested in the Indian tribes and in their duly constituted organs of government.

These powers were not conferred by government, they always existed and, in pure Enlightenment terms, are "endowed" and "inalienable."

But, as Cohen recognized, the fact of conquest modified the pure condition of this indwelling sovereignty, much as John Locke perceived the social compact as modifying pure sovereignty in the transition from a natural to a political state. In having yielded some of their sovereignty to the United States, native people earned certain privileges, protections, and benefits separate from those of others dwelling within the nation's boundaries, whose sovereignty was transferred in different forms through different processes. As summarized by the Institute for the Development of Indian Law, these special rights fell into three broad areas: "(1) protection of Indian trust property, (2) protection of the Indian right to self-government, and (3) provision of social, medical, and educational services for survival and advancement of the Indian tribes." Thus despite Donald Trump's and others' claims concerning "equal treatment under the law," laws affecting Indians and laws affecting everyone else are different laws; equal treatment simply means equally vigorous and equally uncapricious enforcement of each set of laws independently.

As Trump's widely publicized protests made clear, the matter of Indian sovereignty challenged many Americans' understandings of history and due process. Indians were supposed to have vanished long before 1983. To have courts asserting that Indian nations had sovereign power over their own affairs—a special and continuing compact with the United States that superceded any other authority—seemed to defy all sense. But the law was the law, so the struggle shifted to new ground.

Within a year of the *Cabazon* decision, reservation communities around the country began offering a wide variety of gambling games that they claimed were "similar" to those authorized by the state governments in which their reservations were situated. Naturally, controversy ran wild. In deciding as they did that tribes have the right to run gambling games on their properties, which the state permits elsewhere within its confines, the courts opened Pandora's Box, and no amount of shoving was going to push the Furies back in. Fundamental to the issue was the question of what constituted similar games and who had the right to determine similarity. While tribal groups pressed for the most liberal interpretation possible and the authority to determine for themselves what "similar" meant, states lobbied for strict tests and authority vested in state gambling commissions. Congress, ever jealous of protecting its own power from either state or tribal invasion, was caught in the middle. Following the *Cabazon* case, things were moving so fast, money was rolling in in such amounts, and state authorities were so angry and confused that Congress rushed to assert some controls over the growing industry.

In 1988 Congress passed the Indian Gaming Regulatory Act (IGRA), which, by outlining specific federal regulations relating to all forms of gambling, protected federal sovereignty over Indian affairs by pitting the states and the tribes against each other with a regulatory commission and the federal courts designated as referees.

The IGRA began by setting out three distinct classes of gambling activity, each with its own limitations and controls. Class I includes traditional Indian social games and specified that because these were entirely internal and traditional matters, this class fell completely under tribal control. Class II includes games such as bingo and "non-banking" card games like poker. In the case of these games, it was fairly easy to determine whether or not similar games were permitted to non-Indians under state legal codes, so controls followed the precedents outlined in *Seminole* and *Cabazon*. Class III, though, was the sticking point. Designed as a catch-all category, it covers lotteries, banking card games like blackjack and baccarat, slot machines, and other electronic games such as video poker, where the definition of similarity to what was permitted under state law was hazy. Rather than risking a localist backlash by allowing tribes to decide about Class III issues, or a tribal backlash by allowing state regulatory commissions to rule, Congress insisted that the two groups work out a mutual accommodation in the form of a formal compact, binding on both sides. Recognizing that the states had the upper hand in any negotiations, Congress also ruled that the states had to negotiate in good faith. If a state was stonewalling, federal authorities could impose the same sort of arbitration process allowed under the National Labor Relations Act and sit on the parties until accord was reached.

After the passage of the IGRA, Indian gambling became a high-flying growth industry. As of the summer of 1994, a mere six years after Congress approved it, seventy-two tribes were operating gaming facilities in twenty-five states, and several others had successfully negotiated compacts that would permit them to begin operations as soon as the initial capital was raised and facilities prepared. It was estimated that these establishments were grossing in excess of $1.5 billion per year. Although this amounted to only a small percentage of the estimated $330 billion Americans spent on legal gambling— "more," one commentator observed, "than on books, movies, amusement arcades, and recorded music put together,"—it was still an enormous amount.

The Indian take was more than three times what Americans nation-wide spent for movie tickets in that year.

But none of this was accomplished without a lot of political infighting, on and off reservations. States have consistently lobbied Congress and the courts in an effort to tone down the federal role in negotiating compacts with local tribal groups, while organizations like the National Indian Gaming Association have worked equally as hard to shift the balance the other way. And many local Indian groups have found themselves caught in the crossfire. In 1998, for example, the Pala Band of Mission Indians worked out a compact with the State of California that allows the Palas to offer video slot machines, something forbidden to other tribal groups. The catch is that these machines are based on an experimental technology that gets around California's ban on "banking games": high pay-out slot machines like those in Nevada pay out of a house bank rather than out of a player pool. The former is illegal in California, but the latter falls in a negotiable gray area. Although eleven tribes currently operate more than 7,000 video slot machines, federal authorities have resisted imposing California law, arguing that they would wait until the state found common ground in a negotiated compact before acting. The Pala accord creates such a precedent. Speaking for the eleven tribal groups running questionable slot machines, Mark Macarro, chairman of the Pechango tribal council, proclaimed governor Pete Wilson "the best governor that Nevada ever had." "How nice this is for Nevada," Cahuilla spokesman Richard Milanovich said, pointing out that this compact will prevent California tribes from pressing for high pay-out slots and that disgruntled gamblers will take their business elsewhere.

Still, given the amount of money involved and the pressure from state and local forces, tension between tribal groups has been surprisingly rare. In 1993, for example, the *New York Times* reported an upsurge in intertribal cooperation in an effort to protect fragile gambling operations from incursions by organized crime and unorganized hucksterism. And organizations like the National Indian Gaming Association have fostered cooperation and mutual support.

But tensions within tribal communities over the issue of casino gambling have grabbed headlines and encouraged state, local, and federal authorities to question Indian sovereignty. At the heart of the public perception of these conflicts lies one of the key controversies in the history of relations between Indians and non-Indian authorities: assimilation.

It certainly appears that assimilation was the issue when conflict arose on the Navajo Reservation over whether the tribe should join the casino movement. So-called "progressive" leaders in the community largely favored gambling and other resort-like enterprises that would bring increased employment and capital to the reservation, allowing Navajos to stay home rather than migrating to the cities. More "traditional" leaders protested, pointing out that this would bring strangers and outside pressures to an already troubled community.

Assimilation also seemed to be the issue in a particularly disturbing and well-publicized conflict in New York. In the spring of 1990, conflict over casino gambling on the Mohawk's Akwesasne-St. Regis Reserve led to two shooting deaths and a hard core of bad feelings. On one side were people described as "traditional." On the other were the so-called "bingo chiefs."

Lying partly in Canada and partly in New York, the Akwesasne-St. Regis Reserve comes under the authority of one state, two provincial, and two national governments. In addition, five political factions all vied with each other for control on the reservation itself. The Mohawk Nation Council and the Saint Regis Tribal Council were recognized by New York State and by Washington, D.C., while the Akwesasne Tribal Council was recognized by Ottawa, Ontario, and Quebec. The other two, the Mohawk Sovereignty Security Force (the so-called "Warriors"), and entrepreneurial Mohawks, that is, cigarette smugglers (often called "butt-leggers"), and casino owners and operators (the so-called "bingo chiefs"), were not recognized by any non-Indian authorities, but had large followings on the reserve.

Membership in these factions was not mutually exclusive. When the *Seminole* decision first made high-stakes bingo legal for reservation Indians in 1983, pro-gambling interests controlled the Saint Regis Tribal Council, which aligned with the entrepreneurial faction to build casinos in the New York portion of the reservation. They then forged an alliance with the "Warriors" to defend the operations against hostile New York authorities and equally hostile antigambling Mohawks. Those in the antigambling camp, consisting of the majorities in the Mohawk Nation Council and the Akwesasne Tribal Council, aligned with New York, Ontario, and Quebec officials. They also appealed to the large congregation of Long House Religion members on the reservation, whose creed, formulated by the prophet Handsome Lake in the early nineteenth century, is utterly opposed to nontraditional forms of gambling.

In both cases, the popular press and the scholarly community pointed to casino gambling and the IGRA as yet another manifestation of assimilationist forces assaulting Indian tradition. But the actualities are more complicated than popular perceptions allow. In the case of the Mohawks, both sides claimed to be walking in the ways of tradition and tribal autonomy. Antigambling advocates challenged the claims to tradition made by the Warriors and leaned heavily on the religious rhetoric emanating from the Long House and also moralistic and legalistic rhetoric flowing out of Albany. For their part, pro-gambling advocates pointed out the close connection between their opponents and government officials, accusing them of bartering tribal sovereignty for government favors. They also pointed out that the Long House

Religion was relatively new and syncretic (hence an "assimilationist) belief, not a traditional Mohawk one.

In the midst of all the confusion, one of the major players in the Akwesasne conflict, casino entrepreneur Guilford White, asserted that the battle was "not about craps or blackjack or bingo; it is about control of the reservation." Similarly, an assistant to Navajo Nation president Peterson Zah reported, "The real concerns are not cultural." "Gambling is part of Navaho culture, . . . [but] when you have such a large population with high unemployment, all kinds of poverty and related problems like alcoholism, and you put a casino in the middle of it, what kinds of problems do you have?" Similar concerns plagued the Oglala Lakota, who were divided on the issue of building a casino on the Pine Ridge Reservation in South Dakota. Here the question of the reservation's relative remoteness from non-Indian communities raised the anxiety that people from the reservation itself, one of the poorest in the country, would be the casino's only customers; hence the only losers would be tribal members.

Such division only enhanced the perception that Indians could not manage their own affairs. In fact, the expectation that Indian communities should somehow be united behind a common vision, behind a universal traditional response, seems to be the central prop in the growing political, journalistic, and scholarly opposition to the Indian casino gambling movement, and interferes with the emergence of disparate Indian communities into contemporary consciousness. Somehow such conflicts are seen as "un-Indian," and as such undermine claims of special legal consideration. "If gambling operators lack Indianness," one academic observer asked, "where does a true Indianness reside?"

Commenting on the matter of universal traditional Indian responses, Modoc ethnohistorian Michael Dorris pointed out, " 'United Fronts' are difficult to achieve even within tribes, where competing factions (clan versus clan, "traditionalists" versus "progressives," and so on), each believing that it represents the best interest of the group, vie for ascendancy and influence." "If nothing else," he continues, "it was widely recognized in Indian tribes throughout North America in the precontact period that tribal members had pervasive and inherent rights to make individual choices."

By educating people to such discontinuities in the Indian past, ethnohistorians can help to break down one of the stereotypes that threatens contemporary Indian autonomy. But another, and perhaps more difficult question also needs to be addressed. "In a new tribal world of consumer economics, federal subsidies, and wage labor," one writer asked, "what can be recognized as authentically Indian?" Critics have pointed to the "bingo chiefs" as the personifications of the worst sort of assimilation: individuals willing to trade Indian tribalism for Mafia brotherhood, and, in the words of one Tuscarora spokesman, "[religious] prophets for [gambling] prophets." What was at stake, at least in the public's eye, was the question of which were the real Indians.

Of course at some level everyone knows that "Indianness," like the word "Indian" itself, is the product of viewpoints originating far from Native American communities. Lakota writer, scholar, and freelance wit Vine Deloria, Jr. observes that " 'Indianness' has been defined by whites for many years. Always they have been outside observers looking into Indian society from a self-made pedestal of preconceived ideas coupled with an innate superior attitude toward those different from themselves."

Picking up on the same thread, Michael Dorris commented on the "Indian" of the imagination—the stereotypical model for such "Indianness." "In popular and persistent folk belief," Dorris explains,

The Indian is, among other things, male, red-skinned, stoic, taciturn, ecologically aware, and a great user of metaphor. Or, he is cunning, mercurial, wild, lusty, and a collector of blond scalps. At nightfall he silhouettes himself in the sunset, or dances, shrieking, around his campfire. Before vanishing, he was prone to skulking, sneaking, and sundry other double-dealings. Rather than defend himself, he "uprose"; rather than resist the occupation of his land, he "outbroke"; rather than defeat a foe, he "massacred."

And anyone who does not resemble the model is somehow not authentically Indian. "Some people feel that Indians can do anything they want as long as they're doing Indian stuff," observes Indian activist Suzan Shown Harjo. "When they go beyond that, somehow they're taking something away from the white people."

Ethnohistorians know that what is being taken away from white people is what some social scientists call "nostalgic imperialism." One commentator defines this as "an unconscious sentimentalizing and romanticizing of that which a dominant culture has destroyed. It is a fascination with indigenous people and culture, *exclusively* from an historical and artistic point of view." Deloria comments that such sentimentalizing is so pervasive within the scholarly community that "many times anthropologists and sociologists have acted as if we couldn't do anything if they didn't first understand it and approve of it." And by this way of thinking, any departure from the stereotype is a departure from "Indianness." Thus "others in the culture can gamble," one astute observer commented, "but not the 'noble American Indian.' "

This is another stereotype that ethnohistorians are equipped to challenge. One of the first issues that must be dealt with is the fact that issues like "Indianness" and non-Indianness are historical artifacts. Ethnohistorian James Axtell, for example, points out that early European colonists seldom described Indians as being racially distinct from Europeans, and his colleague Karen Ordahl Kupperman argues persuasively that European settlers equated

Indians with their own peasant classes culturally. Indians, too, seem to have been largely unconscious of genetic or serious cultural distinctions between themselves and European newcomers. In fact, George Hamell and I argued some time ago that it was perceived similarity rather than a perceived dissimilarity that led Indians to welcome Europeans during the opening phases of contact. Rachel Buff suggests that such lack of distinction persisted into the nineteenth century. "Since the idea of 'red' and 'white' people as distinct entities contradicts much traditional Shawnee thinking," Buff points out, "Tenskwatawa was invoking historical exigency rather than some authentic, pre-existing cultural practice" when he "articulated a pan-Indian vision."

R. David Edmunds, a mixed-blood Cherokee and well-respected ethnohistorian, points out the dilemma:

Obviously, during much of the early colonial period, issues of identity were almost non-existent, since everyone in a tribal community knew everyone else or at least was familiar with an individual's kinship affiliations. . . . One saw oneself first as a member of the Fox clan, then as a Mesquakie. If captives or other outsiders were adopted into a family, they became part of the clan and consequently were part of the "tribal community." Under such conditions, tribal membership was communally self-determined. Regardless of one's origin or ethnicity, if the Shawnees said you were Shawnee, you *were* Shawnee.

"At the end of the twentieth century," however, Edmunds points out, "questions of Native American identity continue to plague both Indian history and Indian politics."

As soon as these distinctions in identity were first articulated they began to plague the special relations between Indian groups and the federal government. Speaking of Indian/federal relations during the 1830s, Edmunds points out that

although people of mixed lineage generally were accepted as Native Americans by their tribal communities, they were highly suspect to federal officials, who often based their definition of ethnicity on an individual's willingness to cooperate with the government. If mixed-blood leaders acquiesced in federal demands for land cessions, they were described as legitimate "chiefs and spokesmen" for the tribal communities, but if they opposed federal policy they were denounced as "degraded white men."

And so the problem continues. If, as some critics say, Indian casino advocates are nothing more than "degraded white men"—people stripped of their special Indian nature, their identity as Indians—then what right do they have to the special constitutional relationship afforded to Indians alone; what right to sovereignty?

Here again, modern ethnohistorians have something to offer. By restoring time depth and historicity to the Indian world, ethnohistorians can suggest not only the patterns of discontinuity suggested above, but also patterns of continuity that can help forge a more dynamic and useful definition of "Indianness" for public consumption. Michael Dorris, for example, suggests that the one consistent element in Indian experience during the past five hundred years has been "simple survival." Not just biological survival, though this has been an essential component, but also holding "the fabric of their kin-based political systems together." This fabric is what Vine Deloria, Jr. calls "tribalism," a world view that "looks at life as an undifferentiated whole. Distinctions are not made between social and psychological, educational and historical, political and legal. The tribe is an all-purpose entity that is expected to serve all areas of life." But this tribal fabric must be flexible enough to permit Indians too, in Dorris' words, "make a proper response to a growing and increasingly aggressive invading force of foreigners." The question then becomes whether the purveyors of reservation-based casino gambling meet such a historically and culturally dynamic and complicated definition of "Indianness."

A comprehensive examination of spending by casino communities seems to indicate that they do. Among the Mashantucket Pequots, a major portion of the profits on the estimated $800 to $900 million grossed at their Foxwoods Casino in 1994 was invested in diversified income- and job-producing enterprises designed to provide economic support for the Pequot community as a whole. Early in 1995, the tribal council, a seven-member executive board that has absolute discretion over the tribe's earnings, invested in a silica mine, a large printing plant, a historic colonial restaurant and inn, and manufacturing sites formerly owned by the Electric Boat shipyard, a major contractor in the construction and maintenance of the United States' nuclear submarine fleet.

Describing the Pequots' investment strategy to the *New York Times*, A. Searle Field, one-time chief of staff to former Connecticut governor Lowell Weicker and chief advisor for Pequot non-casino investments, announced that the tribe would concentrate its capital locally and would focus on investments that would allow it to maintain its sizable income even if the casino was "not delivering."

Similar strategies have been adopted by other gambling-enriched tribes. For example, the Oneida Tribe of Wisconsin, which runs a 2000-slot-machine complex outside Green Bay, has invested in an industrial park, a printing company, a bank, a convenience store chain, a $7 million factory, and a high-tech research-and-development firm. The Choctaws, who opened a high-stakes bingo parlor in Durant, Oklahoma, have invested in resort hotels, manufacturing operations, and the Choctaw Nation Travel Plaza, a full-service travel center that brought in over $1.4 million per month in 1992.

While such long-term economic planning provides evidence of a broad-based concern about community economic survival, can it truly be called "tribal?" Have they helped to protect the fabric of their kin-based systems? It certainly appears that casino communities believe that is what they are doing. The Grand Ronde's Spirit Mountain Casino advertising pamphlets proclaim that "The casino provides new economic opportunities and benefits programs for housing, education, and heritage." A similar pamphlet advertising the Wisconsin Oneidas' Mystic Lake Casino concludes that, "Tribal governments realize that casino gaming is not an end in itself. It is a means to achieve what no other federal economic development program has been able to in more than 200 years—the return of self-respect and economic self-sufficiency to Indian people."

Many non-Indian analysts agree. Observing the spending patterns among the Oneidas, the prestigious financial journal *The Economist* noted that "spending is not confined to economic development." The magazine went on to report that the tribe was following the advice of hired consultant Stephen Covey, author of "The Seven Habits of Highly Effective People," by spending money to improve the "general quality of life." "Tribal government outlays have surged from $40m to $250m in the past ten years," the journal observed, "to provide services from subsidized housing to health care and student counseling." Similarly, Choctaw gambling profits have not only been used to diversify the nation's economic base, but have also been used to subsidize health-related assistance not funded by the Indian Health Service, especially for the treatment of diabetes and arthritis, diseases endemic in the community. Additional Choctaw funds have been used to construct community centers, fund scholarship programs, provide nutrition counseling to the elderly, and create emergency aid programs.

In addition to such financial and social capital, the casino communities are investing in cultural capital as well. In a 1994 radio interview, Ovide Mercredi, spokesman for Canada's 600,000 First Nations people, announced a cultural agenda that seems to be shared by tribal groups throughout North America. "We're growing stronger," Mercredi observed. "We will win it back, buy it back, the land that was taken from us." Such reacquisition of tribal land bases appears to be a high priority on casino-enriched reservations. *The Economist* reported that the Wisconsin Oneidas spent an estimated $11 million in 1995 to purchase lands lost through various agreements, treaties, and sales. Washington State's Suquamish are also using their casino proceeds to purchase back reservation lands that were long ago taken away by state and federal policies. And the land-buying practices of the Mashantucket Pequots have come under severe criticism: ironically, their non-Indian neighbors describe the ten-fold expansion of their reservation boundaries through repurchasing former tribal lands as "modern-day imperialism."

The reacquisition of land is important for more than economic or nostalgic reasons. The combination of economic opportunity with extended land holdings is making it possible for reservation communities to reverse the pattern of diaspora that characterized Indian life during most of the nation's history. Again to quote Michael Dorris,

Since World War II, an increasingly sizable Indian population migrated to urban areas in search of employment and other opportunities, encouraged by the somewhat ill-conceived federal Urban Relocation Program initiated in the 1950s. In the past twenty years alone over two hundred thousand Indians have left their reservations and moved to such metropolitan centers as Los Angeles, Minneapolis, the Bay Area, Seattle, Denver, Chicago, Boston, New York, and Buffalo. Today nearly one half of the total Native American population in the United States could be classified as urban, though studies strongly suggest that the majority of these migrants maintain significant ties with their home communities.

The Mashantucket Pequots, for example, experienced consistent population loss during the three-hundred years between their relocation to western Connecticut in the 1660s and the 1960s, when only one family remained on the impoverished and shrinking reserve. However, as Dorris goes on to report, "Research conducted among Indians . . . indicates that the vast majority would prefer to return to their reservations if work were available there." This has certainly been true in western Connecticut, where the combination of reacquired reservation land and consistent employment has lured tribal members back from nearby cities. Since 1986, the Pequot reservation population has increased eight-fold. Vine Deloria, Jr. calls this process "recolonization," and places enormous emphasis on it as a means for recovering and maintaining tribal existence and identity.

As formerly estranged tribal members return to communities, tribes find themselves having to reacculturate the newcomers while at the same time trying to preserve or reinvigorate dying cultural practices. On the Wisconsin Oneida reservation, casino money has been spent to revive and preserve the tribe's language and folklore: experts have been hired to produce a written form of the Oneida language, and the tribe has begun production of a compact disk on which elders tell ancestral tales in the Oneida language. The Mashantucket Pequots entered into an agreement with a neighboring school, which includes having a tribal member on the board of directors and a regular program of Indian cultural offerings. The Pequots have also entered into a partnership with the Groton campus of the University of New Haven, where adults can enroll in a special program designed to teach them necessary job and management-related skills, but at the same time get instruction in tribal culture. Other cultural education programs for both adults and children have been adopted at community centers, and a burgeoning number of community colleges are being built with casino money on reservations around the country.

Cultural capital is also being created through other means. At Foxwoods, a gigantic statue of the Pequot culture-hero Rainmaker dominates the entrance; an architectural plan for a projected Mohegan casino calls for gamblers to enter through the mouth of a wolf, the tribe's sacred animal; and on the Wisconsin Oneida reservation, some casino proceeds have been spent to build a new elementary school in the shape of a turtle, a sacred creature in Oneida mythology. Religious historian Jon Butler calls such symbolic manipulation "sacralizing the landscape," that is, building structures that remind observers, even subconsciously, of cultural mores held sacred by the community, thus reinforcing communal values in a subtle but imposing way.

At the Grand Ronde community's Spirit Mountain Casino, the seemingly comic figure of Coyote similarly sacralizes the environment as a cultural symbol. But Coyote is more than that: ethnohistorical analysis informs us that he is also a powerful metaphor. Throughout the western half of the continent, Indians portray Coyote as the creator spirit's special agent. The Okanagon Indians of the Columbia Plateau, for example, call him *Sinkalip*, meaning "trickster" or "imitator," and explain that the Great Spirit gave him that name and his imitative powers for a grand purpose: he continually transforms the world so that it is useful to mortal beings, and teaches his imitative tricks to mortal beings so they can better live in the world. "Northwest Indian mythology portrays Coyote as 'the Changer' who transformed the ancient world into a modern one," a Spirit Mountain pamphlet explains. "Spirit Mountain's logo features Coyote as a symbol of the positive change taking place throughout the Confederated Tribes of The Grand Ronde Community," it concludes.

For the Indians at Grand Ronde, Coyote is alive, just as the kin-based structure of their community is alive, and they intend to use the casino to keep it that way. Coyote symbolizes continuity through change, and thus is a metaphor for the sort of "Indianness" that avoids commonplace or scholarly stereotypes, the sort of "Indianness" that can only be appreciated through the sensitive ethnohistorical consideration of the Indian past and present. And hopefully, as partnerships between scholars and Indian communities continue, the only "vanishing Indian" will be the "male, red-skinned, stoic, taciturn, ecologically aware, . . . cunning, mercurial, wild, lusty, . . . collector of blond scalps." Then, perhaps, the real, dynamic, and historically functional survivors revealed by ethnohistory can find a permanent place in popular contemporary American consciousness.

17

The Demand for Natural Resources on Reservations

Donald L. Fixico

More than 100 years ago, Indian tribal leaders were forced to negotiate with white Americans and the U.S. government for possession of Indian lands. To-day's tribal leaders face a similar situation, due to the growing energy crisis and increased demands for natural resources. Depletion of America's mineral reserves has caused energy companies to look toward reservation lands to replenish needed oil, coal, gas, and uranium supplies. Even water has become a precious resource for transporting coal in slurry pipelines. In almost every western state, Indian and white interests are competing for this priceless commodity. And as a result of the increasing demand for natural resources, conflict between tribal reservation leaders and white Americans has intensified.

Today, more than half of the nation's coalfields are west of the Mississippi River. One-third of the western fields exist on lands of twenty-two tribes, and large portions of most of these tribes' reservations will be disrupted during mining operations. The Northern Cheyenne, whose 440,000-acre reservation stands over a rich coal vein in southeastern Montana, will have approximately fifty-six percent of their land mined. The Crow Reservation, adjacent to the Cheyenne, will suffer similar disturbances, reducing the land available for the Crow's own use. In Montana and North Dakota, coalfields are estimated to contain fifteen times the energy reserves of the Alaska North Slope oil and gas

Reprinted from Donald L. Fixico, *The Invasion of Indian Country in the Twentieth Century: American Capitalism and Tribal Natural Resources*, Boulder: University Press of Colorado, 1998, pp. 143–155, by permission of the University Press of Colorado.

fields. The Jicarilla Apache Reservation, in New Mexico, contains 154 million barrels of oil and 2 trillion cubic feet of gas. Overall, geologists report that twenty-five to forty percent of America's uranium, one-third of its coal, and approximately five percent of its oil and gas are on Indian reservations in the West.

Large-scale mining on reservation lands has occurred since the late nineteenth century. In the late 1800s and early decades of the twentieth century, for example, coal was mined on Choctaw and Chickasaw lands in southeastern Oklahoma. Water was vied for on the Fort Belknap Reservation in Montana in the early 1900s, and non-Indians aggressively pursued Pueblo irrigated lands in the 1920s. Oil was pumped from wells on the lands of the Osage, Creek, and Seminole in Oklahoma during the 1920s and 1930s. In the 1950s, tons of coal were mined on the Crow and Northern Cheyenne Reservations in Montana. In the 1960s, Peabody Coal Company and Shell Oil operated coal mines on the Crow Reservation, and the latter made a record bid of $1.1 million for prospecting rights on 83,000 acres of Crow land. In the late 1960s, the Department of the Interior encouraged the Navajo and Hopi Tribes to provide water and to forgo taxing non-Indians on their reservations so that a power plant using coal could be built at Page, Arizona. The Bureau of Indian Affairs convinced tribal leaders that nuclear power would replace the need for Indian coal in the area. But in the next few years, the coal industry raced to its highest profits ever, and the Navajo and Hopi were locked into contracts for many years.

Mining operations on Indian lands can be monetarily beneficial; consequently, tribes bestowed with large mineral deposits on their reservations receive large royalty payments. Such revenue enables the tribes to promote various programs and to improve their economies. The western tribes faced a grave dilemma, however. Should they allow mining development of their reservations? In 1977, Peter MacDonald, chairperson of the Navajo Nation, noted in a speech before the western attorneys general in Seattle that "the history of Indian resource development reaches far into our past. Before the white man came to our lands, Indians developed their resources for their own needs. Our people used only what they needed, and they were very careful not to destroy the land. The railroads, trucks and powerlines transport this material (resources) off the reservation to provide Americans with a better life." "At the same time, most Indians still live in poverty, without such 'luxuries' as water and electricity, which most Americans regard as the barest necessities of life."

The Indians' reaction to the demand for their energy resources is twofold: reluctance to allow the mining operations to continue, on one hand, and a progressive attitude toward increased mining to help develop tribal programs, on the other. Among the western tribes, factions for and against mining have developed among the Native peoples. Conservative traditionalists oppose mining. Progressives, especially tribal leaders, favor mining, but they are in the minority. Nevertheless, tribal leaders control their tribes' affairs, and they sometimes negotiate with energy companies without their peoples' consent.

Generally, the conservative blocs consist of the tribal elders. They see their traditional cultures threatened, leading them to believe that after the mining companies are gone, their lands will never be the same. David Strange Owl, one of thirty-six Northern Cheyenne on a fact-finding mission, visited the mining operations on the Navajo Reservation in the spring of 1977. He confessed, "Before, I didn't know much about coal." Observing the mining operations aroused in him feelings of repugnance: "What I've seen between the Navajo and Hopi is a sad thing, to see the strip-mining, on their reservations—our lives, our culture." Possessing a deep attachment to the land, traditionalists view themselves as a part of that land. According to Native tradition, the earth is mother to all, and no harm should come to her; in fact, the "Mother Earth" concept is one of the few universal concepts among American Indians. Those who still hold to this concept say that tribal members who want to exploit the land are no longer Indians.

By 2025, more than 250,000 acres of Plains soil will be torn up by huge, steam-powered shovel machines called draglines that are as tall as a 16-story building, weigh 27 million pounds, and are able to move 220 cubic yards (325 tons) of "overburden"—earth—in a single pass. In the path of the draglines are croplands, wildlife refuges, and former residential areas. On the average, the steam shovels rip down through 100 to 150 feet of soil just to reach the coal veins.

Many traditionalists bitterly oppose energy companies wanting to exploit their lands. They do not understand or care about the growing energy crisis. As one young Hopi Indian put it, "Don't tell me about an energy crisis. I don't even have electricity in my village."

Mining operations are lending credence to the traditionalists' fears. As their machines scar Mother Earth and jeopardize the relationship between nature and mankind, the companies bring more non-Indians onto the reservation. Soon, the non-Indians may outnumber the Native people on their own lands. If current mining operations continue on the Northern Cheyenne Reservation, for instance, twenty non-Indians will be brought in for every Cheyenne living there. Many Indians charge that tribal leaders are abusing not only their land but also their people and their culture by cooperating with energy companies.

Conversely, tribal leaders believe that they can improve the welfare of their people by generating revenues and funding programs from mining arrangements. They deem that now is the time to take advantage of the energy companies. And with the increasing demand for natural resources, there is no doubt that revenue received from mining companies will mean further changes in Indian lifestyles. For some Native people, social changes are already taking place.

Residents of reservations who work at off-reservation jobs, for instance, are familiar with the mainstream society.

The progressive Indian nations have elected to improve their situation socially, politically, and economically. Peter MacDonald asserted that his people have chosen to change: "We are an emerging nation. Like other underdeveloped countries with rich but exhaustible supplies of fuel and minerals, we realize we must use our natural resources to create jobs for our people and put us on the road to economic self-sufficiency. Otherwise, we will not have anything left when our resources are gone. That's why we are demanding more from the people who want to exploit our wealth."

Speaking on behalf of the 4500 members of the Crow tribe whose reservation possesses some fourteen to eighteen billion tons of coal, former chairperson Patrick Stands Over Bull said, "I'm for coal development, but I'm for control." Stands Over Bull asserted that his tribe needed time to develop plans for land use and to pass zoning regulations and tax laws.

Navajo and Crow tribal members hesitate to allow mining companies onto their lands. In fact, many do not trust their own leaders, some of whom, they allege, have put tribal moneys into their own pockets. Moreover, lack of knowledge about mining techniques, operations, and legalities has made tribal members suspicious of their leaders. How to estimate the resources on their lands and how to judge their value are problems beyond the expertise of most reservation residents. Instances of mismanagement have upset them, and even though tribal members themselves do not understand the intricacies of mining, they blame their officials for any mishaps or miscalculations, especially for long-term leases that force the tribes to "give away" reservation minerals to mining companies.

Tribal leaders have been forced to rely upon non-Indian lawyers and non-Indian advisers who are experts in energy development areas and the legalities of leasing contracts. This dependency has been reduced in recent years as the number of trained Indian lawyers has grown, but lawyers still demand large fees for their services. Past relations with attorneys and non-Indian experts have caused tribal members to be distrustful of everyone.

Even without the support of their tribespeople, Indian leaders are confident that they can supervise mining operations and develop their own tribal mining companies. But the lack of training and, especially, of capital has hindered and sometimes discouraged them. Addressing the Indians' lack of mining knowledge, the late John Woodenlegs, a Northern Cheyenne, said, "Coal has been under the Cheyenne reservation a long time, and it can stay there until we know the best thing to do."

Tribal leaders protest that the royalty payments from leases are too low and that tribes are locked into poorly negotiated leases for long periods of time. Because the secretary of the interior is empowered by law to approve leases, the energy companies can control Indian lands by entering into agreements with the Department of the Interior. Supposedly, the tribes will benefit from such agreements, but Indians criticize the government for failing to advise tribes correctly and for not protecting them from being victimized. Tribes endowed with energy resources are also angered by the lack of proper supervision by the Bureau of Indian Affairs in protecting Indian interests and by the bureau's urging of tribes to accept inadequate leases.

The Northern Cheyenne have alleged that from 1969 to 1971, the U.S. government misadvised them repeatedly. During this period, Peabody, Amax, and Chevron were given exploration and mining leases for over half of the reservation's 450,000 acres. The tribe did not realize how unfair the ill-advised agreements were until 1972, when Consolidation Coal Company offered the tribe $35 an acre, a royalty rate of $.25 per ton of coal, and a $1.5 million community health center. After further investigation, the Cheyenne Tribal Council charged the federal government with thirty-six violations of leasing procedures.

The tribe petitioned Rogers Morton, then secretary of the interior, to cancel all of their leases with energy companies. Instead, the secretary suspended the leases until a "mutual agreement" was worked out between the companies and the tribe. But the Northern Cheyenne demanded cancellation. "We don't negotiate with the companies until they tear those leases up in front of us and burn them," said tribal chairman Allen Rowland. "And we can start over on our terms, not theirs."

Government and industry officials have responded that, although some mistakes have been made, most leases were negotiated fairly. In 1974, Secretary Morton told Northern Cheyenne leaders that they would have to abide by lease agreements with Peabody, Consolidation, and other companies. Later that same year, however, Northern Cheyenne leases were suspended, and leasing was conducted by negotiation or competitive bidding.

The Crow have charged the secretary of the interior with violating the National Environmental Policy Act and have said that, as a result, their coal leases do not comply with federal regulations. Since the government represents the tribes, through the BIA and the secretary of the interior, there are conflicting attitudes within the federal government, and the tribes are caught in between. The Omnibus Tribal Leasing Act of 1938 authorized the Department of the Interior to approve leases between the tribes and the mining companies. "The government is the trustee of the Indians and the coordinator of national energy policy. That is a conflict of interests," stated Thomas J. Lynaugh, an attorney for the Crow Tribe. Hopi chairperson Abbott Sekaquaptewa summed up the situation when he commented, "The energy situation has put us in a much better posture. We are going to make our decisions on whether to develop our resources, when it will be done, and how."

Indian leaders are currently taking a more active role in the negotiations for their natural resources. In some instances, tribal officials are suing against long-term leases that underpay their tribes, especially because the American dollar has shrunk since these leases were originally signed. The Crow Indians are trying to regain control of some 30,000 acres in southeastern Montana leased to Shell Oil Company and 14,000 acres held by Amax Coal Company. In addition, Peabody Coal Company controls 86,122 acres of Crow land, and Gulf Oil Company holds 73,293. If the Crow are successful in obtaining a favorable decision from the courts, new leases will benefit their tribal economy tremendously.

Another possible alternative for the Crow is to establish joint ownership by forming a new company with an energy firm. Instead of accepting the traditional royalty payments, Crow tribal leaders are asking for a percentage of the production results in raw material or profit. On April 4, 1983, Secretary of the Interior James Watt approved a coal-mining agreement between the Crow and Shell Oil Company to mine an estimated 210 million tons of coal from the reservation's Youngs Creek area. The tribe negotiated $12 million in preproduction and royalty payments. The agreement also provided the tribe with a fifty percent participation in a profit-sharing plan to be implemented after twenty years of mining operations. A decline in coal prices forced Shell to negotiate with the Crow, but negotiations broke off in December 1985. In 1988, the Crow and Shell renewed agreements, and a total of sixty-seven contracts had been made between tribes and energy companies for coal, gas, oil, and uranium.

As early as 1971, the tribes, the Bureau of Indian Affairs, and mining companies began to work on agreements for training and employing Native Americans in the mining industry. The Northern Cheyenne in a community action program proposed a joint venture to the Indian Bureau through which they would work with Peabody Coal Company to produce "trained and well qualified" Indians to enter the construction and mining businesses.

The Indian Mineral Development Act of 1982 allows tribes to enter into joint agreements to establish companies for developing oil, gas, and other mineral resources. The measure was passed during a lame-duck session of Congress with the expectation that President Ronald Reagan would sign the bill into law. Tribes endowed with energy resources—the so-called energy tribes—could now venture into business enterprises to develop their resources. A contract between the Assiniboine, the Sioux, and the U.S. Energy Corporation was the first approved joint company under the new legislation. Assistant Secretary of the Interior Ken Smith stated that the contract "accords perfectly with [the] President's recently issued Indian policy which calls for the development of reservation economies and the strengthening of tribal governments." Under this particular agreement, the company will bear the entire cost of drilling and operating the first well; afterward, the company and the tribes will share the net proceeds from production.

In another case, the Blackfeet formed a joint ownership with Damson Oil Corporation, a small energy firm. Once the company strikes gas on the Blackfeet Reservation, the tribe will receive 58 percent of the profits after paying operational expenses. The Blackfeet also entered into another agreement, forming a joint company with Blocker Drilling Ltd. Distribution of the drilling company's profits will be based upon the tribe's fifty-one percent ownership and Blocker's forty-nine percent, with the understanding that 90 percent of the company's net cash flow will first be used for purchasing equipment for the company to operate. The agreement also includes an on-the-job training program for tribal members in both roughneck work and management. The joint company worked out as promised, although the Blackfeet hoped for more control of the management.

The Chippewa-Cree Indians and other Native groups are exploring the joint venture idea, yet some tribes want to form their own energy companies in the future. "Up to now, we've always been satisfied in exchange for mineral rights," said Navajo leader Peter MacDonald. "That is no longer enough. We want a share of the income instead of the royalties. Eventually, we plan to go it alone in development of our natural resources."

The Jicarilla Apache of New Mexico began drilling their own oil and gas wells, using their tribal funds. The Assiniboine and Sioux tribes of the Fort Peck Reservation in Montana did the same in developing their own oil and gas wells.

In an effort to protect reservation resources, leaders of twenty-five western Indian tribes united in 1975 to form the Council of Energy Resource Tribes (CERT). CERT is controlled by an executive board consisting of eight tribal chairpersons and a ninth chairperson who serves as the executive director. With one-third of all coal in the West located on Indian lands, CERT takes an aggressive business approach toward energy firms to bargain in the best interests of the tribes. It sought advice in the late 1970s from several members of the Organization of Petroleum Exporting Countries (OPEC) over the U.S. government's disapproval. To halt further OPEC assistance, the federal government awarded CERT grants totaling $1,997,000 from the Department of Energy (DOE), the BIA, and the Department of Health, Education, and Welfare. Initially, CERT opened offices in Denver, Colorado, and Washington, D.C., but it closed the doors of the Washington office when its 1982 budget of $6 million was cut to $3.1 million in 1983. The council educates tribes in evaluating their energy sources, in the technology of mining natural resources, and in the development of human resources; it also provides management studies and computer services. To prevent further exploitation of Indian lands, CERT has established a broad Indian policy "so that energy companies won't be able to pick us off one by one," according to Charles Lohah, the acting secretary for CERT.

It should be added that despite its success, the organization has hardly been immune from criticism. In recent years, CERT has been severely criticized by Indians who charge that it is too "pro-development" regarding reservation resources. CERT has also been accused of holding "glittery, black-tie galas for federal officials and energy company brass."

Today, coal is considered a key natural resource to meet the recurring energy crises, and mining companies are eager to develop reservation minerals. The nation's energy resources east of the Mississippi have been severely depleted, and mining firms look to the West for new fields of coal and other natural resources. Economic reasons have also forced companies westward because strip mining is more economical than shaft mining in the East. Vast reserves of coal in beds up to 100 feet thick lie just below the surface, and over half of the 225 billion tons of coal in the West is available by strip mining. In the West, draglines can strip-mine 100 tons of coal per man-day of labor, more than eight times the rate from the deep Appalachian shaft mines. Health and safety conditions are also more favorable in western strip mining, allowing coal to be mined at $3 to $5 per ton, as compared with $9 to $14 in the East.

The list of corporations on Indian lands in the West is long. In the Black Hills of South Dakota alone, 26 multinational corporations have obtained state prospecting leases for over one million acres. Other examples include several energy companies working in the Four Corners area on the Navajo and Hopi reservations, mining for coal and uranium. In Oklahoma, the Sac and Fox, Osage, Creek, Choctaw, Chickasaw, and other tribes have leases with energy companies extracting oil, gas, or coal.

Until recent years, energy firms have had easy access to Western coalfields. The Department of the Interior could persuade tribal officials to lease lands to companies, thereby easing the exploitation of Indian lands. As a result, the Utah International Mining Company has been operating the largest strip-mining project in the world in the Four Corners region on Navajo land. In response to growing pressure to renegotiate with the Crow Tribe, Westmoreland Resources renegotiated its mining leases with the Crow in November 1973. The Crow Tribe formed the Crow Mineral Committee, which was elected by the tribal council and entrusted to negotiate directly with Westmoreland officials. As of 1975, of the entire Crow Reservation of 2,226,000 acres, Westmoreland leased 30,876 acres, Shell Oil leased 30,248 acres, Peabody Coal leased 86,122 acres, and Gulf Minerals Resources leased 73,292 acres. A 1975 survey prepared by Rural Research Associates of Missoula and Edgar, Montana, estimated that the Crow Reservation contained four to five and a half billion tons of strippable coal, plus six to twelve billion tons of coal that would be more costly to mine.

Today, as Native American officials who conduct negotiations with energy company officials, tribal leaders are developing a new image for themselves. Unlike their forebears, today's tribal leaders understand the complexities of handling land negotiations. Company and government officials have noticed the transition from the old tribal leadership; the new leaders are adamant in their demands and cognizant of white ways of dealing for land.

Reservation leaders have become more successful in negotiations, and the future looks brighter for Plains and Southwest tribes. With the increased knowledge and understanding of white ways, tribal leaders are also initiating and developing new programs to help their people. In this context, it is appropriate to cite the advice of the Sioux leader Sitting Bull. When the mighty Sioux Nation was in decline, mostly because of white influence, Sitting Bull warned: "Take the best of the white man's road, pick it up and take it with you. That which is bad, leave it alone, cast it away. Take the best of the Indian ways—always keep them. They have been proved for thousands of years. Do not let them die."

The younger tribal leaders of the western reservations are making tremendous strides in improving the tribes' status. Beginning at the level of Third World nations, Indian groups are progressing rapidly toward parity with white American society. With competent leadership and additional aid from the Bureau of Indian Affairs, energy tribes have been able to develop successful industries. Federal funds have been appropriated to finance such tribal ventures as Yatay Industries, Sandia Indian Industries, Apache Indian Industries, and Ute Fabricating, Ltd. Other tribal industries include Northern Pueblo Enterprises, Navajo Indian Wood Products, Zuni Enterprises, and White Eagle Industries. These business ventures are the result of careful planning, and they exemplify the entrepreneurial quality of modern Indian achievement.

Partly because such new tribal programs are highly visible, a resurgence of Indian nationalism is developing among western tribal nations. Damson Oil president Barrie M. Damson has contended that this Native nationalism will grow and that energy companies need to recognize this.

As Indian Americans entered the 1980s, some problems remained unresolved. A 72-page report from the Minerals Management Service of the Department of the Interior stated that $119.2 million in royalties had reportedly been paid to Indians in 1980. The next year, some $16.4 million in royalties went to Indians. Unfortunately, in one known case, the royalty checks never reached the people. In Wyoming, seventy allottees from the Wind River Reservation have filed a lawsuit against Amoco Production Company for not paying royalties on 1.3 million barrels of crude oil taken from the Lander Oil Field between 1971 and 1982. The allottees, who have coalesced into the Wind River Allottees Association, petitioned their case to a federal court because they felt that the government would not act soon enough on their behalf. The group seeks either a return of the oil or payment at the current value, an estimated $41 million, plus compensation for punitive damages.

An area of new importance opened after a court decision of 1982 in which the U.S. Supreme Court ruled that the Jicarilla Apaches could charge energy companies a severance tax for mining on their land. Two other tribes, the Shoshone and the Arapaho of Wyoming, are attempting to impose a four percent severance tax on oil and gas, pending approval by the secretary of the interior. With state governments also taxing the mining companies, the energy firms now face double taxation. Although the state taxes are generally higher, the energy companies are challenging the right of the tribes to tax them. The 1982 ruling has opened up a new source for tribal income, but it is one that reservation leaders will have to fight to keep.

Many tribal leaders and reservation peoples, however, face serious problems. Some Americans assume that Indians are getting rich from royalty payments, though actually only fifteen percent of the Indian population has natural resources on tribal lands. In 1982, the BIA reported that royalties on reservations totaled more than $396 million, but if the royalties were distributed to the entire Indian population of 1.3 million (according to the 1980 census), the per capita payment would be only $290 for each person. For their oil, tribes received on the average $2 a barrel in royalties at a time when OPEC nations were demanding and receiving $40 a barrel. Four of the largest energy resource deposits are on the Blackfeet, Crow, Fort Peck, and Wind River Reservations in Montana and Wyoming. In 1980, more than 1200 wells on the four Plains reservations produced 6.1 million barrels of oil. As for coal, in early 1981, when American coal was being sold to foreign buyers for $70 a ton, the Navajo were receiving only $.15 a ton from Utah International Mining Company and less than $.38 a ton from Pittsburgh and Midway Coal Company. These two companies negotiated leases with the Navajos in 1953, 1964, and 1966.

In negotiations with the energy companies, tribal leaders were historically at a disadvantage, but conditions have changed in the 1990s. Their governments once could not pay for equipment to evaluate their natural resources, but with the assistance of CERT and their own resources, tribes now have a very good idea of the natural resources on their lands. During the late 1970s, the requisite trained personnel and exploratory data were in short supply, forcing tribes to give up a major share of their potential wealth by leasing their lands or entering into joint ventures with energy companies. This has also changed in the 1990s.

Nonetheless, despite these improvements, Indian affairs continue to have a low priority in Washington, and the entire budget appropriated for Indian affairs would buy just one aircraft carrier. Even worse, the BIA is a frequent hindrance to tribal leaders because it also lacks the expertise that the mining firms possess in the highly competitive business of energy development. For example, on January 25, 1982, ruling in favor of the Jicarilla Apaches, the Supreme Court maintained that Indian tribes "have the inherent power" to impose severance taxes. Nevertheless, a few months later, the BIA wrote regulations for the severance taxation, and in doing so, it invited the opinions of representatives from the oil and gas industry. Indian criticism forced the BIA to withdraw its regulations, and guidelines were substituted. The bureau's actions prompted additional criticism from U.S. Representative Sidney Yates, who chaired the House appropriations subcommittee that handles Indian affairs. Yates chided, "Tell me why an oil and gas industry association should be allowed to formulate guidelines by which the tribes will be able to tax members of that industry."

Today's tribal leaders, unlike their ancestors, have had to adopt a hurried "get-tough" attitude in a businesslike, modern, "ruthless" way. Such behavior is foreign to the traditional nature of Indian leadership, and it is an obstacle that tribal representatives must overcome if their people are to survive. Although the leaders can probably use more expertise in running their reservation governments like corporations, they know how to hire such expertise. In a very short time, they have become educated in the high-finance business world, and they are experienced in dealing with the bureaucracy of the federal government. Contemporary Indian leaders are sophisticated and forceful in order to protect their people and their reservations—lands that were deemed worthless in the nineteenth century.

The energy crises and the industrial demand for natural resources on Indian lands imply serious repercussions for the tribes' future. The anticipated outcomes are both positive and negative and will have tremendous impact on Indian leaders, tribal members, and reservation lands. The mining operations, the gasification plants to convert coal into gas, and the facilities necessary to produce electricity are extensive and cover large areas of land; as a result, reservation supplies of nonreplaceable natural resources are being severely deleted. In addition, land formations that have religious significance to the people are permanently damaged. Even with reclamation attempts to restore the land to its original state, it will never be the same to the traditional Indian.

Perhaps the fears of the tribal elders who oppose the mining of their Mother Earth are justified. While tribal leaders are trying to improve their tribes' economies through new programs, schools, and jobs, perhaps a greater harm will come to their people. Aside from the exploitation of their lands, the trend to adopt white ways may also mean that much of the tribal cultures will be forgotten.

Can Indians live with one foot in the traditional world and the other in the white world? Many are doing it now, but how much of their tribal heritage do they remember, and how successfully have they assimilated into white American society? Currently, more Indians than ever are receiving the same education as whites and are moving rapidly into the mainstream society. Indians who live on reservations are becoming more aware of the functions of white society as they travel to and from their reservation. Once living in poverty, many Native people have now raised their economic level and have become successful American citizens according to white standards. Perhaps it is premature to judge whether the Indian has opted for social change at the cost of losing Native identity. Certainly, the next generation will provide better answers.

America's need for natural resources to heat family homes, operate automobiles, and run industries continues to grow. As a result, coal mining in Wyoming has become a $1.2 billion industry, and the Kerr-McGee operation in the Powder River Basin is now the fourth largest coal mine in the country. By 1996, Wyoming was the nation's largest producer of low-sulfur coal, mining 279 million tons a year; West Virginia and Kentucky followed at 170 and 149 million tons, respectively. With typical houses dependent upon coal for heating, the annual demand is seven tons. Clearly, the demand for natural resources has not abated.

At the present time, the growing demand for natural resources on Indian lands has acted as a catalyst in forcing Indians, especially tribal leaders, to choose a new lifestyle for their peoples. They are confronted with the dilemma of making a social transition from the traditional world to the white society's lifestyle. It is ironic that today's Indian leaders are negotiating with white Americans and the federal government for tribal lands just as their ancestors did more than one hundred years ago.

For Further Reading

ON AMERICAN INDIAN WOMEN

Allen, Paula Gunn. *The Sacred Hoop: Recovering the Feminine in American Indian Tradition.* Boston: Beacon Press, 1986.

Babb, Genie. "Paula Gunn Allen's Grandmothers: Toward a Responsive Feminist-Tribal Reading of *Two Old Women*." *American Indian Quarterly* 21, 1997.

Bataille, Gretchen M. and Kathleen Mullen Sands. *American Indian Women: Telling Their Lives.* Lincoln: University of Nebraska Press, 1984.

Bolt, Christine. "Indian Women in Fancy and Fact." In *American Indian Policy and American Reform.* London: Allen and Unwin, 1987.

Bowker, Ardy. *Sisters in the Blood: The Education of Women in Native America.* Newton, MA: WEEA Publishing Center, Educational Development, 1993.

Crow Dog, Mary with Richard Erdoes. *Lakota Woman.* New York: Harper Perennial, 1991.

Green, Rayna. *Native American Women: A Contextual Bibliography.* Bloomington: University of Indiana Press, 1983.

———. "Review Essay: Native American Women." *Signs: Journal of Women in Culture and Society* 6, 1980.

Gridley, Marion E. *American Indian Women.* New York: Hawthorn Books, 1974.

Hoikkala, Paivi. "The Hearts of Nations: American Indian Women in the Twentieth Century." In Frederick E. Hoxie and Peter Iverson, eds., *Indians in American History: An Introduction.* Wheeling, IL: Harlan Davidson, 1998.

James, Caroline. *Nez Perce Women in Transition, 1877–1990.* Moscow: University of Idaho Press, 1996.

Klein, Laura F. and Lilian A. Ackerman. *Women and Power in Native North America.* Norman: University of Oklahoma Press, 1995.

LaFramboise, Teresa, Anneliese Heyle, and Emily Ozer. "Changing and Diverse Roles of Women in American Indian Cultures." *Sex Roles* 22, 1990.

Mathes, Valerie Sherer. "Nineteenth Century Women and Reform: The Women's National Indian Association." *American Indian Quarterly* 14, 1990.

Medicine, Bea. "North American Indigenous Women and Cultural Domination." *American Indian Culture and Research Journal* 17, 1993.

Mihesuah, Devon. *Cultivating the Rosebuds: The Education of Women at the Cherokee Female Seminary, 1851–1909.* Urbana: University of Illinois Press, 1993.

Perdue, Theda. "Writing the Ethnohistory of Native Women." In Donald L. Fixico, ed., *Rethinking American Indian History.* Albuquerque: University of New Mexico Press, 1997.

Peters, Virginia Bergman. *Women of the Earth Lodges: Tribal Life in the Plains.* Norman: University of Oklahoma Press, 2000.

Riley, Glenda. "The Historiography of American Indian and other Western Women." In Donald L. Fixico, ed., *Rethinking American Indian History.* Albuquerque: University of New Mexico Press, 1997.

Schweitzer, Marjorie M., ed. *American Indian Grandmothers: Traditions and Transitions.* Albuquerque: University of New Mexico Press, 1999.

Van Kirk, Sylvia. "Towards a Feminist Perspective in Native History." In William Cowan, ed., *Papers of the Eighteenth Algonquian Conference.* Ottawa: Carleton University Press, 1987.

Welch, Deborah. "American Indian Women: Reaching Beyond the Myth." In Colin Calloway, ed., *New Directions in American Indian History.* Norman: University of Oklahoma Press, 1988.

Wilson, Angela Cavender. "Grandmother to Granddaughter: Generations of Oral History in a Dakota Family." *American Indian Quarterly* 20, 1996.

Woodsum, Jo Ann. "Gender and Sexuality in Native American Societies: A Bibilography." *American Indian Quarterly* 19, 1995.

ON REPATRIATION, REBURIAL, AND PRESERVATION OF SACRED LANDS

Churchill, Ward. "The Black Hills Are Not For Sale: The Lakota Struggle for the 1868 Treaty Territory." In *Struggle for the Land: Indigenous Resistance to Genocide, Ecocide and Expropriation in Contemporary North America.* Monroe, ME: Common Courage Press, 1993.

Echo-Hawk, Roger C. and Walter R. Echo-Hawk. *Battlefields and Burial Grounds: The Indian Struggle to Protect Ancestral Graves in the United States.* Minneapolis: Lerner Publications, 1994.

Gulliford, Andrew. *Sacred Objects and Sacred Places: Preserving Tribal Traditions.* Boulder: University Press of Colorado, 2000.

Lame Deer, John (Fire) with Richard Erdoes. *Lame Deer: Seeker of Visions.* New York: Simon and Schuster, 1972.

Lazarus, Edward. *Black Hills, White Justice: The Sioux Nation versus the United States, 1775 to the Present.* New York: HarperCollins, 1991.

Mallouf, Robert J. "The Unraveling Rope: The Looting of America's Past." *American Indian Quarterly* 20, 1996.

Mander, Jerry. "Desecration of Sacred Lands: The Case of the Native Hawaiians." In *In the Absence of the Sacred: The Failure of Technology and the Survival of the Indian Nations*. San Francisco: Sierra Club Books, 1991.

Mihesuah, Devon A., ed. "Repatriation: An Interdisciplinary Dialogue." Special issue of *American Indian Quarterly* 20, 1996.

———, ed. *Repatriation Reader: Who Owns American Indian Remains?* Lincoln: University of Nebraska Press, 2000.

Moore, Steven C. "Sacred Sites and Public Land." In Christopher Vecsey, ed., *Handbook of American Indian Religious Freedom*. New York: Crossroad, 1991.

Ripani, Michael N. "Native American Free Exercise Rights in Sacred Land: Buried Once Again." *American Indian Law Review*, 1991.

Swidler, Nina et al., eds. *Native Americans and Archaeologists: Stepping Stones to Common Ground*. Walnut Creek, CA: Alta Mira Press, 1997.

United States Congress, Senate Committee on Indian Affairs. *Native American Graves Protection and Repatriation Act*. Washington, D.C.: Government Printing Office, 1999.

Walker, Deward E., Jr. "Protection of American Indian Sacred Geography." In Christopher Vecsey, ed., *Handbook of American Indian Religious Freedom*. New York: Crossroad, 1991.

Washburn, Wilcomb E. *Against the Anthropological Grain*. New Brunswick, NJ: Transaction Press, 1998.

Worster, Donald. "The Black Hills: Sacred or Profane." In *Under Western Skies: Nature and History in the American West*. New York: Oxford University Press, 1992.

ON INDIAN RESERVATION GAMING AND CASINOS

Benedict, Jeff. *Without Reservation: The Making of America's Most Powerful Indian Tribe, and Foxwoods, the World's Largest Casino*. New York: HarperCollins, 2000.

Chenault, Venida. "Indigenous Gaming: Economic Resources for Social Policy Development in First Nations Country." *Indigenous Nations Studies Journal* 1, 2001.

Faiman-Silva, Sandra. "Decolonizing the Choctaw Nation: Choctaw Political Economy in the Twentieth Century." *American Indian Culture and Research Journal* 17, 1993.

Frey, James H. *Gambling: Socioeconomic Impacts and Public Policy*. Thousand Oaks, CA: Sage Periodicals Press, 1998.

Gabriel, Kathryn. *Gambling Way: Indian Gaming in Mythology, History, and Archaeology in North America*. Boulder: Johnson Books, 1996.

Hsu, Cathy H.C. *Legalized Casino Gambling in the United States: The Economic and Social Impact*. Binghampton, NY: Haworth Hospitality Press, 1999.

Indian Gaming Magazine, all issues, 1990–.

Kickingbird, Kirke. "American Indians, Bingo, and the Law." *American Indian Journal* 9, 1986.

Mason, W. Dale. *Indian Gaming: Tribal Sovereignty and American Politics*. Norman: University of Oklahoma Press, 2000.

Mirkovich, Thomas R. and Allison A. Cowgill. *Casino Gaming in the United States: A Research Guide.* Lanham, MD: Scarecrow Press, 1997.

National Indian Gaming Association. "Historical Review of Indian Gaming." In *A Historical Review of Gaming in the United States.* Washington, D.C.: National Indian Gaming Assoc., 1993.

Peroff, Nicholas. "Indian Gaming and American Indian Tribal Sovereignty." Conference paper, "American Indian Leaders: Red Power and Tribal Politics," Lawrence, KS, 15 Sept. 2000.

Stein, Wayne J. "American Indians and Gambling: Economic and Social Impacts." In Dean Morrison, ed., *American Indian Studies: An Interdisciplinary Approach to Contemporary Issues.* New York: Peter Lang, 1997.

Vizenor, Gerald. "Gambling on Sovereignty." *American Indian Quarterly* 16, 1992.

———. "Minnesota Chippewa: Woodland Treaties to Tribal Bingo." *American Indian Quarterly* 13, 1989.

ON NATURAL RESOURCES IN INDIAN COUNTRY

Ambler, Marjane. *Breaking the Iron Bonds: Indian Control of Energy Development.* Lawrence: University Press of Kansas, 1990.

Baden, John, Richard Stroup, and Walter Thurman. "Myths, Admonitions, and Rationality: The American Indian as Resource Manager." *Economic Inquiry* 19, 1981.

Barry, Tom. "An Energy Dichotomy for the 80's." *American Indian Journal* 6, 1980.

Barsh, Russel Lawrence. *The Washington Fishing Rights Controversy: An Economic Critique.* Seattle: University of Washington Press, 1979.

Burnham, Philip. *Indian Country, God's Country: Native Americans and the National Parks.* Covelo, CA: Island Press, 2000.

Churchill, Ward. *Struggle for the Land: Indigenous Resistance to Genocide, Ecocide, and Expropriation in Contemporary North America.* Monroe, ME: Common Courage Press, 1993.

Cohen, Fay G. *Treaties on Trial: The Continuing Controversy over Northwest Indian Fishing Rights.* Seattle: University of Washington Press, 1986.

Fixico, Donald L. *The Invasion of Indian Country in the Twentieth Century: American Capitalism and Tribal Natural Resources.* Boulder: University Press of Colorado, 1998.

Folk-Williams, John A. *What Indian Water Means to the West: A Sourcebook.* Santa Fe: Western Network, 1982.

Gedicks, Al. *The New Resource Wars: Native and Environmental Struggles Against Multinational Corporations.* Boston: South End Press, 1993.

Grinde, Donald A. and Bruce E. Johnson. *Ecocide of Native America: Environmental Destruction of Indian Lands and Peoples.* Santa Fe: Clear Light Publishers, 1995.

Harris, Richard R., Greg Blomstrom, and Gary Nakamura. "Tribal Self-Governance and Forest Management at the Hoopa Valley Indian Reservation, Humboldt County, California." *American Indian Culture and Research Journal* 19, 1995.

Iverson, Peter. *We Are Still Here: American Indians in the Twentieth Century.* Wheeling, IL: Harlan Davidson, 1996.

Jorgensen, Joseph G. *Native Americans and Energy Development.* Cambridge, MA: Anthropological Research Center, 1978.

———. *Oil Age Eskimos.* Berkeley: University of California Press, 1990.

Keller, Robert H. and Michael F. Turek. *American Indians and National Parks.* Tucson: University of Arizona Press, 1998.

LaDuke, Winona. *All Our Relations: Native Struggles for Land and Life.* Boston: South End Press, 1999.

Lewis, David Rich. "Native Americans and the Environment: A Survey of Twentieth-Century Issues." *American Indian Quarterly* 19, 1995.

Lipton, Charles J. "The Pros and Cons of Petroleum Agreements." *American Indian Journal* 6, 1980.

McCool, Daniel. *Command of the Waters: Iron Triangles, Federal Water Development, and Indian Water.* Berkeley: University of California Press, 1987.

McPherson, Robert S. and David A. Wolff. "Poverty, Politics, and Petroleum: The Utah Navajo and the Aneth Oil Field." *American Indian Quarterly* 21, 1997.

Parman, Donald L. "Inconsistent Advocacy: The Erosion of Indian Fishing Rights in the Pacific Northwest, 1933–1956." *Pacific Historical Review* 53, 1984.

Stevens, Stan. "The Legend of Yellowstone." In Stan Stevens, ed., *Conservation through Cultural Survival: Indigenous Peoples and Protected Areas.* Covelo, CA: Island Press, 1997.

Vecsey, Christopher and Robert W. Venables, eds. *American Indian Environments: Ecological Issues in Native American History.* Syracuse: Syracuse University Press, 1980.

Wallace, Mary. "The Supreme Court and Indian Water Rights." In Vine Deloria, Jr., ed., *American Indian Policy in the Twentieth Century.* Norman: University of Oklahoma Press, 1985.

Weaver, Jace, ed. *Defending Mother Earth: Native American Perspectives on Environmental Justice.* Maryknoll, NY: Orbis Books, 1997.

Wilkinson, Charles F. *Message from Frank's Landing: A Story of Salmon, Treaties, and the Indian Way.* Seattle: University of Washington Press, 2000.

Afterword

Speaking to a group of Soviet students at Moscow State University in the summer of 1988, President Ronald Reagan, in what has become a rather famous statement on his beliefs about American Indians, commented that the United States erred in setting up reservations rather than completely assimilating Indians into American society: "Maybe we should not have humored them in that, wanting to stay in that kind of primitive life style. Maybe we should have said 'No, come join us. Be citizens along with the rest of us.' " The statement was of course picked up by the media, and sent shock waves throughout Indian Country. It did not bode well for the Reagan administration's policies of stressing tribal self-government and to continue self-determination programs, which later were underfunded anyway, due to the Republican administration's belief in a smaller federal government. But perhaps the statement and its underlying philosophy are reflective of the shifting governmental policies toward American Indians in the past one hundred thirty years—a swinging pendulum between assimilation and sovereignty, which has been shown in this book.

More important, self-determination survived the Reagan years, and American Indians have continued to retain an active presence in American society at the dawn of the twenty-first century. "Tribal communities [have] continued to build their political, legal, cultural, and economic institutions," as Alvin Josephy explained in his book *Red Power: The American Indians' Fight for Freedom* (p. 128), and have benefited from legislation on Indian gaming, religious freedom, and repatriation. A recent (June 2001) example of the latter is that officials at Chicago's Field Museum of Natural History agreed to return a twenty-seven-foot totem pole—one of its most prized possessions—to the Tlingit Nation of southeast Alaska. Under the direction of the 1990 Native American Graves Protection and Repatriation Act, the museum has also returned a carved wheel, beads, and eagle feathers to the Arapaho Indians. Other tribes have been less fortunate. In Blaine, Washington, bulldozers cleared away and destroyed many bones and artifacts from a sacred burial ground of the Lummee Nation for the construction of a new water treatment facility.

Other struggles persist. American Indians in the twenty-first century are faced with a wide range of issues, some of which, due to space constraints, were not addressed here. Readers should know that they can try to keep abreast of such issues through the journals *Indian Country Today* and *American Indian Report.* One of the greatest problems overall is the continuing struggle for recognition of sovereignty and self-governance by the U.S. government and the American people in general. Sovereignty issues such as fishing and hunting rights, including that of the limited taking of whales by the Makah Tribe of Washington, are indicative of the larger problem of natural resource management in general in Indian Country, which continues to be controversial. Many tribes and individuals have worked for years for such rights. Billy Frank, Jr., a Nisqually Indian leader from Washington and chairman of the Northwest Indian Fisheries Commission has fought for fishing rights since the 1960s and continues to work for salmon recovery. "We don't just want salmon up in the spawning beds," he was quoted by the Tacoma, Washington, *News Tribune* (18 March 2000, p. A16). "We want salmon we can all eat." The fish has also been at the center of controversy in the Klamath River Basin of southern Oregon and northern California. There, enforcement of the Endangered Species Act has allowed less water to be detained up-river for irrigation agriculture to ensure proper stream flows for salmon recovery. It is also a victory for the Yurok Indians, whose reservation lies along the Klamath River and who depend on salmon fishing for economic and cultural resources.

Wildlife issues are important to other Native Americans as well. The Nez Perce Indians, for example, are the first tribe in the United States to oversee the statewide reintroduction of an endangered species—the wolf, which to the Nez Perce symbolizes wisdom, strength, and family unity—in the mountains of Idaho. When the Idaho legislature barred the state fish and game department from taking part in the federal wolf recovery program, the Nez Perce approached the federal government and volunteered to do it. Their efforts have been successful, with now almost 200 wolves running freely in the state, and with tribal members working with federal authorities to help track them in Idaho's wilderness areas. Likewise, the Pyramid Lake Paiutes have helped to restore the endangered cui-cui fish in Nevada's Pyramid Lake. And in Montana, the Blackfeet have worked with the group Defenders of Wildlife to reintroduce the swift fox, the Gros Ventre and Assiniboine tribes have cooperated with the U.S. Fish and Wildlife Service to reintroduce endangered black-footed ferrets and black-tailed prairie dogs, and the Salish and Kootenai Confederated Tribes have worked with the Federal Highway Administration to create wildlife overpasses for endangered grizzly bears.

Other natural resource issues continue to vex American Indian tribes. The Hopi and Navajo reservations in northern Arizona have been particularly hard hit with a steadily decreasing supply of water due to the Peabody Coal Company's operation of a slurry pipeline that uses 3.3 million gallons of water a day pumped from an aquifer beneath Black Mesa. The Black Mesa Trust reports that Peabody's plans to continue pumping until 2032 will result in a loss of 70 billion gallons of water, or enough to sustain 30,000 Navajo and Hopi people for 170 years. The Trust (*www.blackmesatrust.org*) based in Kykotsmovi, Arizona, is working to halt Peabody's pumping and to educate the public about the matter. People form all over the United States have joined in the group's on-site protests to draw attention to the crisis.

But there are important success stories too. One is that American Indian tribes in and around protected areas are starting to have a larger role in land management. The Ojibwe Tribe has now taken over the management of the Grand Portage National Monument, which is located within their reservation in northern Minnesota. The arrangement opens up resource protection projects and the creation of a museum. Similarly, the Yurok Tribe reached an agreement with the National Park Service in September 2001 that allows the tribe to work with the NPS on environmental and cultural projects on former Indian land within Redwood National Park on California's north coast. The tribe now has more say in management decisions on watershed restoration and salmon and steelhead recovery projects—the first such agreement between a national park and an Indian tribe in U.S. history. And in Montana, the Salish and Kootenai negotiated a deal with state authorities to oversee hunting, fishing, recreation, and water quality regulations on their reservation in the Flathead Valley. They were also successful in the 1990s in getting the Yellowstone Pipeline removed from their reservation because of repeated petroleum leaks that contaminated groundwater and in settling a $45 million legal case with ARCO which held the legal responsibility for more than one hundred years of mining pollution on the Clark Fork River. The money is being used to rehabilitate streams on the reservation.

The question of blood quantum, status of mixed-blood Indians, and tribal membership is another dilemma many tribes are grappling with while struggling to create ways to perpetuate tribal enrollments and cultural traditions. Under federal law, American Indian tribes make their own rules about tribal membership. Some require a proportion of Indian lineage, others a certain blood quantum, and others use old census reports and historical documents. Because of profits associated with Indian casinos (from which income from gambling is distributed to tribal members), however, some places have witnessed increases in people claiming Indian ancestry. Connecticut, home of the Mashantucket Pequots' Foxwoods Resort—America's largest casino, and one of the world's most profitable gaming resorts—has seen a fifty percent jump in state residents claiming Indian blood.

In seeking to sustain tradition, many tribes are taking active measures to have elders teach youngsters their Native languages, as evidenced by a program recently started on the Hoopa Valley Reservation in northern California. In Oregon, where the state legislature in spring 2001 passed a bill approving Native language instruction in the state's public schools, members of the Warm Springs Confederated Tribes are not only teaching the Ichishkiin language to students, but are also working to create an alphabet to transcribe their oral language into written form. Likewise, the Indigenous Language Institute (*www. indigenous-language.org*), out of Santa Fe, New Mexico, is working to encourage the learning of Native languages across the United States, and the Cherokee Nation of Oklahoma maintains a website complete with downloadable Cherokee language font. "The way to keep a language and culture alive is to adapt to the new technology," said Cherokee spokesperson Mike Miller in an Associated Press news story in August of 2001.

Making equally important in-roads is the work of two other important projects: the Heart of the Earth Survival School, which was started by the American Indian Movement (AIM) as an alternative, culturally based K-12 school, and the Cradleboard Teaching Project—an innovative program developed by Buffy Sainte-Marie, a Cree folk musician, activist, and educator. According to the *American Indian Report* (June 1999, p. 28), the Cradleboard project was designed to teach both Native and non-Native K-12 students the "real deal" about Indians—"information common to all tribes . . . their own culture, as well as the cultures from other tribes in core classes such as science, social studies, history, and geography, all through a Native American perspective." The project, run by the nonprofit Nihewan Foundation for American Indian Education, which Sainte-Marie founded in 1969, develops curricula that now include the use of computers for use with e-mail and live chats between students of different cultures.

Readers should also know about the work toward the advancement of Native America by the Seventh Generation Fund, Inc. (SGF) (*www. 7genfund.org*), which is headquartered in Arcata, California. Founded in 1978 as the Tribal Sovereignty Program, SGF is a pan-Indian, nonprofit "indigenous people's organization dedicated to promoting and maintaining the uniqueness of Native peoples and our nations," according to its literature. It also "provides a dynamic, integrated program of small grants, training and technical assistance, advocacy support, financial management, and leadership development to Native community-based organizations throughout the Americas." Also, a renewal of customs, dances, ceremonies, and powwows is flourishing in Indian Country. These practices have been especially important for many American Indians now living in cities outside or far from their home reservations.

Serious problems, however, like unemployment, alcoholism, increased incidences of sugar diabetes due to poor nutrition, and family violence are ongoing symptoms of the larger dilemma of economic development in Indian Country. In South Dakota, more than half of the Lakota people live below the poverty level, and unemployment has been as high as 80 percent on their reservations. Many American Indians live on remote reservations far from even the availability of electricity and telephone service. According to the National Indian Telecommunications Institute in Santa Fe, New Mexico, in 1998 there was a telephone in seventy-nine percent of the nation's poorest households (annual income less than $5,000), but the rate for the forty-eight largest Indian reservations—at all income levels—was only forty-seven percent. One of the more remote reservations in the continental United States is the Yurok Indian Reservation along the Klamath River gorge of northern California. Although many Yuroks now live in nearby cities and towns, about seventy percent of the reservation still lack telephones and electrical power, and cell phones work only sporadically, meaning there is no 911 service for emergencies. Some residents have gas generators and gasoline-powered appliances; others heat their homes with wood and use kerosene lamps. "It's the Third World," remarked tribal member Bertha Peters in an Associated Press news story (14 August 2000). "It's hard on the school kids—to do their homework . . . all they have is this little light."

New ideas, like reservation gambling, and old ideas, like re-stocking bison herds on reservations on the Great Plains, are plans that are alleviating some of these economic conditions. The InterTribal Bison Cooperative, as quoted in *High Country News* (15 January 2001), for example, is now helping to support fifty different tribes and is running 10,000 bison. Rosebud Sioux member Edward Valandra was instrumental in starting this initiative by researching such county indicators as population figures, degrees of soil erosion, long-term population loss, and low agricultural income to propose a 2.2 million-acre buffalo zone in southwestern South Dakota. Similarly, the Gros Ventre and Assiniboine tribes are running a 600-head herd of bison on the Ft. Belknap Reservation in northern Montana, and are using the animals for meat, trophy hunts, and ceremonial and educational purposes.

Other innovative economic alternatives are booming in Indian Country. In southern New Mexico, the Mescalero Apaches did not stop with a gambling casino, but built a ski area and were the first Indians to establish a golf resort on their reservation. Others, especially various Pueblo tribes that have powerful water rights, quickly followed suit. There are now some twenty-five tribal-owned golf resorts in ten states. Taking advantage of natural resources on their forested lands are the Hupas in northern California and the Mascalero Apaches who have established reservation saw mills or wood-processing plants. Equally innovative are some Lakota members on the Pine Ridge Reservation of South Dakota who have started raising industrial hemp, which is not only one of nature's most versatile fibers used in a variety of products and materials, but also is an excellent nitrogen fixator for soil that can be grown in an ecologically sound and sustainable way. Navajos in Arizona are also considering raising industrial hemp. But showing just how far the U.S. government continues to violate American Indian sovereignty, federal authorities misidentified the Lakotas' hemp field for marijuana (which contains the psychoactive ingredient THC, missing in industrial hemp) in the summer of 2000 and destroyed the crop. According to the SGF newsletter *Sovereignty* (November 2000, p. 1), "twenty-five federal agents with bullet-proof vests in eleven sport utility vehicles, one reconnaissance helicopter, and two small engine planes armed with machine guns came to greet traditional Lakota leader, Alex White Plume, and his family at their home on the Pine Ridge Reservation." The armed agents confiscated White Plume's entire field of hemp just two days before harvest.

Despite such violations, American Indians continue to pursue these and other initiatives that are combining economic development with cultural traditions in creative and beneficial ways. The diversity of cultural traditions, however, determines acceptance or rejection of some of these new plans for economic development. The Onondaga in New York, who issue their own passports and have entered their own lacrosse teams in the Olympics, for example, refuse to accept federal funding and refuse to develop casino gaming. They have stayed away from gambling based on a Seneca chief's visions and teachings in 1799 that warned against it. Some members of New Mexico's Pueblo tribes are opposed to the development of golf resorts which alter the natural environment and use great amounts of scarce water resources. Likewise, many Native Americans oppose nuclear waste dumps on Indian reservations for obvious safety, public health, and environmental reasons.

Another important problem for all Americans to understand is the abuse of American Indian terms and icons as sports mascots and nicknames. From team names such as the Washington "Redskins," to symbols such as the exaggerated stereotype of the Cleveland "Indians," to chants such as the "tomahawk chop," many American Indians are offended and are fed up with the kind of insensitivity displayed toward them, which would never be tolerated against other minority groups in the United States. Suzan Harjo, a Northern Cheyenne, is one of the leading spokespersons working through her organization, the Morningstar Foundation in Washington, D.C., to get sports teams to change their names and symbols, which some universities have done. The University of Oklahoma dropped a mascot character named "Little Red"; Stanford's teams switched from being Indians to the Cardinal; Marquette replaced their Warriors with Golden Eagles; Miami of Ohio changed from the Redskins to the RedHawks; and other schools have made similar changes. But the issue has been perhaps most keenly noted at the University of North Dakota where moves to change the school's Fighting Sioux nickname were halted in the spring of 2001 when a prominent alumnus and major donor to the school's new hockey arena vowed to withhold his multi-million-dollar contributions if the name were changed. The state Board of Higher Education voted to keep the school's seventy-year-old nickname, but adopted a new logo that depicts an Indian with feathers and war paint that was painted by an American Indian artist. And at Florida State University the nickname Seminoles has the support of the American Indian tribe of that name.

All of these economic, environmental, and cultural conflicts in Indian Country are the products of federal and corporate patterns of colonialism that have now persisted for over two hundred years. Maria Yellow Horse Brave Heart, a Lakota traditionalist working for the Takini Network, cites how such colonialism has led to Native peoples suffering from the "effects of a traumatic history across generations." In *Sovereignty* (November, 2000, p. 2–3), she writes how the memory and impacts of massacres, starvation, incarceration, and forced removal of children to boarding schools "have resulted in a historical trauma response, defined as emotional and psychological wounding" through time, signs of which "may include alcoholism, suicidal behavior, depression, anxiety, and health problems." Working to address this vital concern is the Takini Network, based in Rapid City, South Dakota, which has conducted "intensive historical trauma workshops" and "successful community healing interventions with Native communities" from Alaska to New Mexico. Brave Heart writes that the Network's mission is "to help Native people transcend historical trauma and unresolved grief, *hecel lena oyate kin nipi kte* (so that the people may live). To truly transcend—beyond survival and toward the empowerment of Native peoples—we must restore *oyate ptayela* (taking care of the nation)."

Other American Indian leaders are working on similar goals and are bringing attention to Native America. Winona LaDuke (Anishanabe [Ojibwe] from Minnesota) was the vice presidential nominee for the Green Party in 1996 and 2000 and is an in-demand speaker on American Indian issues and cultural restoration. Ada Deer, a member of the Menominee Tribe of Wisconsin, was the first woman assistant secretary for Indian affairs in the Department of the Interior during the Clinton administration where she worked for federal recognition of 220 Alaska Native villages and an increasing number of self-governance tribes. LaDonna Harris (Comanche) was the founder of Oklahomans for Indian Opportunity and Americans for Indian Opportunity, a national Indian organization dedicated to enhancing the cultural, social, political, and economic self-sufficiency of tribes. She also was instrumental in founding the National Women's Political Caucus, the Council for Energy Resources for Tribes, the National Indian Business Association, and INDIANnet. Russell Means (Yankton Sioux), Clyde Bellecourt (Anishanabe), and Dennis Banks (Anishanabe) were co-founders of the American Indian Movement (AIM) in 1968, established to protect the traditional ways of Indian people and to engage in legal cases protecting treaty rights of Natives. They remain active today as activists, lecturers, and authors. Bellecourt was a co-founder of the International Indian Treaty Council and today directs the Peacemaker Center for Indian Youth in Minneapolis and is an organizer of the National Coalition on Racism in Sports and the Media. Banks continues to be involved in American Indian activism as a lecturer and teacher and has appeared in several feature films, including "The Last of the Mohicans," "Thunderheart," and "Incident at Oglala." Appearing with him in the latter two films was John Trudell (Santee Dakota from Nebraska), who also was a leader of AIM and Indians of All Tribes and who helped take over Alcatraz. Trudell, who refers to himself as a "blue Indian" in recognition of the sorrows and problems shared by so many humans living outside the inner circles of corporate and government decision-making, remains active as a spoken word artist and has used his blend of poetry and music to broadcast wake-up calls on Native American issues. Oren Lyons, raised in the traditional ways of the Iroquois on the Seneca and Onondaga reservations of upstate New York, is a lecturer on American Indian traditions, Indian law and history, human rights, and environment and interfaith dialogue. He is an author and activist and was a negotiator between the governments of Canada, Quebec, New York, and the Mohawk Indians in the crisis at Oka, Quebec, during the summer of 1990. He also led a delegation of seventeen American Indian leaders to meet with President George Bush in 1991. Adam Fortunate Eagle, from the Red Lake Chippewa Reservation in Minnesota, was one of the organizers of the Alcatraz Island occupation in 1969 and today is an activist, author, and the spiritual leader of the Keepers of the Sacred Tradition of Pipemakers. He gained worldwide attention when he stepped off a plane in Italy, drove a spear into the ground, and claimed the country for the Native Americans based on the same right of discovery that Christopher Columbus used in the Caribbean! Rosalie Little Thunder (Lakota) is on a personal and spiritual crusade to save the last remaining wild bison herd (free from cattle DNA present in domestic bison) in Yellowstone National Park. The herd, currently at about 3,000 buffaloes, is threatened by sanctioned "hunts" and roundups when the animals cross out of the park during the winter to search for forage on national forest lands leased by ranchers in Montana. Little Thunder and others from her tribal community undertook a 500-mile walk from Rapid City, South Dakota, to Yellowstone in 1999 (commemorated in the documentary film "The Buffalo War") to protest the slaughter of the bison which are sacred to the Lakota and other American Indians. Many others, such as Vine Deloria, Jr. (Standing Rock Sioux), Ward Churchill (Keetowah Band Cherokee), and David Wilkins (Lumbee), are scholars whose work and writings have gone far to promote a better understanding of the cultural and legal aspects of Native America.

But while many gains are being made, there is still much work to be done. When will the United States start living up to its treaty obligations? When will the Black Hills be "returned" to American Indians, who consider them sacred? Why did outgoing President Bill Clinton refuse to grant a presidential pardon to Leonard Peltier, an AIM activist who is in the Leavenworth Federal Penitentiary serving time for the 1975 murders of two FBI agents in South Dakota although he has never been proven guilty? What will be the policies toward a new Republican administration under George W. Bush, especially in terms of a change of values in the Department of the Interior, which has jurisdiction over the BIA? Will Americans of the future be better educated on the history of American Indians and their role in society? It is the hope and mission of this book that they will be.

Index

Index

Index

Index

About the Contributors

Russel Lawrence Barsh is adjunct professor of law at the New York University School of Law. He is the author of *The Washington Fishing Rights Controversy: An Economic Critique* (1979), and co-author of *The Road: Indian Tribes and Political Liberty* (1980).

Liza Black is an assistant professor of history and American culture at the University of Michigan. She teaches American Indian history and is currently writing a book on Indians in movies in the 1940s and 1950s.

Kent Blansett (Cherokee) is a graduate student in history at the University of New Mexico. He is specializing in Native American history and contemporary U.S. history.

Thomas Clarkin received his doctorate in history at the University of Texas and is now an independent scholar living in Lakehills, Texas. He is the author of *Federal Indian Policy in the Kennedy and Johnson Administrations, 1961–1969* (2001).

Roger C. Echo-Hawk (Pawnee) is Repatriation Coordinator for the Native Arts Department at the Denver Art Museum. He is the co-author of *Battlefields and Burial Grounds: The Indian Struggle to Protect Ancestral Graves in the United States* (1994).

Walter R. Echo-Hawk (Pawnee) is a senior staff attorney for the Native American Rights Fund in Denver, Colorado. He is the co-author of *Battlefields and Burial Grounds: The Indian Struggle to Protect Ancestral Graves in* *the United States* (1994), and *Encyclopedia of Native American Religions: An Introduction* (1999).

Sterling Evans teaches history at Humboldt State University in northern California. He has researched and published on the Yaqui Indians, and is completing the book *Bound in Twine: The History and Ecology of the Henequen-Wheat Complex for Yucatan, Sonora, and the American and Canadian Plains.*

Donald L. Fixico (Creek, Sac and Fox, Shawnee, Seminole), CLAS Scholar, is history professor and director of the Indigenous Nations Studies Program at the University of Kansas. Among his works are *Termination and Relocation: Federal Indian Policy, 1945–1960* (1986), *The Invasion of Indian Country in the Twentieth Century: American Capitalism and Tribal Natural Resources* (1998), and *The Urban Indian Experience in America* (2000).

Tom Holm (Cherokee, Creek) is a professor in the American Indian Studies Program at the University of Arizona. He is the author of *Strong Hearts, Wounded Souls: Native American Veterans of the Vietnam War* (1996), and co-editor of *Indian Leaders: Oklahoma's First Statesmen* (1979).

Peter Iverson is a history professor at Arizona State University. He is the author of many books and articles, including *The Navajo Nation* (1981), *When Indians Became Cowboys: Native Peoples and Ranching in the American West* (1994), and *"We Are Still Here": American Indians in the Twentieth Century* (1998).

Elizabeth James-Stern is completing her doctorate in history at Arizona State University, where she is specializing in American Indian history. She has published articles in *Idaho Yesterdays* and in Roger Nichols, ed., *The American Indian: Past and Present*, 5th ed. (1998).

D'Arcy McNickle (Salish-Kutenai) was an influential Native American writer, historian, and activist from the 1930s to the 1970s. He wrote many books and stories, including *They Came Here First: The Epic of the American Indian* (1949), *The Surrounded* (1977), *Runner in the Sun: A Story of Indian Maize* (1987), and *Wind from an Enemy Sky* (1988).

Devon A. Mihesuah (Choctaw) teaches history at Northern Arizona University. She has written *American Indians: Stereotypes and Realities* (1977), *Cultivating the Rosebuds: The Education of Women at the Cherokee Female Seminary, 1851–1909* (1997), and is editor of *Repatriation Reader: Who Owns American Indian Remains?* (2000).

Christopher L. Miller has many published articles and essays and is the author of *Prophetic Worlds: Indians and Whites on the Columbia Plateau* (1985). He teaches history at the University of Texas–Pan American in Edinburg, Texas.

About the Contributors

L.G. Moses is a professor of history at Oklahoma State University. He is the author of *Indian Man: A Biography of James Mooney* (1984), *Wild West Shows and the Images of American Indians, 1883–1933* (1996), and co-author of *Indian Lives: Essays on Nineteenth- and Twentieth-Century Native American Leaders* (1985).

Raymond Pierotti (Comanche) is a professor of biological sciences at the University of Kansas. He has published a variety of articles in such journals as *Ecology, Evolution,* and *American Naturalist,* and in the United Nations book *Cultural and Spiritual Values of Biodiversity* (2000).

Daniel C. Swan, a long-time student of peyote culture, is senior curator of the Gilcrease Museum in Tulsa, Oklahoma. He is the author of *Peyote Religious Art: Symbols of Faith and Belief* (1999).

Margaret Connell Szasz teaches history at the University of New Mexico. She is the author of *Education and the American Indian: The Road to Self-Determination Since 1928* (1974, 1999), *Indian Education in the American Colonies, 1607–1783* (1988), and is editor of *Between Indian and White Worlds: The Cultural Broker* (1994).

Robert M. Utley is an independent historian who lives in Georgetown, Texas. Among his lifetime of works are *Frontiersmen in Blue: The United States Army and the Indian, 1866–1891* (1967), *The Indian Frontier in the American West, 1846–1890* (1984), and *The Lance and the Shield: The Life and Times of Sitting Bull* (1994).

Daniel R. Wildcat (Yuchi, member of the Creek Nation) is a professor of American Indian Studies at Haskell Indian Nations University in Lawrence, Kansas. He has published in *Cultural and Spiritual Values of Biodiversity* (2000), and will be a co-author with Vine Deloria, Jr., in a forthcoming new edition of *American Indian Education.*